MEXICO

Anita Ganeri and Rachel Wright

W
FRANKLIN WATTS
LONDON•SYDNEY

This symbol appears on some pages throughout this book. It indicates that adult supervision is advisable for that activity.

This edition 2007

Franklin Watts
338 Euston Road
London NW1 3BH

Franklin Watts Australia
Hachette Children's Books
Level 17/207 Kent Street
Sydney, NSW 2000

© Franklin Watts 1993, 2003

Editor: Hazel Poole
Designer: Sally Boothroyd
Commissioned photography: Peter Millard
Artwork: John Shackell
Picture research: Juliet Duff

A CIP catalogue record for this book is available from the British Library.

ISBN-13: 978 0 7496 7333 8

Printed in China

Franklin Watts is a division of Hachette Children's Books.

CONTENTS

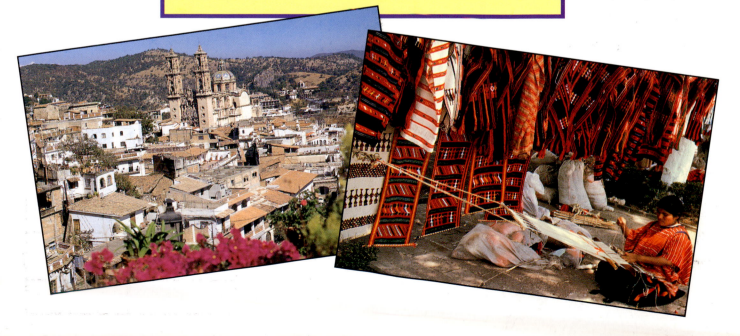

Introducing Mexico

!Buenos días! !Bienvenido!
Hello, and a very warm welcome to Mexico! Before you set off on your travels, here are some fascinating and useful facts about the country.

MEXICO IN THE WORLD

Mexico is a long, thin country in the southernmost part of North America. It covers an area of 1,958,200 square kilometres and has a population of over 100 million. Its capital is Mexico City, one of the largest and most crowded cities in the world. Other major cities include Guadalajara, Netzahualcóyotl and Monterrey. From the map you can see that Mexico has long coastlines on both sides. The Pacific Ocean lies to the west and south-west. The Gulf of Mexico and the Caribbean Sea (parts of the Atlantic Ocean) lie to the east. On land, Mexico has boarders with the USA in the north and with Guatemala and Belize in the south-east.

THE MEXICAN FLAG

The Mexican flag has three vertical stripes in green, white and red. Each colour has a special meaning. Green is for independence; white is for religion and red stands for unity. In the centre of the flag is Mexico's coat of arms. It shows an eagle, perched on a prickly pear cactus, holding a snake in its beak. According to legend, the Aztecs (see page 24) built their capital, Tenochtitlán, on the spot where they saw the eagle eating the snake. Mexico City now stands on the sight of Tenochtitlán. The flag was adopted in 1821, when Mexico gained its independence from Spain.

GOVERNMENT

Mexico's official name is the *Estados Unidos Mexicanos* – the United Mexican States. The country is a republic, divided into 31 states and one federal district. It has a democratic form of government. The president is the head of state and is elected for six years at a time. Parliament is made up of a General Congress, divided into the Senate and the Chamber of Deputies.

MEXICAN MONEY

The Mexican currency is called the *peso*, written as MX$. One *peso* is divided into 100 *centavos*. To stop any confusion with American dollars, prices are sometimes written as $25mn. The "mn" stands for *moneda nacional* (national money).

MEXICAN LANGUAGES

The words in the "Say it in" boxes throughout this book are in Spanish, the official language of Mexico. Mexican Spanish is almost identical to the Spanish spoken in Spain, except that it has Indian words mixed in with it. These come from the Náhuatl language. Other Indian languages still spoken in Mexico include Mixtec, Maya and Zapotec. These date from the days before the Spanish conquest of Mexico in the 16th century. Almost everyone in Mexico speaks and understands Spanish, though.

Say it in Spanish

!Buenos días! – hello, good morning

dinero – money

banco – bank

timbre – stamp

correo – post office

español – Spanish

carta – map

Around Mexico

Mexico is a fascinating country with ancient ruins and remains, modern cities, deserts, jungles and beautiful beaches. With such a variety of sights to see and places to explore, it's not surprising that 20 million tourists visit Mexico each year.

BAJA CALIFORNIA

Baja California is a long, spindly finger of land sticking out into the Pacific Ocean. About halfway down the peninsula lies the town of Guerrero Negro. It is famous for its lagoon, called Scammon's Lagoon. Each year, thousands of grey whales migrate here from the Bering Sea in the Arctic, to breed.

MEXICAN GEOGRAPHY

On the map of Mexico below you can see the different geographical regions, the main mountains, rivers and so on. There are also suggestions for places to visit. Mexico has a wide range of landscapes within its borders. Two thirds of the country is covered with high mountains and hills, including the western and eastern Sierra Madre. The highest mountain is Citlaltépetl at 5,700 metres. It is one of a chain of volcanic mountains running across the south of the country. The main rivers are the Río Grande and the Balsas.

The Mexican climate varies from place to place. The north is mostly hot, dry desert. The south has a tropical climate. The tops of the highest mountains are permanently covered with snow.

MEXICALI

BAJA CALIFORNIA

SCAMMON'S LAGOON

GUERRERO NEGRO

CIUDAD JUAREZ

RIO GRANDE

CHIHUAHUA

COPPER CANYON

SIERRA MADRE OCCIDENTAL

SIERRA MADRE ORIENTAL

MEXICAN PLATEAU

MONTERREY

GULF OF MEXICO

PACIFIC OCEAN

GUADALAJARA

MEXICO CITY

TAXCO

BALSAS

ACAPULCO

TEOTIHUACÁN

Vol. CITLALTÉPETL

VERACRUZ

PALENQUE

CHICHÉN ITZÁ

MERIDA

YUCATAN

MEXICO CITY

Mexico City is a mixture of ancient Aztec temples and palaces, grand Spanish churches and cathedrals and modern high-rise apartment blocks, streets and slums. A huge square, called the Zócalo, lies at the heart of the city. This was also the site of the main square of the Aztec city of Tenochtitlán (see page 24), where the Great Temple and royal palace stood.

THE COPPER CANYON

The Copper Canyon, or Barranca del Cobre, lies in the western Sierra Madre mountains. For the most dramatic view of the Canyon, take the train. The journey lasts for about 12 hours, passing through 86 tunnels and over 39 bridges! But it's worth it. The gorges which make up the Copper Canyon are up to 1,200 metres deep and 1,500 metres wide, carved out of the mountain sides by the Urique River.

ACAPULCO

The city of Acapulco on the south-west coast is Mexico's most famous holiday resort. It has beaches, hotels and restaurants galore. But one of its most amazing attractions are the cliff divers of La Quebrada. They dive off the sheer cliffs, from heights of up to 45 metres, into a narrow inlet of sea below. The water is only 3.5 metres deep here.

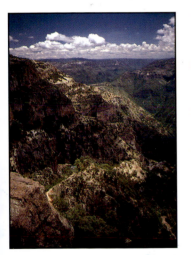

DESERT LIFE

The deserts of north and north-western Mexico are home to some amazing plants and animals. Among them are giant saguaro cacti, which can grow over 12 metres tall, and prickly pear cacti. There are also coyotes, rattlesnakes, prairie dogs and gila monsters, one of only two types of poisonous lizards.

CHICHÉN ITZÁ

The ruins of the ancient Mayan city of Chichén Itzá are to be found on the Yucatán Peninsula in the south-east of Mexico. The city was at its greatest between the 6th and 10th centuries AD. One of the best preserved buildings is a pyramid, El Castillo (The Castle). The temple at the top was reached by a flight of 365 steps, one for each day of the year.

Say it in Spanish
montaña – mountain
volcán – volcano
río – river
ciudad – city
desierto – desert
cacto – cactus
culebra – snake

7

Food and Drink

In Mexico, people eat three meals a day – *desayuno* (breakfast), *comida* (a large lunch) and *cena* (a light supper). The staple foods in the Mexican diet are *tortillas* (corn pancakes), *frijoles* (beans) and *chiles* (chilli peppers). Many Mexicans grow their own food or buy it fresh from the local markets.

TASTY TORTILLAS

Maize (corn) is the most important crop grown in Mexico and the most important source of food. It is ground into meal (like flour) and made into thin, round pancakes called *tortillas*. These can be eaten plain or filled with chicken, meat, cheese or beans. They are called *tacos* if they are filled, folded then fried. They are called *enchiladas* if they are filled, rolled up and covered in spicy sauce. And they are called *tostados* if they are fried and served flat with a topping. Don't worry – you'll soon get the hang of it! *Tortillas* are often stuffed with *frijoles* (beans), or used to scoop up helpings of beans. Many Mexicans eat beans every day, seasoned with hot chilli peppers. You can find out how to make another Mexican speciality, *guacamole*, on the next two pages.

WHAT TO DRINK?

If you are hot and bothered, try a refreshing glass of an *agua fresca*. This is fruit juice mixed with sugar and water. There are many different varieties.

Mexico is famous for its very strong alcoholic drinks which are made from cacti and other desert plants. Tequila is made from the sap of the spiky maguey plant. The sap is pressed out, mixed with sugar, then fermented, distilled and bottled. As a final touch, a worm is added to each bottle! Tequila is traditionally drunk with salt and lime. When the bottle is empty, the worm has to be eaten!

CHOCOLATE MONEY

Chocolate is made from the beans of the cacao tree which originally grew wild in Mexico. The Aztecs valued chocolate so much that they used cocoa beans as currency. They also drank chocolate spiced with peppers. Modern-day Mexicans prefer their chocolate flavoured with sugar and vanilla. A popular dish for special occasions is turkey with *mole*, a sauce made of chocolate, chilli peppers and sesame seeds.

Shopping List

huevos – eggs
pan – bread
mantequilla – butter
carne – meat
pavo – turkey
gazpacho – chilled, spicy vegetable soup
aguacate – avocado pear
elote – corn on the cob
queso – cheese
agua – water
tuña – fruit of the prickly pear cactus

Mexican Dip

The next time you throw a party, why not give it a real Mexican flavour by serving a bowl of guacamole, surrounded by tortilla chips for dipping?

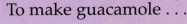

To make guacamole . . .

YOU WILL NEED:

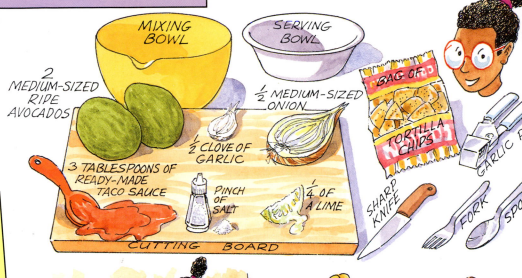

MIXING BOWL
SERVING BOWL
2 MEDIUM-SIZED RIPE AVOCADOS
½ MEDIUM-SIZED ONION
½ CLOVE OF GARLIC
3 TABLESPOONS OF READY-MADE TACO SAUCE
PINCH OF SALT
¼ OF A LIME
CUTTING BOARD
BAG OF TORTILLA CHIPS
GARLIC P
SHARP KNIFE
FORK
SPOO

1. Peel the onion. Chop it up as finely as you can and put it in the mixing bowl. If you have a food processor, ask an adult to show you how to use it to chop up the onion.

2. Crush the ½ clove of garlic into the bowl and add the taco sauce.

3. Squeeze the juice of the lime into the mixing bowl and stir well.

4. Cut the avocados in half and dig out their stones with a spoon. Put the stones to one side.

5. Scoop the flesh of the avocados into the bowl with a spoon. Make sure you scrape the skins well.

6. Chop the avocado flesh roughly with the knife and fork.

7. Using the fork, mash the avocado flesh until it is almost smooth. Add a pinch of salt and stir.

8. Spoon the guacamole into the serving dish. Surround the dish with tortilla chips and crisps or, if you prefer, scrubbed raw vegetables cut into sticks, and leave your guests to help themselves.

Dip Tip
Don't make your guacamole too far in advance otherwise the avocado will darken. To slow down this darkening process, try leaving the avocado stones in the guacamole until you are ready to eat it.

Life in Mexico

PEOPLE AND THEIR ORIGINS

Over 100 million people live in Mexico and the population is getting bigger all the time. Some three-quarters of people live in towns and cities. Only about a quarter live in the countryside. Many people are very poor. Some try to make their way, illegally, across the border into the USA to look for work. Most are caught and sent back again.

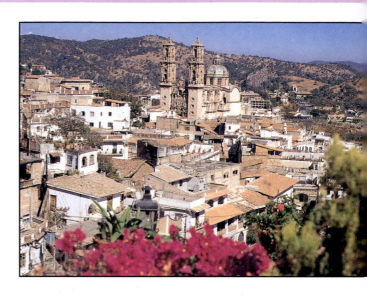

Most Mexicans are descended from Spanish and Indian ancestors. They are called *mestizos*. There are also about 10 million Indians who have kept their traditional customs, culture and languages. The biggest group are the Nahua whose ancestors were the Aztecs.

TRADE AND INDUSTRY

In the last 30 years, Mexico has made great efforts to strengthen its economy and modernise its industries. It manufactures and exports iron, steel and motor vehicles. It also exports sugar and coffee. It is a leading producer of oil (from the Gulf of Mexico) and silver. Tourism is one of Mexico's most important industries. It provides valuable foreign income and jobs.

ON THE FARM

About a quarter of Mexicans live in small villages or on farms. The main crops are maize, coffee, bananas, wheat and potatoes. Avocados, chilli peppers, lemons, tomatoes and vanilla are also grown. Cattle are raised for beef and milk. Farmers take their produce to market to sell or trade for other goods. Many farms are very small and very poor. There are also *ejidos*, community farms worked by groups of farmers, and large *haciendas*, country estates owned by rich landowners.

GOING TO SCHOOL

All Mexican schools used to be under the control of the Roman Catholic Church. Today the government is in charge of education. By law, children have to go to school from the age of six to 14. In the countryside, however, many children leave school early to help their parents in the fields. The oldest university in Mexico is the National Autonomous University of Mexico, in Mexico City. It was founded in 1551.

WHAT PEOPLE WEAR

In the towns and cities, most Mexicans wear western-style clothes. In the villages, however, people wear more traditional clothes. They wear wide-brimmed *sombreros* to protect them from the hot sun. *Ponchos* or *serapes* (shawls) are worn in cold weather. You can find out how to make your own poncho on pages 15–17. Clothes are hand-woven and embroidered in bright colours. Each region has its own distinctive set of colours and designs.

Say it in Spanish
fábrica – factory
granja – farm
pueblo – village
escuela – school
mercado – market
plata – silver
café – coffee
azúcar – sugar

Arts and Crafts

If you visit a market in Mexico, you'll find a wide range of locally made handicrafts. You'll be able to buy hand-woven baskets and embroidered cloth, pottery, carpets and silverware. Market prices are not usually fixed, so be ready to barter!

MAGIC CARPETS

Carpets are woven in brightly coloured wools on large looms. Their designs include ancient symbols such as the sun and moon which represent the forces of nature, and animals and birds which represent life. A medium-sized carpet takes four people about 30 days to make and uses at least 140,000 knots.

MODERN ART

One of modern Mexico's most famous artists was Diego Rivera (1886–1957). He painted bold, colourful murals of scenes from Mexican life, many of which had historical events, such as the Mexican Revolution, and social problems as their themes.

A Diego Rivera mural of an Aztec market.

BEAUTIFUL POTS

Mexico is famous for its decorative pottery. Pots are often brightly painted with scenes from ancient myths and legends as well as everyday people and places.

Patterned Ponchos

Mexican ponchos or *jorongos* are often striped and colourful.

YOU WILL NEED:

THREADS

WOOL

PEN

SCISSORS

NEEDLES

PINS

RULER

CARD

The edges of the poncho on page 17 are covered with blanket stitch. To sew a row of blanket stitches . . .

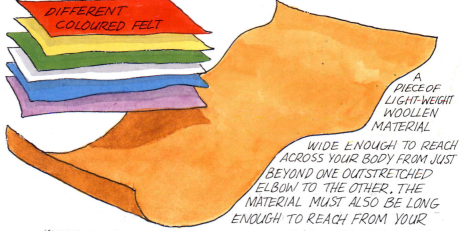

DIFFERENT COLOURED FELT

A PIECE OF LIGHT-WEIGHT WOOLLEN MATERIAL

WIDE ENOUGH TO REACH ACROSS YOUR BODY FROM JUST BEYOND ONE OUTSTRETCHED ELBOW TO THE OTHER. THE MATERIAL MUST ALSO BE LONG ENOUGH TO REACH FROM YOUR KNEES OVER YOUR SHOULDER TO THE BACK OF YOUR KNEES.

1. Push a threaded needle through some material from back to front. Then, working from left to right, push the needle through to the back of the material and bring it out between the material and thread.

2. Pull the thread through the loop. Start again at step 1.

3. Try to keep your stitches the same length and the same distance apart.

15

4. Fold the woollen material in half, as shown, and cut a slit about 14 cm long into the centre of the folded edge.

5. Using the slit as a base line, draw a triangle about 10 cm high. Cut out this triangle, slip the poncho over your head and check that the neck opening is the right size.

6. Turn in the raw edges along the neck opening and pin them down. Thread a needle with a length of wool and, using blanket stitch, sew narrow hems. Remove the pins.

7. Turn in the raw edges along the bottom and sides of the poncho and pin them down. Sew the edges down with blanket stitch and remove the pins.

8. Decide how long you want your tassel to be and cut a piece of card to the same length. Wind some wool around the card. Thread a needle and pass it under the top of the tassel a couple of times. Tie the thread in a knot.

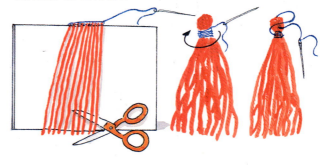

9. Cut the tassel through at the bottom. Wind the thread around the tassel, near the top. Pull it through the top of the tassel and tie in a knot to finish. Make more tassels and sew them onto the bottom of your poncho.

To decorate the poncho

10. Find some simple Mexican designs that you like and copy them onto the pieces of felt. Cut out these designs and pin them onto your poncho. Sew them into place and remove the pins.

11. Before you wear your poncho for the first time, iron all its blanket-stitched hems.

Ponchos are also worn in other countries such as Peru and Bolivia.

Sport and Leisure

Sport has been an important part of Mexican life for hundreds of years. Like everything else in the country, the sports followed are a mixture of ancient and modern and show Indian, Spanish and American influences.

FOOTBALL CRAZY

Mexicans are mad about football. Although it has never won the World Cup, Mexico has hosted it twice, in 1970 and 1986. On each occasion, the final was played in the 100,000-seater Azteca Stadium in Mexico City. The top national clubs are América (of Mexico City) and Guadalajara. Football is also shown on television.

BASKETBALL OLD AND NEW

Basketball is a very popular sport in modern Mexico. It was a favourite of the Maya, too. They played their own version of the game, called *ollamalitzli.* Players had to get a solid rubber ball through a small stone ring set in the wall of the ball court. They were only allowed to touch the very hard ball with their knees, hips and elbows. This caused a lot of injuries.

OLYMPIC CITY

The 1968 Olympic Games were held in Mexico City. The main stadium was the Estadio Olimpico Mexico 68 which holds 80,000 spectators and is designed to look like the cone of a volcano. There is a mosaic by Diego Rivera (see page 14) over the main entrance.

BULLFIGHTING

Because of the Spanish influence on Mexico, bullfighting has become the country's national sport. There are two bullrings in Mexico City, including the largest in the world which seats about 55,000 people. The bravest matadors (bullfighters) become great heroes. Sunday is bullfighting day in the capital.

JAI ALAI

Jai alai is a game rather like squash, based on the Spanish game, pelota, and played on a long court. The players have curved, basket-like raquets attached to their arms. They use these to hit the ball very hard against the walls. Jai alai is a fast, furious and very exciting game to watch.

Say it in Spanish
toro – bull
futbol – football
balón – soccer ball
pelota – ball (eg tennis ball)
deporte – sport
equipo – team
televisión – television

Festival Time!

There are holidays, festivals and fiestas throughout the year in Mexico. Many of them have religious themes. About 90 per cent of Mexicans are Roman Catholics. Some Indians still follow their ancient religions which are based around the worship of the spirits of nature. There are also festivals to celebrate good harvests. (You can find out more about the festival of the Day of the Dead on page 22).

INDEPENDENCE DAYS

Mexico's independence days are celebrated on 15 and 16 September each year. Mexico gained its independence from Spain in 1821. The biggest fiesta takes place in Mexico City. The president recites a special hymn to freedom in the Zócalo, then the celebrations begin with fireworks, folk dancing, music and horse races.

GUADALUPE DAY

The most important religious festival is Guadalupe Day, celebrated on 12 December. It is the feast day of the patron saint of Mexico, Our Lady of Guadalupe. According to legend, this was the day in 1531 on which the saint appeared to a local Indian girl on Tepeyac Hill in Mexico City.

Fiesta time in Mexico.

Independence celebrations in the Zócalo.

Mexican boy trying to break open the piñata.

MEXICAN HAT DANCE

Music and dancing are vital parts of any fiesta. One of the most popular folk dances is the Mexican hat dance, the *jarabe tapatio*. The women dancers wear a costume called a *china poblana*, made up of a red and green beaded skirt, an embroidered short-sleeved blouse and a colourful sash. The story goes that this costume is named after a Chinese princess who was sold as a slave in Mexico. She dedicated her life to helping the poor and wore this costume as she worked.

MUSIC TO THE EARS

Mexico is famous for its bands of strolling musicians, called *mariachis*. They sing and play guitars, violins and trumpets. There are also marimba bands who play instruments resembling large, wooden xylophones. Some Indian groups still play the ancient music of their ancestors, on traditional instruments such as gourd rattles, wooden flutes and seashells.

CHRISTMAS CHEER

On the nine days before Christmas Day, children all over Mexico act out Mary and Joseph's journey to Bethlehem. These special parades are called *posadas*. After each night's posada, the children break open papier-mâché models, called *piñatas*. These are full of sweets, toys and fruit. On Twelfth Night (6 January), parents also fill their children's shoes with gifts.

Say it in Spanish
fiesta – festival
música – music
baile – dance
juguete – toy
Día de Navidad – Christmas Day
regalo – present, gift

Day of the Dead

The Day of the Dead, which is celebrated on 1 and 2 November, is Mexico's most fantastic festival. It marks the time when the souls of the dead come back to Earth for just a few brief hours.

During the festival tables are set up in the family home and decorated with flowers, fruits, candles and pictures of the saints. At the appropriate time, they are also covered with a feast of food and drink. Attracted by the scent of the flowers and incense, the souls of the dead return to their families, usually unseen and unheard, to take up the essence of the food. After that, they go back to their resting place and the living family share the feast with their friends.

Many Mexicans also take flowers and candles to the graves of their loved ones during the festival, as well as more food and drink.

During the Day of the Dead festival, children buy sugar skulls bearing the names of their friends, to give as presents.

SUGAR SKULLS

1. Roll the marzipan into a ball and then shape it into a skull. (If the marzipan sticks to the palms of your hands, sprinkle it with a little icing sugar.)

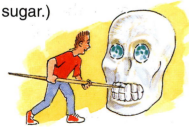

2. Press two eye sockets into the skull with the end of a wooden spoon and put a paste jewel in each hole. Carve teeth and other features with a cocktail stick.

A LITTLE ICING SUGAR

A TUBE OF COLOURED ICING

AND NOZZLES

PASTE JEWELS ETC. TO DECORATE

250 g. READY-MADE WHITE MARZIPAN

COCKTAIL STICK

WOODEN SPOON

YOU WILL NEED:

3. Decorate the skull with icing, coloured foil or anything else you like, and write or stick your name on it.

Mexico's history is long and fascinating. It can be split into two periods, before and after the arrival of the Spanish *conquistadors* (conquerors) in 1521. Before this date, a series of Indian civilisations grew up in Mexico. They were highly advanced, with great cities, counting systems and calendars. You can find out about some of them below. There is more about the history of Mexico after the Spanish conquest on page 28.

THE OLMECS

The first great Mexican civilisation was that of the Olmecs from 1200–400BC. Their name means "people from the land of rubber". The Olmecs are famous for the huge stone heads they carved out of basalt. Some of the heads are 3 metres tall and weigh over 20 tonnes. They probably show ruler-priests of the Olmecs.

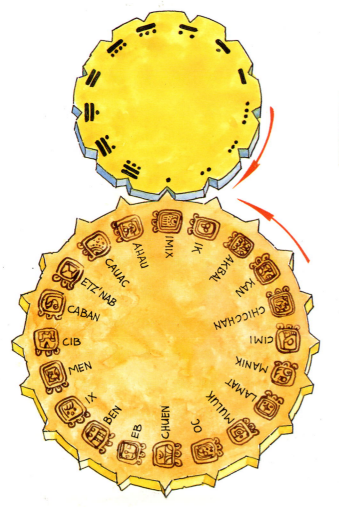

THE MAYA

The Maya civilisation of southern Mexico lasted from 500BC–AD1450. Its greatest cities were built at Chichén Itzá (see page 7) and Tikal. The Mayans were skilled astronomers and mathematicians. They devised an accurate 365-day solar calendar, made up of 18 months of 20 days each and five days spare. They had a separate calendar for religious events. The Maya also had a complicated system of picture writing, with some 500 symbols.

THE TOLTECS

The war-like Toltecs flourished from 950–1200AD. Their capital was the city of Tula. The main god of the Toltecs, and of many other Indian groups, was the plumed serpent, Quetzalcoatl. He was the god of nature, air and earth, symbolised by a serpent with quetzal bird feathers. Emperors and people of high rank were also permitted to wear quetzal feather headdresses as status symbols. Quetzals still live in the jungles of Central America but are very rare.

The sacred quetzal bird.

THE AZTEC EMPIRE

The Aztecs were at the height of their powers from 1300–1521AD. Originally a wandering tribe, they established a huge, well-organised capital city on the site of modern Mexico City. Tenochtitlán was built on an island in Lake Texcoco (later drained by the Spanish). Three great causeways linked it to the mainland. In its heyday, the city was home to 100,000 people.

SACRIFICES TO THE SUN

The Aztecs believed that human sacrifice was needed to make sure the sun rose every day. The victims were killed and their hearts and blood offered to the sun god. Most of the victims were prisoners of war.

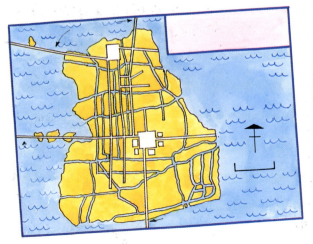

Mosaic Masks

Aztec craftsmen made beautiful mosaic masks which may have been worn by priests during religious ceremonies. This mask of the god Quetzalcoatl is decorated with small pieces of turquoise.

To make a similar mask . . .

YOU WILL NEED:

TRACING PAPER

DARK COLOURED THIN CARD

WHITE OR CREAM COLOURED THIN CARD

SHEETS OF DIFFERENT COLOURED STICKY-BACKED PAPER

A STRIP OF FLAT ELASTIC

PENCIL

GLUE

SCISSORS

CRAFT KNIFE

RULER

STAPLER

1. Trace the template on page 27 onto some dark coloured card and cut it out. If your face is longer than the template, alter the length of your tracing before you copy it onto the card.

2. Hold the cut-out mask against your face and ask a friend to check that the eye and mouth holes are in the right place before you cut them out. Check the position of the nose hole too, then cut along the dotted lines and open out the flaps.

3. Cut out two pieces of cream coloured card, big enough to cover the mask's eyeholes. Draw a small circle in the middle of each piece. Cut out both circles and glue the pieces of card to the back of the eyeholes.

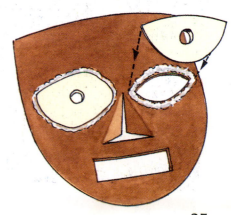

25

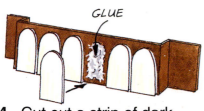

4. Cut out a strip of dark card, slightly longer than the mask's mouth. Glue some card teeth onto this strip, and bend it twice at each end as shown.

5. Snip away the corners of the strip and glue it to the back of the mask's mouth, as shown.

6. Fold a piece of dark coloured card in half and draw a nose on it. Make sure that the centre of the nose is along the fold and that the outside edge is longer than the flaps on the mask.

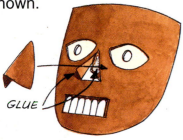

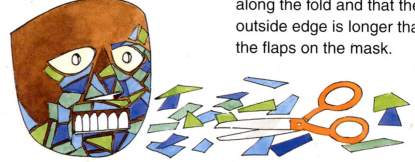

7. Cut around the nose, open it out and glue it to the flaps.

8. Cut the sticky-backed paper into small shapes. Stick the shapes, one by one, onto the mask until it is completely covered.

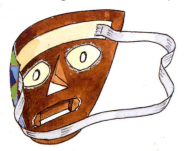

9. To strengthen the forehead, glue a band of card to the back of the mask, just above the eyeholes. Before you staple the strip of elastic to this band, check that the elastic is long enough to reach from one side of your head, round the back to the other side. If you pull the mask around your face too tightly, the paper shapes may peel off.

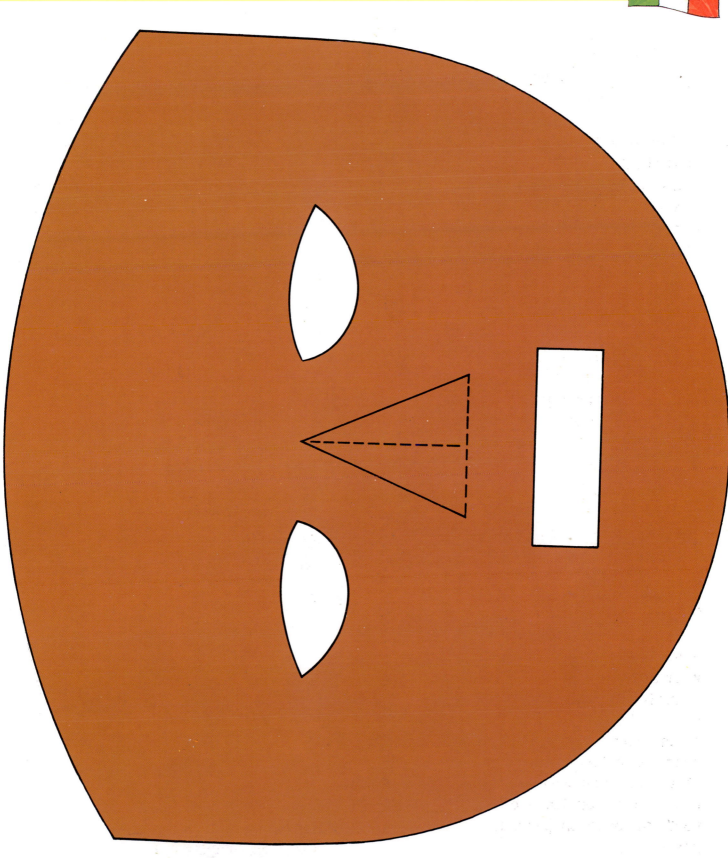

Mexican History 2

THE SPANISH ARRIVE

The Spanish discovered Mexico, and the wealth of the Aztecs, in 1517. In 1519, Hernando Cortés arrived in Mexico. The Aztec emperor, Moctezuma, sent gifts for Cortés, believing him to be the god, Quetzalcoatl. In return, he was taken hostage. It was not long before the Spanish, with the help of their own horses and cannon, and the Aztecs' Indian enemies, had destroyed this great empire.

UNDER SPANISH RULE

King Charles I of Spain allowed the Indians to keep their own languages and some of their own form of government. But he insisted that they pay a tax, called a tribute, and convert to the Roman Catholic religion. Many of the Spanish conquistadors behaved very cruelly, killing any Indians who resisted them.

THE FIGHT FOR INDEPENDENCE

On 15 September 1810, a priest called Miguel Hidalgo y Costilla called upon all Mexicans to rebel against Spanish rule and fight for control of their own country. The speech he made that night is the one repeated by the Mexican president every year on independence day. He won some support but was soon captured and killed by Spanish troops. In 1820, however, another group of rebels had more success. Mexico finally gained its independence from Spain in 1821.

D. MIGUEL HIDALGO,
Cura del pueblo de Dolores en la provincia de Guanajuato.

THE MEXICAN REVOLUTION

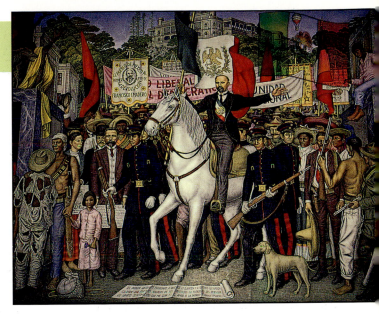

In 1910, a wealthy landowner, Francisco Madero, led a campaign to overthrow the unpopular president, Porfirio Díaz. Bands of revolutionaries fought against government troops all over Mexico. In 1911, Díaz was forced to resign, to stop any further bloodshed. Madero became president but he himself was assassinated in 1913.

MEXICAN EARTHQUAKE

In September 1985, Mexico City was hit by a terrible earthquake. More than 8,000 people died and thousands more were left homeless. Among the hundreds of buildings destroyed was the city's maternity hospital. Against the odds, about 50 babies survived being buried under the dust and rubble.

TIME BAND	
c.2000BC	The first villages develop in Mexico
1200–400BC	The Olmec civilisation
500BC–AD1450	The Maya civilisation
AD950–1200	The Toltec civilisation
1300–1521	The Aztec civilisation
1350s	The Aztecs found their capital city, Tenochtitlán
1519	Hernando Cortés arrives in Mexico
1521	The last Aztec emperor surrenders
1810–1821	The struggle for independence
1821	Mexico gains its independence
1846–1848	The Mexican War – America wins large areas of Mexican land
1910	The Mexican Revolution
1985	Earthquakes hit Mexico City

Say it in Spanish
historia – history
emperador – emperor
rey – king
calendario – calendar
dios – god
temple – temple
iglesia – church
caballo – horse
soldado – soldier

Picture Pairs

Play Picture Pairs and see how many of the Spanish words in this book you actually remember! The instructions given here are for two to four players, but as your Spanish vocabulary increases, you might like to make more cards and include more players.

YOU WILL NEED:

OLD MAGAZINES

WRAPPING PAPER

METAL RULER

GLUE

SCISSORS

STIFF PAPER

THICK CARD

CUTTING BOARD

PAINTS OR CRAYONS

PENCIL

CRAFT KNIFE

To make the cards

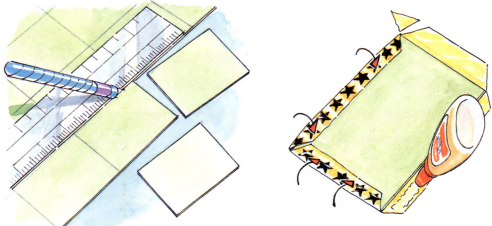

1. Draw 50 rectangles of the same size onto the card and carefully cut them out using the craft knife.

2. Draw another 50 rectangles onto the wrapping paper and cut them out too. These rectangles should be about 2 cm longer and wider than the card ones.

3. Cut the corners of the paper rectangles as shown and glue them onto your cards.

4. Draw 25 rectangles, slightly smaller than your cards, onto the stiff paper and cut them out.

5. Choose 25 Spanish words from this book and write them down with their English translations. (Keep this list beside you when you play the game.)

6. Look through the magazines and cut out any photographs which illustrate the words you have chosen. If you can't find suitable pictures, cut out some more rectangles from stiff paper and paint pictures of your words on them.

El Pan

La Montaña

El Regalo

El Baile

La Culebra

7. Stick each photograph or picture onto the front of one of your cards. Glue the stiff paper rectangles onto the rest of the pack and write a Spanish word from your list on each one.

To play the game
The object of Picture Pairs is to collect pairs of cards made up of words and their matching picture.

Each player starts the game with seven cards. The rest of the pack is placed face down on the table. If you have any pairs, put them on the table in front of you.

Then ask one of the other players if he/she has a card that you need to make a pair. If that player has the card requested, he/she must hand it over and you win the pair and have another turn. If he/she does not have the card, you take a card from the pack in the middle and the turn passes to the next person.

All word cards must be translated into English. If you cannot remember the translation of the word, look it up and miss your next go.

The player who pairs all his cards first is the winner.

Index

Additional Photographs:
AA Photo Library P. 17; A.G. Formenti P. 21; All Sport Photographic Ltd. P. 18; Bridgeman P. 14; J. Allan Cash Ltd.; Bruce Coleman P. 24; P. 14; Gamma P. 9; Robert Harding P. 9, 12, 14, 24, 29; Hutchison P. 4, 7, 12, 13, 22; Mexicolore P. 22, 29; South American Pictures P. 19, 20; Frank Spooner P. 19, 20; Werner Forman Archive P. 23, 25; Zefa P. 6, 7, 8, 15, 20 Cover.

CHRISTIAN COUNSEL MANUAL

THIS WORK CONTAINS VIEWPOINTS, THAT MANY READERS HAVE NOT HEARD IN THEIR REGULAR CHRISTIAN FELLOWSHIPS. IT IS HOPED, THAT AN OPEN SPIRIT WILL BE BLESSED IN THE READING.

(It is suggested, that the reader read the first 11 pages before getting into the various subjects of the Manual.)

**COUNSEL
IS
MINE
And
SOUND
WISDOM**
(Proverbs 8:14)

<u>Acts 5:38-39</u> ...for if this counsel or this work be of men,
it will come to nought:
But if it be of God, ye cannot overthrow it; lest haply ye be found
even to fight against God.

**Bro. Ray Chiasson
Stand Fast Ministries**

PRESS

Christian Counsel Manual
by Bro. Ray Chiasson – Stand Fast Ministries

Printed in the United States of America

ISBN 1-594672-28-8

Unless otherwise indicated, Bible quotations are taken from the King James Version.

Xulon Press
www.XulonPress.com

Xulon Press books are available in bookstores everywhere,
and on the Web at www.XulonPress.com.

SUGGESTIONS ON THE USE OF THIS MANUAL

1. The blank side of each page is for notes the reader may want to make as regards the page being perused. This could mean the addition of scripture verses, the making of notes, the citing of agreements or disagreements with Manual content and/or whatever.

2. This Manual does not replace God's Word as the Truth and authority - God forbid. No comments cited here by the author are meant to decide how God's Word may, or may not, speak to your spirit. My added comments are only meant to share how God's Word speaks to my spirit.

3. This Manual "uses" only the King James Bible as the main reference source for cited scripture verses. This Bible speaks the loudest to my spirit as being the true translation - as prepared by the commission appointed by King James in the early 1600s. (A discussion of the KJ Bible appears in this work.) Unless otherwise indicated, Bible quotations are taken from BibleGateway.com - King James Bible. Copyright 1995-2003. Many publisher sources used by BibleGateway.com.

The Bible commands the following:

Romans 12:16 Be of the same mind one toward another

1 Corinthians 1:10 Now I beseech you, brethren, by the name of our Lord Jesus Christ, that ye all speak the same thing, and that there be no divisions among you; but that ye be perfectly joined together in the same mind and in the same judgment.

2 Corinthians 13:11 Finally, brethren, farewell. Be perfect, be of good comfort, be of one mind, live in peace; and the God of love and peace shall be with you.

1 Peter 3:8 Finally, be ye all of one mind

You will have to agree, that today's religious climate has done little or nothing to bring the body of Christ in line with these verses - actually the opposite exists today. We have as many different attitudes and postures as there are denominational and non-denominational fellowships. We can thank God, that all this will eventually be to His Glory - thank God, that the playing field will be leveled out, when Christ returns for his bride. We will then be finally one body in Christ—as God has provided for us in His perfect plan.

What we need is less interpretation of God's Word (s), and more obedience to what they tell us to do.

In His Name, Power and Service,

Bro. Ray Chiasson
Stand Fast Ministries
P.O. Box 156
South Lyon, MI 48178
e-mail: ccmrbook@ccahq.com
Web Site: http://www.ccahq.com/~ccmrbook (Manual Digest and Biblical Chat and Counsel Room.

DEDICATION

<u>ACTS 5:38-39</u>

...for if this counsel or this work be of men, it will
come to nought; But if it be of God, ye cannot
overthrow it, lest haply ye be found even to fight
against God.

This counsel, this work, is dedicated to God the Father, His Son
Jesus Christ, and His Holy Spirit. To God be all the glory, now
and forevermore.

TABLE OF CONTENTS

SUMMARY

How does one summarize such a glorious subject as salvation through Jesus Christ of Nazareth, our Lord and Savior-our Lord, Father, and God? Many have tried, and have done very well. My humble contribution follows, and will go against much that has been offered and practiced by denominational "religions". This will not be a criticism or judgment of what they have put forth, because of **Philippians 1:18**. My understanding has nothing to do with pity-parties, complaining, moaning, groaning, and praying for deliverance from all kinds of challenges and the like. It has to do with accepting the peace of Jesus Christ-praising, thanking, and rejoicing in and for all things-much as the angels did that were round about the throne as depicted in **Revelation 5:11-14**. It has to do with being thankful with a constant and joyous attitude of gratitude.

My summary follows the theme of a story recently related to me by a Christian brother, who speaks before various Christian groups. My decision to take a small poetic license with the story as he tells it will be forgiven-I'm sure.

In his talks, the brother tells the story of the underdog American hockey team that met the favored Russian team in the Olympic Gold Medal game some years ago. He nervously watched the first two periods-never knowing what the outcome would be. He witnessed missed shots, penalties, botched-up plays, sloppy passing, crunching body checks, and all the other things, that make up the game of hockey. He lived through, and agonized, over every one of the facets of the game-constantly on edge.

Before the start of the third period, the announcer reported that the game being presented was a tape-delayed broadcast-the Americans had already won. Can you imagine the attitudinal change of my brother as he watched the third and final period? There was no change on the ice-the same array of happenings was going on as they would in any normal hockey game. However, the brother was at peace-he was no longer perched on the edge of his chair (his heart was no longer troubled). He was relaxed, because the result was already a given fact-the battle was won, and the victory was ours. He watched the third period with a thankful and praise-filled spirit, because he knew, that he knew, that he knew.

Now, let us consider the average Christian walk through this valley of the shadow of death-this 70-plus years of life that God has given us here on earth (Ps 90:10). Our walk is filled with all kinds of problems-we look at these things, and are traditionally encouraged to pray for deliverance. We seem to almost enjoy wallowing in the circumstances-while praying to God for relief. We live much of our lives in the flesh, as my dear brother suffered through the first two periods of the hockey game-sitting on the edge of our spiritual seats.

We either forget, or do not fully accept, and stand in faith, on what happened over 2000 years ago on Calvary's cross. Jesus Christ took upon himself the problems of the world, and reconciled us to His Father by his redeeming death on the cross. He gave us a 2000-year tape-delayed victory (if you will). We can now look at the life around us, and regardless of what is going on, we can relax - we can be at peace, because we know, that we know, that we know. We don't have to look at temporal things-we can bask in the spiritual things, because they are eternal. We can now accept and endure all the facets of life's "hockey game", because we know the outcome-we know that they are only a part and parcel of our ultimate victory in Christ. We can now look at life's challenges merely as rungs in the ladder of eternal peace-we can now be thankful and full of worship and praise to God.

We can now actively practice here what we will be doing when we don the white robes of righteousness, and join the "ten thousands times ten thousand, and thousands" of angels-blessing, worshipping, and praising God for all eternity in New Jerusalem. WOW!!

THE VICTORY IS OURS. THE GOLD IS OURS. LET'S ACT LIKE IT!

GALATIANS 5:25 "IF WE LIVE IN THE SPIRIT, LET US WALK IN THE SPIRIT".

PREFACE

1 Corinthians 12:18 But now hath God set the members every one of them in the body, as it hath pleased him.

1 Corinthians 15:10 But by the grace of God I am what I am:

Colossians 4:17 Take heed to the ministry which thou hast received in the Lord, that thou fulfil it.

1 Corinthians 7:24 Brethren, let every man, wherein he is called, therein abide with God.

Galatians 4:16 Am I therefore become your enemy, because I tell you the truth?

Ephesians 4:7 But unto every one of us is given grace according to the measure of the gift of Christ.

1 Corinthians 3:11 For other foundation can no man lay than that is laid, which is Jesus Christ.

1 Corinthians 3:12 Now if any man build upon this foundation gold, silver, precious stones, wood, hay, stubble;

1 Corinthians 3:13 Every man's work shall be made manifest: for the day shall declare it, because it shall be revealed by fire; and the fire shall try every man's work of what sort it is.

1 Corinthians 3:14 If any man's work abide which he hath built thereupon, he shall receive a reward.

1 Corinthians 3:15 If any man's work shall be burned, he shall suffer loss: but he himself shall be saved; yet so as by fire.

Romans 14:5 Let every man be fully persuaded in his own mind.

Romans 15:7 Wherefore receive ye one another, as Christ also received us to the glory of God.

John 13:34 A new commandment I give unto you, That ye love one another;

Colossians 3:12 Put on therefore, as the elect of God, holy and beloved, bowels of mercies, kindness, humbleness of mind, meekness, longsuffering; Col 3:13 Forbearing one another, and forgiving one another,

Matthew 7:1 Judge not, that ye be not judged.

John 8:7 He that is without sin among you, let him first cast a stone at her.

Notes

<u>Acts 5:38</u> And now I say unto you, Refrain from these men, and let them alone: for if this counsel or this work be of men, it will come to nought: Acts 5:39 But if it be of God, ye cannot overthrow it; lest haply ye be found even to fight against God.

<u>Hebrews 4:12</u> For the word of God is quick, and powerful, and sharper than any twoedged sword, piercing even to the dividing asunder of soul and spirit, and of the joints and marrow, and is a discerner of the thoughts and intents of the heart.

<u>Isaiah 55:11</u> So shall my word be that goeth forth out of my mouth: it shall not return unto me void, but it shall accomplish that which I please, and it shall prosper in the thing whereto I sent it.

TO GOD BE THE GLORY

SIMPLICITY

You have heard the old story about a committee, that was appointed to draw a picture of a horse. After hours of deliberation, they came up with a picture of an elephant. The point here is that men can complicate almost anything, if given only half a chance. Men have even complicated the Bible-God's Word. Thank God that his Word endureth forever, and will stand pure and perfect regardless of men's efforts to cause otherwise. The simplicity of God's Word is wonderful as indicated in the following verses:

Ecclesiastes 12:13-14 Let us hear the conclusion of the whole matter: Fear God, and keep his commandments: for this is the whole duty of man. For God shall bring every work into judgment, with every secret thing, whether it be good, or whether it be evil.

2 Corinthians 11:3 But I fear, lest by any means, as the serpent beguiled Eve through his subtlety, so your minds should be corrupted from the simplicity that is in Christ.

2 Corinthians 1:12 For our rejoicing is this, the testimony of our conscience, that in simplicity and godly sincerity, not with fleshly wisdom, but by the grace of God, we have had our conversation in the world, and more abundantly to you-ward.

1 Timothy 1:5 Now the end of the commandment is charity out of a pure heart, and of a good conscience, and of faith unfeigned:

Question: (Since faith cometh by hearing, and hearing by the Word of God—is it possible, that God's Word is the only true key to faith?)

Romans 13:8 Owe no man any thing, but to love one another: for he that loveth another hath fulfilled the law.

Galatians 5:14 For all the law is fulfilled in one word, even in this; Thou shalt love thy neighbour as thyself.

Romans 14:17 For the kingdom of God is not meat and drink; but righteousness, and peace, and joy in the Holy Ghost.

Notes

1 Corinthians 2:2 For I determined not to know any thing among you, save Jesus Christ, and him crucified.

Galatians 6:14 But God forbid that I should glory, save in the cross of our Lord Jesus Christ,

Philippians 3:8 Yea doubtless, and I count all things but loss for the excellency of the knowledge of Christ Jesus my Lord:

Micah 6:8 He hath showed thee, O man, what is good; and what doth the LORD require of thee, but to do justly, and to love mercy, and to walk humbly with thy God?

SIMPLE—ISN'T IT?

PS. There are surely many other verses that speak to the simplicity that is in Christ Jesus- please feel free to search the scriptures, and add those gems to the list.

Believer's Simplicity

There is a company of believers in the Lord Jesus Christ, who do not recognize denominational, non-denominational and/or boundaries or sectarian limitations, that limit the freedom God has provided for their walk with Him. They strive to avoid the non-essential questions, that cause division and controversy.

They refuse as unscriptural all denominational and/or non-denominational names and systems for church"order." Believing that the church is one body, composed of all believers, they refuse to take any name that is not common to all Christians. They meet regularly to study the Scriptures, to fellowship together, to break bread in remembrance of their Lord, and to pray (**Acts 2:42**).

They seek to assemble in the name of the Lord Jesus Christ, and to maintain the apostolic pattern and simplicity, which marked the churches in the days of the apostles (**Romans 12: 4-8).** They seek by God's grace to honor the Lord Jesus, and worship God "in Spirit and in truth" (**John 4:23-24**). They assemble every "first day in the week" to "break bread" (**Acts 20:7**). They desire to eliminate ritual and a stated order of service, however, they want to be led entirely by the Holy Spirit in the order of worship and ministry. They do not wish to silence any of the brethren present, who may be led by the Spirit to pray and offer praise, to give out a hymn, to read or minister the Word, to exhort or to pass the elements of the Lord's Table. No one man presides—only the LORD "in the midst" (**Matthew 18:20**), presides with the leading of the Holy Spirit. They seek to carry out a *scriptural* order of meeting, worship and discipline.

Anyone who, is a child of God through faith in Christ's atoning work on the cross for sin and reception of Him as his own personal Savior, has a right to eat at the Lord's Table— provided he is not living in sin and in deliberate disobedience to God's Word (**Romans 15:7; 1 Corinthians 5:11; 2 John 9-11).**

They adhere to the Scriptures in "not giving flattering titles to men," as "Reverend" and "Father" (**Psalm 111:9**; **Matthew 23:8**). Distinction between "clergy" and "laity" is not recognized (**Revelation. 2:6 & 10**). But they recognize that God bestows gifts to men in His body as He wills. They aim to do away with the traditional custom of a one-man ministry. They refuse all thought of a stipulated remuneration for preaching the Gospel, but hold themselves responsible to help those who are in the Lord's work (**3 John 7**). They take no collections at public meetings.

The Bible being a record of what "holy men of old spake as they were moved by the Holy Ghost," there is consequently "no private interpretation" of the Bible. They are concerned with having the mind of the Spirit in matters of interpretation, because the Spirit has only one interpretation of God's Word. Hence they consider men's creeds as unnecessary.

However, they have certain belief in the doctrines as unfolded in the Scriptures: man's fall and total depravity; his guilty, lost and hopeless condition; the amazing love of God in providing a Savior in His Only Son; the perfection of Christ in His divine and human nature; reconciliation to God through Christ's shed blood, by which alone man is redeemed and not by works, law-keeping, or reformation; Christ's resurrection as proof that God

Notes

accepted His atonement.

They believe that the Christian should have full assurance of his eternal salvation, and that this assurance comes not through those who do not obey the Gospel, who will have their part "in the lake of fire," which is the "second death," eternal punishment, not extinction or restoration. Therefore, they believe in the earnest and loving dissemination of the Gospel of God's Grace.

Ephesians 6:19 And for me, that utterance may be given unto me, that I may open my mouth to make known the mystery of the gospel.

They are not moved by feelings or experiences, but by the Word of God. They see that being saved by Christ's work once for all, a believer can never be lost, but is as safe as though he were in the Holy City New Jerusalem already (**1 John 3:2**). They see, however, that Scripture guards against an abuse of this teaching, because it insists on good works as the fruit of being saved; it teaches the believer to reckon himself dead to sin and alive to God; it clearly shows that the Christian life should be one of devotedness to Christ, and of separation from the way of the world.

They see the hope of Christians is not the betterment of this world system, but the coming of Christ for His own. He will raise the dead and change the living, who will then be caught up to meet Him in the air. Then God will cleanse the world by judgment preparatory to Christ's millennial reign on earth when He will "rule the nations with a rod of iron." But His church will always be with Him (**1 Thessalonians 4:17**).

This is what these Christians believe and practice - what do you believe and *practice*?

INTRODUCTION

1 Corinthians 1:1-13

[1] Paul called to be an apostle of Jesus Christ through the will of God, and Sosthenes our brother,

[2] Unto the church of God which is at Corinth, to them that are sanctified in Christ Jesus, called to be saints, with all that in every place call upon the name of Jesus Christ our Lord, both their's and our's:

[3] Grace be unto you, and peace, from God our Father, and from the Lord Jesus Christ.

[4] I thank my God always on your behalf, for the grace of God which is given you by Jesus Christ;

[5] That in every thing ye are enriched by him, in all utterance, and in all knowledge;

[6] Even as the testimony of Christ was confirmed in you:

[7] So that ye come behind in no gift; waiting for the coming of our Lord Jesus Christ:

[8] Who shall also confirm you unto the end, that ye may be blameless in the day of our Lord Jesus Christ.

[9] God is faithful, by whom ye were called unto the fellowship of his Son Jesus Christ our Lord.

[10] Now I beseech you, brethren, by the name of our Lord Jesus Christ, that ye all speak the same thing, and that there be no divisions among you; but that ye be perfectly joined together in the same mind and in the same judgment.

[11] For it hath been declared unto me of you, my brethren, by them which are of the house of Chloe, that there are contentions among you.

[12] Now this I say, that every one of you saith, I am of Paul; and I of Apollos; and I of Cephas; and I of Christ.

[13] Is Christ divided? was Paul crucified for you? or were ye baptized in the name of Paul?

John 13:34 A new commandment I give unto you, That ye love one another; as I have loved you, that ye also love one another. John 13:35 By this shall all men know that ye are my disciples, if ye have love one to another.

Ephesians 5:2 And walk in love, as Christ also hath loved us,

Notes

1 John 3:11 For this is the message that ye heard from the beginning, that we should love one another.

John 15:12 This is my commandment, That ye love one another, as I have loved you.

1 Thessalonians 4:9 for ye yourselves are taught of God to love one another.

1 Peter 1:22 see that ye love one another with a pure heart fervently:

1 John 4:21 And this commandment have we from him, That he who loveth God love his brother also.

1 John 4:7 Beloved, let us love one another: for love is of God;

1 Peter 2:17 Honour all men. Love the brotherhood.

Hebrews 13:1 Let brotherly love continue.

Romans 13:8 Owe no man any thing, but to love one another:

1 John 4:11 Beloved, if God so loved us, we ought also to love one another.

1 John 4:18 There is no fear in love; but perfect love casteth out fear:

GOD IS LOVE - 1 John 4:8 & 16

KING JAMES BIBLE - PREFERRED

My dear brethren in the Lord,

The following is a sharing of why I stand fast on the King James Bible as the only true inspired Word of God. Much of what follows is taken from the offerings of others as regards this subject; along with some of my own thoughts as well. As you already know my spirit, I added some of my own thoughts along the way. Please take the time to read these many pages, that deal with the comparison of the various bible versions. The exercise may, or may not, speak to your spirits - this is left in the hands of the Holy Spirit, who is our Teacher and Comforter. There are many, who have kept their spirits open to the message given by the King James Bible - that it is the truly inspirational Words of God. I began playing the drums in school bands from the 5th grade through my 2-year Army stint. As a percussionist, there is felt a spiritual beat (a tempo, if you will) threading its way through the King James Bible - I felt no such beat in any other versions.

> **"I am the LORD, I change not."**
> **Malachi 3:6**

God is unchangeable. God's Word is unchangeable too. In **Matthew 24:35**, the Lord Jesus said, "Heaven and earth shall pass away, but my words shall not pass away."

Why then are we so ready to accept changes to God's word in the form of different Bible versions? (That is all they are - versions of an already perfect work, which is the King James Bible) The Authorized King James Bible text has faithfully served the body of Christ for almost 400 years. During this time, and during its translation, it has been viciously and relentlessly attacked. I now hear Christians attacking it too! I've heard preachers and lay people say things like, "it's too hard to read", or "it doesn't properly reflect the true meaning of the original Greek", or "Let's rid ourselves of the thys, thous, and all the eth endings, and such." Another

Notes

point, why all the fuss about the original Greek - which Greek? There are Greek manuscripts galore, including the corrupted manuscripts that the Roman Catholic religion uses. The snide remarks and attacks against this utterly reliable text, the King James Bible, are unfounded. Please note, that I call it the "King James Bible", and not the King James "version" - this is the true Bible, and all the others are merely corrupted "versions."

We must remember, that the Bible is a spiritual book and is understandable only to those, who are led by God's Spirit. It is not possible for the natural man to understand it **(I Corinthians 2:14)**- hence paraphrasing or simplifying it will do no good. Even if we had complete understanding, we are told not to lean on our own understanding. The Bible is not supposed to read like a fairy tale—Peter said, "for we have not followed cunningly devised fables" **(II Peter 1:16**). The words of the Authorized King James Bible are not laborious to read, they are beautiful and full of God's power - there is a wondrous spiritual beat that courses through it. Even the world knows it—the Authorized King James Bible has been listed on Norton Anthology's list of "the world's best literature" for decades.

The new versions have also come up with some dangerous changes to the scriptures - since God is not the Author of confusion, from where are these versions originating?. The Lord God gives us stern warnings about changing His Word:

Revelation 22:18-19, If any man shall add unto these things, God shall add unto him the plagues that are written in this book: And if any man shall take away from the words of the book of this prophecy, God shall take away his part out of the book of life, and out of the holy city, and from the things which are written in this book.

Proverbs 30:5-6, Every word of God is pure: he is a shield unto them that put their trust in him. Add thou not unto his words, lest he reprove thee, and thou be found a liar.

Look at this change in the niv: **John 3:16**, For God so loved the world that He gave his *one and only Son...*

The authorized King James Bible says, **John**

Notes

3:16, For God so loved the world that He gave his *only begotten Son.*

In this instance, the niv changes the scriptures by saying that Jesus is God's "one and only" Son instead of His only begotten Son. This change causes a contradiction in the word of God because God has more than one son according to both the King James (**Genesis 6:2, Job 1:6, John 1:12**) and, lo and behold even in the niv (**Genesis 6:2**). (Is the niv contradicting itself? Sure looks like it, doesn't it?)

I do not buy the line that the inerrant word of God is found only in the originals— which nobody has. I know that God has the power to preserve His Word, and that he wouldn't leave us out in the dark with an "imperfect" translation. In the authorized King James Bible God assembled, and moved with His Spirit, a team of some of the world's best scholars to translate His Word into the world's most popular language, English.

The complete translator's notes of the Authorized King James Bible scholars are not included in today's publishings. This is unfortunate because these notes say a lot about these men— they were humble, loved the word of God, loved the King, were berated by the catholic religion, and they desired a translation for the common man, who was kept in darkness. Some of the translators where killed for their faith. This book was forged in blood, sweat, and tears.

I've heard folks make a big to-do about the italics in the Authorized KJ Bible. Well, unlike many of today's translators, the authorized KJV translators let us know which words they had to add in translating in order to give the full meaning of the original text (these are the words in italics in the KJ Bible). Other translators have added words too—but they don't tell you what they've added. I speak a French and a little Italian, and know that it is oftentimes necessary to rearrange or add words so that the translation makes sense. These men went through the extra trouble of identifying which words they added. That's real scholarship and integrity - their additions did not corrupt the truth of the text.

Let's accept and love only the Authorized KJ Bible, and stand on it. Let's get down to business and read the Word, and stop spending so much time

Notes

reading what others have to say about the Word in other versions, commentaries, Greek lexicons, study bibles, etc. We want the Holy Spirit to talk to us, and he can only speak and teach through the inspired Word of God - the King James Bible.

How many classes have you been in where every student has a different textbook? None. It just doesn't make good sense on a very practical level. We all need to be on the same sheet of music so that we are in harmony - so that we can truly be of one accord. Let's not confuse our brethren by teaching/preaching from the all the other sources, that claim to be the truth - this serves only to confuse, and we know that God is not the Author of confusion. We also know who is the confusion author.

Let's not accept the premise, that the tried and true Authorized King James Bible is somehow outdated, and is to be replaced by other versions, because they are, in fact, only that - versions of the true Bible. A standard test determined the Authorized KJ Bible reading level to be 5th grade because it contains mostly one and two-syllabic words making it one of the easiest to read. We know, that people do not get saved by reading a bible, but we also know, that, once saved, the inspired Word of God is found in the King James Bible - that it contains the Word of life whereby we are to live and grow. The King James Bible is truly the inspired Word of God - why go to corrupted versions for what they purport as truth.

KING JAMES BIBLE COMPARISON
INFORMATION
(MODERN TRANSATIONS ARE A
DECEPTION)

ALL VERSIONS ARE NOT SAYING THE SAME
THING
(VERSES ARE BEING OMITTED AND /OR
OFFERING DIFFERENT SHADES OF
MEANING)

MANY CHRISTIAN BELIEVERS RECOGNIZE
AND ADVERTISE THE JEHOVAH'S WITNESS
"BIBLE" AS THE CORRUPT WORK,

THAT IT IS.

WHAT MOST BELIEVERS DO NOT RECOGNIZE AND ACCEPT IS THE FACT, THAT THE SAME CORRUPTION EXISTS IN THE VARIOUS SO-CALLED "MODERN" VERSIONS OF THE CHRISTIAN BIBLE

(WHAT FOLLOWS IS NOT BY ANY MEANS A COMPLETE COMPARISON, BUT IT IS ENOUGH TO MAKE THE POINT WE ARE SHARING HERE - THE KING JAMES BIBLE IS THE PURE TRUTH - THE INSPIRED WORD OF GOD.

MODERN VERSIONS (NIV & NEW AMERICAN STANDARD) Vs. KING JAMES BIBLE AS REGARDS JESUS CHRIST

I will first cite the King James wording. In the parenthesis following will be found the NIV and NAS wording in that order; if the NIV and NAS are the same, it will be so indicated. The words in **bold print** in the KJ wording are left out of the other two. Is this adding or subtracting from the Word of God? Could this say that Jesus is not the Christ and Lord?

<u>Matthew 1:25</u> she had brought forth her first-born son: and he called his name **JESUS.**
(The other two say "a son")
<u>Matthew 8:29</u> What have we to do with thee, **Jesus, thou** Son of God? (both say: "Son of God.)
<u>Matthew 16:20</u> that they should tell no man that he was **Jesus** the Christ. (Both say only, "the Christ.")
<u>Luke 4:41</u> Thou art **Christ** the Son of God (both say, "You are the son of God."
<u>Luke 7:31</u> And the Lord said (OMITTED in both.)
<u>Luke 22:31</u> And the Lord said (OMITTED in both.)
<u>Luke 23:42</u> And he said unto Jesus, **Lord,** remember me (both say, "Jesus, remember me")
<u>John 4:42</u> **Christ**, the Saviour (Both say only,

Notes

"the Savior")

John 6:69 Christ, **the Son** of the living God. (Both say, "Holy One of God")

John 9:35 Son of **God?** (Both say, "Son of Man")

Acts 16:31 Lord Jesus **Christ** (Both say only, "Lord Jesus")

Romans 1:16 gospel **of Christ** (Both say only "gospel")

1 Corinthians 16:22 Lord **Jesus Christ** (Both say only "Lord")

2 Corinthians 4:6 Jesus Christ (Both omit the word, "Jesus")

2 Corinthians 11:31 Lord Jesus **Christ** (Both say only "Lord Jesus")

Ephesians 3:9 who created all things **by Jesus Christ**: (both say, "created all things")

Ephesians 3:14 the Father **of our Lord Jesus Christ** (The other two versions say only, "Father")

2 Corinthians 4:6 & 5:18 Jesus Christ. (Both say only "Christ")

Colossians 2:1 Lord Jesus Christ. (OMITTED in both)

Colossians 1:28 Christ **Jesus:** (Both say only "Christ")

1 Thessalonians 2:19 Lord **Jesus** Christ (Both omit "Lord Jesus")

There are many more like examples of changes made by the various "modern" versions, but the above should suffice to make the point taken here. "Lord Jesus Christ" in the same reference being made? Hmmm!! **Question:** Why is it, that the various modern versions have such a problem in combining the words "Lord, Jesus and Christ?

MORE COMPARISONS

Let us look at some other comparisons made between the King James Bible and the NIV—the KJ will appear first; followed by the NIV.

Mathew 9:13 for I am not come to call the righteous, but sinners to repentance. (**NIV:** for I have not come to call the righteous but sinners.

Matthew 18:11 For the Son of man is come to save that which was lost. (**NIV**: OMITTED)

Matthew 19:17 Why callest thou me good (**NIV**: Why do you ask me What is good?)

Matthew 25:13 ye know neither the day nor the hour wherein the Son of man cometh. (**NIV**: You do not know the day or the hour)

Matthew 10:24 how hard is it for them that trust in riches to enter into the kingdom of God! (**NIV**: How hard it is to enter the kingdom of God)

Luke 2:33 And Joseph and his mother (**NIV**: the child's father and Mother)

Luke 4:4 That man shall not live by bread alone, but by every word of God. (**NIV**: Man does not live on bread alone.)

Luke 4:8 Get thee behind me, Satan (**NIV**: OMITTED)

John 6:47 He that believeth on me hath everlasting life. (**NIV**: He that believeth on me hath everlasting life.

John 8:9 And they which heard it, being convicted by their own conscience, went out (**NIV**: those who heard began to go away)

John 9:4 I must work the works of him that sent me (**NIV**: We must do the works of him that sent me)

John 10:30 I and my Father are one. (**NIV**: I and the Father are one)

Acts 2:30 that of the fruit of his loins, according to the flesh, he would raise up Christ to sit on his throne; (**NIV**: he would place one of his descendants on his throne)

Acts 8:37 If thou believest with all thine heart, thou mayest. And he answered and said, I believe that Jesus Christ is the Son of God. (**NIV**: OMITTED)

Acts 23:9 let us not fight against God. (**NIV**: OMITTED)

Romans 13:9 Thou shalt not bear false witness (**NIV**: OMITTED)

Colossians 1:14 In whom we have redemption through his blood, even the forgiveness of sins: (**NIV**: In whom we have redemption, the forgiveness of sins)

1 Timothy 3:16 God was manifest in the flesh (**NIV**: He appeared in the flesh)

1 Timothy 6:5 Perverse disputings of men of

Notes

corrupt minds, and destitute of the truth, supposing that gain is godliness: from such withdraw thyself. (**NIV**: "from such withdraw thyself" is OMITTED)

1 Peter 1:22 Seeing ye have purified your souls in obeying the truth through the Spirit (**NIV**: "through the Spirit" is OMITTED)

1 John 4:3 And every spirit that confesseth not that Jesus Christ is come in the flesh is not of God (**NIV**: But every spirit that does not acknowledge Jesus is not from God)

Revelation 5:14 four and twenty elders fell down and worshipped him that liveth for ever and ever. (**NIV**: The elders fell down and worshipped)

Revelation 20:9 and fire came down from God out of heaven (**NIV**: Fire came down from heaven)

Revelation 21:24 And the nations of them which are saved shall walk in the light of it (**NIV**: The nations shall walk by its light)

This is only a small sample of the many differences found in the NIV and NAS versions. Multiply these by the many other versions in existence, and what do we find? We find confusion, and we know that God is not the Author of confusion. It is left up to you dear readers just who the author of confusion is, and why this confusion has been foisted on believers in Christ Jesus. You may contact me directly for my input here.

The above Comparison exercises show the reasons for the changes and alterations made by the "modern" bible versions:

1. They color and/or change the emphasis placed on the true KJ Bible words;
2. They even change words;
3. They add and/or detract from the KJ bible'
4. They bring the emphasis away from God and upon ourselves;
5. The desire is to cause confusion in the one body of Christ.

THE FOLLOWING SHOWS AT LEAST 200 CHANGES EXAMINED

Why is there so much controversy about the

King James Bible? Modern Christian scholarship minds (in their high-toned attitudes) hve changed the Greek Textus, from which the King James translation was translated—it was done in at least 6000 places. This is why we have so many omissions, and changes of the KJ text as found in the modern versions of the Bible. The moderns counted as not authentic the KJ words, that were found in brackets; that were in parentheses; that were italicized.

The following is a list of at least 200 of these changes. Compare them to the ones changed in your Bible. If nothing else, it may rekindle your interest in reading your Bible more and more. This might help you in putting more of your faith in God's Word than what you might hear from any other source.

MATTHEW

1:25—(FIRSTBORN) is out. Speaking of the Lord Jesus.
5:44— (BLESS THEM THAT CURSE YOU) is out.
6:13—(KINGDOM, POWER, GLORY) is out.
6:27—(STATURE) is changed to span of life.
6:33—(OF GOD) is out. Referring to the kingdom-
8:29—(JESUS) is out. As Son of God.
9:13—(TO REPENTANCE) is out. Calling sinners—
12:35—(OF THE HEART) is out. Good treasure—
12:47—(VERSE IS OUT) About Christ's mother.
13:51—(JESUS SAID UNTO THEM and LORD) is out.
15:8 —(DRAWETH UNTO ME WITH THEIR MOUTH) is out.
16:3 —(O YE HYPOCRITES) is out.
16:20—(JESUS) is out.
17:21—(VERSE IS OUT). About prayer and fasting.
18:11—(VERSE IS OUT). Tells Jesus came to save.
19:9 —(LAST 11 WORDS ARE OUT). About adultery.
19:17—(GOD) is out. None good but (God).
20:7 —(WHATSOEVER IS RIGHT RECEIVE) is out.

Notes

20:16—(MANY BE CALLED BUT FEW CHOSEN) is out.

20:22—(BAPTIZED WITH CHRIST'S BAPTISM) is out.

21:44—(VERSE IS OUT) About Christ the stone.

23:14—(VERSE IS OUT) Woe scribes and hypocrites.

25:13—(WHEREIN THE SON OF MAN COMETH) is out.

27:35—(FULFILLED SPOKEN BY THE PROPHET) is out.

27:54—(THE SON OF GOD) is A SON of God.

28:2 —(FROM THE DOOR) is out.

28:9 —(THEY WENT TO TELL HIS DISCIPLES) is out.

MARK

1:1 —(SON OF GOD) is out in Williams, Godspeed, Panin, Nestle, New World, Westcott & Hort.

1:14—(OF THE KINGDOM) is out. Jesus gospel—

1:31—(IMMEDIATELY) is out. The fever left—

2:17—(TO REPENTANCE) is out. Call sinners—

6:11—(MORE TOLERABLE FOR SODOM & GOMORRHA) is out.

6:16—(FROM THE DEAD) is out. John is risen—

6:33—(HIM) is changed to them.

7:8 —(WASHING OF POTS AND CUPS) is out.

7:16—(VERSE IS OUT) About having an ear to hear.

9:24—(LORD) is out. A believer called Him Lord.

9:42—(IN ME) is out. Little ones that believe—

9:44—(VERSE IS OUT) About fire not quenched.

9:46—(VERSE IS OUT) Where worm dieth not.

9:49—(EVERY SACRIFICE SHALL BE SALTED) is out.

10:21—(TAKE UP THE CROSS) is out. Jesus said—

10:24—(FOR THEM THAT TRUST IN RICHES) is out.

11:10—(IN THE NAME OF THE LORD) is out.

11:26—(VERSE IS OUT) If ye do not forgive, etc.

13:14—(SPOKEN BY DANIEL THE PROPHET) is out.

13:33—(AND PRAY) is out, or in italics.

Notes

14:68—(AND THE COCK CREW) is out.

15:28—(VERSE IS OUT) Scripture was fulfilled, etc.

15:39—(THE SON OF GOD) is A SON of God.

16:9-20—(12 VERSES ARE OUT) in some Bibles.

LUKE

1:28—(BLESSED ART THOU AMONG WOMEN) is out.

2:33—(JOSEPH) is changed to father.

2:43—(JOSEPH AND HIS MOTHER) is changed to parents.

4:4 —(BUT BY EVERY WORD OF GOD) is out.

4:8 —(GET THEE BEHIND ME SATAN) is out.

4:41—(THE CHRIST) is out. The Son of God.

6:48—(FOUNDED UPON A ROCK) is well built.

7:31—(AND THE LORD SAID) is out.

9:54—(EVEN AS ELIJAH DID) is out.

9:55—(YE KNOW NOT WHAT MANNER OF SPIRIT) is out.

9:56—(SON OF MAN IS COME TO SAVE LIVES) is out.

11:2-4—(MUCH IS OMITTED FROM THE LORD'S PRAYER)

11:29—(THE PROPHET) is out. About Jonah.

17:36—(VERSE IS OUT) One taken, another left.

21:4 —(CAST IN UNTO THE OFFERINGS OF GOD) is out.

22:20—(VERSE IS OUT) Out in NEB, and RSV.

22:31—(AND THE LORD SAID) is out.

22:64—(THEY STRUCK HIM ON THE FACE) is out.

23:17—(WHOLE VERSE IS OUT) in many Bibles.

23:38—(LETTERS OF GREEK, LATIN, HEBREW) is out.

23:42—(LORD) is out. Remember me, etc.

23:45—(SUN WAS ECLIPSED) in Moffatt and NEB.

24:3 —(OF THE LORD JESUS) is out.

24:12—(VERSE IS OUT) Peter's testimony.

24:40—(VERSE IS OUT) Christ showed them hands, feet.

24:49—(OF JERUSALEM) is out.

24:51)CARRIED UP INTO HEAVEN) is out.

24:6 —(HE IS NOT HERE, BUT IS RISEN) is out.

Notes

JOHN

1:14—(BEGOTTEN) is out in 1:18, 3:16, 3:18.

1:27—(PREFERRED BEFORE ME) is out. Jesus is)

3:13—(WHICH IS IN HEAVEN) is out.

3:15—(SHOULD NOT PERISH) is out.

4:42—(THE CHRIST) is out.

5:3 —(WAITING FOR MOVING OF THE WATER) is out.

5:4 —(VERSE IS OUT) Pool of Bethesda.

6:47—(ON ME) is out. He that believes—

6:69—(THAT CHRIST THE SON) is out.

7:53—(TO 8:11) is out, in brackets or italics.

8:36—(FATHER) is out. Changed to He.

9:35—(SON OF GOD) is out. Is Son of Man.

11:41—(WHERE THE DEAD WAS LAID) is out.

16:16—(BECAUSE I GO TO THE FATHER) is out.

17:12—(IN THE WORLD) is out.

20:29—(THOMAS) is out.

ACTS

2:30—(ACCORDING TO FLESH RAISE UP CHRIST) is out.

7:30—(OF THE LORD) is out. Angel—

7:37—(HIM SHALL YE HEAR) is out. Christ—

8:37—(VERSE IS OUT) or in brackets, or italics.

9:5-6—(MUCH IS OMITTED) Concerning God's call.

10:6 —(WHAT THOU OUGHTEST TO DO) More is out.

15:18—(KNOWN UNTO GOD HIS WORKS) More is out.

16:31—(CHRIST) is out.

17:26—(BLOOD) is out.

20:25—(OF GOD) is out. The kingdom—

20:32—(BRETHREN) is out.

23:9 —(LET US NOT FIGHT AGAINST GOD) is out.

24:6-8—(MUCH IS OMITTED) or in brackets or italics.

24:15—(OF THE DEAD) is out. Resurrection—

28:16—(HALF OF VERSE IS OUT) in italics or brackets.

28:29—(VERSE IS OUT) in italics or brackets.

ROMANS

1:16—(OF CHRIST) is out or in italics, brackets.
1:29—(FORNICATION) is out.
5:2 —(BY FAITH) out in Moffatt, RSV, and NEB.
8:1 —(LAST 10 WORDS ARE OUT) or in italics.
9:28—(IN RIGHTEOUSNESS) is out.
10:15—(OF PEACE) is out. Gospel—
10:17—(OF GOD) is out. Christ is substituted.
11:6 —(LAST 18 WORDS ARE OMITTED)
13:9 —(SHALL NOT BEAR FALSE WITNESS) is out.
14:6 —(15 WORDS ARE OUT) Regarding the day.
14:21—(OFFENDED, MADE WEAK) is out.
15:29—(OF THE GOSPEL) is out.
16:24—(WHOLE VERSE IS OUT) in italics or brackets.

I CORINTHIANS

1:14—(I THANK GOD) is out in many Bibles.
5:7 —(FOR US) is out. Christ sacrificed—
6:20—(LAST 7 WORDS ARE OUT) Your spirit, etc.
7:5 —(FASTING) is out. Joined with prayer.
7:39—(BY THE LAW) is out. The wife is bound—
10:28—(THE EARTH IS THE LORD'S) is out, and more.
11:24—(TAKE EAT) is out. This is my body—
11:29—(LORD'S) is out, referring to the body.
15:47—(THE LORD) is out. Lord from heaven.
16:22—(JESUS CHRIST) is out.
16:23—(CHRIST) is out.

II CORINTHIANS

4:6 —(JESUS) is out.
5:10—(THE LORD) is out.
5:18—(JESUS) is out, or in italics.
11:31—(CHRIST) is out, or in italics.

GALATIANS

1:15—(GOD) is out.
3:1 —(THAT YE SHOULD NOT OBEY TRUTH) is out.
3:17—(IN CHRIST) is out.
4:7 —(THROUGH CHRIST) is out.
6:15—(IN CHRIST JESUS) is out.

Notes

33

Notes

6:17—(LORD) is out.

EPHESIANS
3:9 —(BY JESUS CHRIST) is out. God created—
3:14—(OF OUR LORD JESUS CHRIST) is out.
5:30—(OF HIS FLESH AND OF HIS BONES) is out.
6:1 —(IN THE LORD) is out. Obey parents—
6:10—(MY BRETHREN) is out.

PHILIPPIANS
3:16—(LET US MIND THE SAME THING) is out.

COLOSSIANS
1:2 —(THE LORD JESUS CHRIST) is out.
1:14—(THROUGH HIS BLOOD) is out, or in italics.
1:28—(JESUS) is out.
2:11—(OF THE SINS OF) is out.
3:6 —(SONS OF DISOBEDIENCE) is out.

I THESSALONIANS
1:1 —(FROM GOD OUR FATHER AND LORD JESUS) is out.
2:19—(CHRIST) is out.
3:11—(CHRIST) is out, or in italics.
3:13—(CHRIST) is out, or in italics.
II THESSALONIANS
1:8 —(CHRIST) is out, or in italics.

I TIMOTHY
1:17—(WISE) is out. The only wise God.
2:7 —(IN CHRIST) is out, or in italics.
3:16—(GOD) is out. Manifest in the flesh.
4:12—(IN SPIRIT) is out.
6:5 —(FROM SUCH WITHDRAW THYSELF) is out.

II TIMOTHY
1:11—(OF THE GENTILES) is out.
4:1 —(LORD) is out.
4:22—(JESUS CHRIST) is out, or in italics.

TITUS
1:4 —(THE LORD) is out, or in italics.

Notes

PHILEMON
1:6 —(JESUS) is out.
1:12—(RECEIVE HIM) is out.

HEBREWS
1:3 —(BY HIMSELF) is out. Purged our sins—
2:7 —(SET HIM OVER THE WORKS OF THY HANDS) is out.
3:1 —(CHRIST) is out.
7:21—(AFTER ORDER OF MELCHIZEDEK) is out.
10:30—(SAITH THE LORD) is out.
10:34—(IN HEAVEN) is out.
11:11—(WAS DELIVERED OF A CHILD) is out. Sarah—

JAMES
5:16—(FAULTS) is changed to SINS. (Wrong Greek text.)

I PETER
1:22—(THROUGH THE SPIRIT) is out.
4:1 —(FOR US) is out. Christ suffered—
4:14—(LAST 15 WORDS ARE OUT) or in italics.
5:10—(JESUS) is out, or in italics.
5:11—(GLORY AND DOMINION) is out of some Bibles.

II PETER
2:17—(FOREVER) is out, or in italics.
3:9 —(US IS CHANGED TO YOU) Destroys meaning.

I JOHN
1:7 —(CHRIST) is out.
2:7 —(FROM THE BEGINNING) is out.
4:3 —(CHRIST IS COME IN THE FLESH) is out.
4:9 —(BEGOTTEN) is out in some versions.
4:19—(HIM) is out, or in italics. We love—
5:7-8—(MANY WORDS ARE OUT OR CHANGED)
5:13—(LAST 13 WORDS ARE OUTJUDE
1:25—(WISE) is out. Referring to God.

Notes

REVELATION

1:8 —(THE BEGINNING AND THE END) is out.

1:11—(TEN WORDS ARE OUT) Alpha and Omega, etc.

2:13—(THY WORKS) is out.

5:14—(HIM THAT LIVETH FOREVER AND EVER) is out.

6:1 —(AND SEE) is out in 3, 5, 7 also.

8:13—(ANGEL IS EAGLE) Greek text says "angel."

11:17—(AND ART TO COME) is out.

12:12—(INHABITERS OF) is out. The earth.

12:17—(CHRIST) is out.

14:5 —(BEFORE THE THRONE OF GOD) is out.

16:17—(OF HEAVEN) is out.

20:9 —(GOD OUT OF) is out. Fire came from—

20:21—(GOD IS CHANGED TO THRONE)

21:24—(OF THEM WHICH ARE SAVED) is out. Nations—

24 BIBLE VERSIONS EXAMINED

Words omitted, in brackets, parentheses, or italics are counted as not

Authentic according to BRAINWASHED modern versions.

New English New Testament (Omissions)......197 out of 200

New International Version.................195 out of 200

Revised Standard New Testament.............189 out of 200

Berkeley Version New Testament.............185 out of 200

Weymouth's in Modern Speech N.T............184 out of 200

New American Standard New Testament........183 out of 200

Good News for Modern Man N.T...............182 out of 200

Williams' New Testament....................180 out of 200

Ivan Panin's Numeric New Testament.........180 out of 200

Goodspeed's American Translation N.T.......179 out of 200

Moffatt's New Translation N.T..............175 out of 200

Wuest's Expanded Translation N.T...........169 out of 200

Amplified New Testament....................165 out of 200

Twentieth Century New Testament............161 out of 200

Phillip's New Testament....................142 out of 200

Darby's Translation New Testament..........138 out of 200

Living New Testament Paraphrased...........130 out of 200

New Confraternity New Testament............119 out of 200

Norlie's New Translation N.T.............. 62 out of 200

Lamsa's Eastern Text New Testament......... 49 out of 200

John Wesley's Translation N.T.............. 43 out of 200

Martin Luther's German New Testament....... 0 out of 200

King James Version New Testament........... 0 out of 200

Textus Receptus (King James Greek) N.T..... 0 out of 200

(Almost all of the above comparison information was garnered from other writers - it is hoped, that they will suffer this use of their work.)

(NOTE: Anyone interested in more comparison information needs only to contact me - my address information is found on the Instruction page)

Notes

Notes

COUNSEL IS MINE

This effort addresses Christian counseling. It seems that more and more believers are seeking counseling. Today's fast-moving world seems to affect many Christians negatively, and they seek counseling in order to be delivered from the things that are bothering them. You, the reader of this Manual, can be assured of one thing-there is no magical answer involved. The answer is at everyone's disposal, and is as close as your Bible. God has provided *all* answers in His Word.

Before we delve into the various challenges for which believers seek counseling, let us look at this thing called "counseling". Just what is Christian counseling (or what should it be?) Counsel is defined as advice, instruction, deliberate purpose, design, intent, plan. For the Christian believer, all of these definitions fit the spirit of God's Word. It speaks to us that Christian counseling is no different than preaching, teaching, ministering, exhorting,, evangelizing, or any other activity that a believer is called upon to fulfill. All of these ministries should have one single aim; to rightly divide the Word of Truth, the Word of God. **2 Timothy 2:15** tells us to rightly divide the Word of Truth. To divide means to distribute, to share, to give of, to pour out and/or spread, to send out, to circulate, to disseminate, to scatter. In all our research we have not found one definition, that even hints at interpreting of passing opinion on, or the like. This is why you will find, that we counsel with God's Words—not man's. God said, that his Word shall not return to him void—we haven't found this attributed to the words of men anywhere. In a work such as this comments are often made to explain how certain scriptures speak to my spirit as regards clarification. Although this is done in order to make easy the dividing of the truth, you are free to decide for yourself—to be fully persuaded in your own mind. We often find, that the reason many believers remain in bondage is, that they have accepted another's opinion (s) about scripture. We share comments in order to give our view—we do not ask, that you accept as truth how the scriptures speak to us. We only ask, that you filter out what you have been previously led to believe by others, and truly allow the Holy Spirit to speak directly to you through God's Word—not the words of others (including me.)

There are many scriptures that talk about counsel, counseling, and counselor. It speaks to me, that God's Word clearly states, that he is the Counselor—His Word is the only true counsel.

1 Peter 4:11 If any man speak, let him speak as the oracles of God;

Comment: An oracle is the way by which God reveals his hidden knowledge, or makes known his divine purpose. God does this through his Word, and his Holy Spirit provides the understanding. God's Word is his oracle. If we are to speak as the oracles of God, then any ministry, which we are called upon to fulfill, *must* be carried out using God's Word—this includes Christian counseling.

Please allow the sharing of scripture verses that support this position:

Proverbs 8:14 Counsel is mine, and sound wisdom: I am understanding; I have strength.

Isaiah 9:6 and his name shall be called Wonderful, Counsellor,

Isaiah 46:10 My counsel shall stand,

Question: Is this saying that man's counsel will not stand?

Psalm 119:24 Thy testimonies also are my delight and my counsellors.

Psalm 73:24 Thou shalt guide me with thy counsel,

Question: Where does it say that man's counsel will guide us?

Proverbs 19:21 There are many devices in a man's heart; nevertheless the counsel of the LORD, that shall stand.

Acts 20:27 For I have not shunned to declare unto you all the counsel of God.

Ephesians 1:11 In whom also we have obtained an inheritance, being predestinated according to the purpose of him who worketh all things after the

Notes

counsel of his own will:

Psalm 33:11 The counsel of the LORD standeth for ever,

Question: Is he saying here again that man's counsel will not stand?

Proverbs 20:18 Every purpose is established by counsel:

Note: Only God's Word can establish a purpose-counsel must be God's Word.

Hebrews 6:17 Wherein God, willing more abundantly to show unto the heirs of promise the immutability of his counsel, confirmed it by an oath:

Comment: Immutability means unchangeability—only God's Word is forever.

Isaiah 5:19 let the counsel of the Holy One of Israel draw nigh and come,

Isaiah 28:29 This also cometh forth from the LORD of hosts, which is wonderful in counsel,

Question: Does scripture say, that any man is wonderful in counsel?

Jeremiah 32:19 Great in counsel, and mighty in work: (Speaking of God).

Jeremiah 23:22 But if they had stood in my counsel, and had caused my people to hear my words,

Comment: Counsel and his Words are joined.

The above scriptures speak loudly, that God is the Counselor—His Word is the counsel. It is this understanding that tells us to advise believers, who are seeking counsel, to find scriptures that apply to their challenge—then stand on them in faith. We also encourage believers to stand on God's Word, because of: **Hebrews 4:12** For the word of God is quick, and powerful, and sharper than any twoedged sword, piercing even to the dividing asunder of soul and spirit, and of the joints and marrow, and is a discerned of the thoughts and intents of the heart. Do you know of anywhere in the Bible, where men's words are described in like manner? In counseling we share many scriptures with the believer, who is seeking counsel. Then we suggest that the believer settle on scripture (s) that speaks to him, and stand fast.

The believer knows where to find the answer to any problem.

The unbeliever knows only to find problems in any answers.

Isaiah 55:11 So shall my word be that goeth forth out of my mouth: it shall not return unto me void, but it shall accomplish that which I please, and it shall prosper in the thing whereto I sent it.

Proverbs 30:5 Every word of God is pure: he is a shield unto them that put their trust in him.

Proverbs 30:6 Add thou not unto his words, lest he reprove thee, and thou be found a liar.

Question: Are we being told to look for our answers only in God's Word?

We also suggest that the scriptures be recited aloud, for "out of the abundance of the heart the mouth speaketh" (**Matthew 12:34**). Saying what you claim aloud will speak more strongly to your heart and spirit, and will eventually become your belief and deliverance. If you utter words according to the Word of God, his Will can become alive in your spirit.

We always start our counseling with a few questions.

A. Are you saved?

If the answer is "no", we state that this their main challenge. Their other problems are nothing compared to not being born-again. We then witness Jesus Christ.

B. If they are saved, we ask: "Do you believe that God wrote the Bible:? If they answer "no", we offer our belief that the Bible is the inspired Word of God. He did The "writing", and inspired men put the Words on paper. If we believe, that men wrote the Words, then we can argue with what the Words say. If we accept, that God wrote the Words, there can be no argument—only obedience.

C. Do you believe your answer is in the Bible? If the answer is an insistent "no", we lovingly advise the seeker to look to someone else for help. We always go to God's Word for the answers—if

Notes

Notes

the believer does not accept his answer is in the Bible, we can't help him.

After setting the scene, we then ask if the believer has thanked God. Very few have done so—in fact, this question surprises them. They usually ask if they are supposed to thank God for their problem. Our answer is "no"—the Word tells us in **Ephesians 5:20**, **Colossians 3:17**, and **1 Thessalonians 5:18** to give thanks in and for all things. A simple, "Thank you, Father, in the Name of Jesus" will suffice to put one in line with God's Word. When we are in line with God's Will, his promises are manifested in our lives.

We are now going to share various challenges and problems brought by believers seeking relief. Most of the requests for counseling fall into certain categories-we will address them with the appropriate scriptures, which will provide the answers. We will share comments, when led to do so—indicating how they speak to us in relation to any problems presented. As we do in all our ministering, we begin by claiming: **Psalm 141:3** Set a watch, O LORD, before my mouth; keep the door of my lips. **Acts 5:38** And now I say unto you, Refrain from these men, and let them alone: for if this counsel or this work be of men, it will come to nought: **Acts 5:39** But if it be of God, ye cannot overthrow it; lest haply ye be found even to fight against God. We are content to give God all the glory. The fact that God has ordained this as part of his Will grants us the boldness needed to launch this particular boat into deeper waters. As our Lord said in: **Mark 4:35** Let us pass over unto the other side.

WELCOME ABOARD.

REJOICE

We find many believers walking around with their chins on the ground. Their faces show a sadness, which reflects a fleshly response to happenings around them. Look around you, when you are assembled with believers. If you see sadness, exhort to rejoice in the Lord. When believers come to us seeking deliverance from sadness, we first get vocal agreement on the thank-you scriptures (**Ephesians 5:20; Colossians 3:17; 1 Thessalonians 5:18**)—then we share the following:

1 Thessalonians 5:16 Rejoice evermore.

Philippians 3:1 Finally, my brethren, rejoice in the Lord.

Philippians 4:4 Rejoice in the Lord always: and again I say, Rejoice.

Psalm 118:24 This is the day which the LORD hath made; we will rejoice and be glad in it.

Romans 5:2 By whom also we have access by faith into this grace wherein we stand, and rejoice in hope of the glory of God.

1 Peter 4:13 But rejoice, inasmuch as ye are partakers of Christ's sufferings; that, when his glory shall be revealed, ye may be glad also with exceeding joy.

Philippians 2:16 Holding forth the word of life; that I may rejoice in the day of Christ,

Deuteronomy 26:11 And thou shalt rejoice in every good thing which the LORD thy God hath given unto thee

Psalm 2:11 Serve the LORD with fear, and rejoice with trembling.

Matthew 5:12 Rejoice, and be exceeding glad: for great is your reward in heaven

Revelation 19:7 Let us be glad and rejoice, and give honour to him

Habakkuk 3:18 Yet I will rejoice in the LORD, I will joy in the God of my salvation.

Psalm 119:14 I have rejoiced in the way of thy testimonies, as much as in all riches.

Comment: Please note that there are no conditions listed in our rejoicing - we are not exhorted to

Notes

rejoice only when things are going well. When a believer claims aloud the rejoice verses, it will be impossible to be other that joyful regardless of circumstances. Does it say anywhere in God's Word, that we are to moan and groan? When we stand fast on this position and posture, we are often met with the following verse in rebuttal:

12
James 4:9 Be afflicted, and mourn, and weep: let your laughter be turned to mourning, and your joy to heaviness.

This verse seems on the surface to be in conflict with James the rejoice scripture verses cited earlier - they are not. We believe, that God's Word is perfect - there are no conflicts, disagreements and contentions in the Words of the Holy Bible. Would our perfect God give us an imperfect Book of Instructions to follow? He would and did not! Let's complete the statement in **James 4:9** with: **James 4:10** Humble yourselves in the sight of the Lord, and he shall lift you up.

It speaks here, that the key is the end result. In other words, it is acceptable to cut the proverbial engine for a short while. However, the time comes, when we must once again power up and rejoice. It is easier to rejoice in the face of adversity, when we stand fast in faith on **Philippians 4:8**. Do you remember this verse? Just in case you forgot, here it is: **Philippians 4:8.** Finally, brethren, whatsoever things are true, whatsoever things are honest, whatsoever things are just, whatsoever things are pure, whatsoever things are lovely, whatsoever things are of good report; if there be any virtue, and if there be any praise, think on these things. **Note**: The only things, that are true, honest, just, pure, lovely, and are of good report are The Words of God - found in the Holy Bible.

THERE ARE OVER 1100 SCRIPTURE VERSES, THAT TELL US TO REJOICE, BE GLAD, BE HAPPY, BE JOYFUL. (How times must we be told)

JUST WHO ARE WE IN CHRIST JESUS ?

1. We are saved

<u>Acts 16:31</u> And they said, Believe on the Lord Jesus Christ, and thou shalt be saved, and thy house.

<u>Romans 8:24</u> For we are saved by hope:

<u>Romans 10:9</u> That if thou shalt confess with thy mouth the Lord Jesus, and shalt believe in thine heart that God hath raised him from the dead, thou shalt be saved.

<u>Romans 10:13</u> For whosoever shall call upon the name of the Lord shall be saved.

<u>Titus 3:5</u> Not by works of righteousness which we have done, but according to his mercy he saved us, by the washing of regeneration, and renewing of the Holy Ghost;

11. We are born again.

<u>2 Corinthians 5:17</u> Therefore if any man be in Christ, he is a new creature: old things are passed away; behold, all things are become new.

<u>Galatians 6:15</u> For in Christ Jesus neither circumcision availeth any thing, nor uncircumcision, but a new creature.

<u>Ephesians 2:5</u> Even when we were dead in sins, hath quickened us together with Christ, (by grace ye are saved;)

<u>James 1:18</u> Of his own will begat he us with the word of truth,

<u>1 Peter1:23</u> Being born again, not of corruptible seed, but of incorruptible, by the word of God, which liveth and abideth for ever.

111. We are chosen.

<u>1 Peter 2:9</u> But ye are a chosen generation, a royal priesthood, an holy nation, a peculiar people;

<u>Ephesians 1:4</u> According as he hath chosen us in him before the foundation of the world.

1V. We are heirs of God, and joint-heirs with Christ.

<u>Romans 8:17</u> And if children, then heirs; heirs of God, and joint-heirs with Christ;

Notes

V. We are the light of the world.

Matthew 5:14 Ye are the light of the world. A city that is set on an hill cannot be hid.

VI. We are the salt of the earth.

Matthew 5:13 Ye are the salt of the earth:

VII. We are free.

John 8:32 And ye shall know the truth, and the truth shall make you free.

Galatians 5:1 Stand fast therefore in the liberty wherewith Christ hath made us free,

Romans 8:2 For the law of the Spirit of life in Christ Jesus hath made me free from the law of sin and death.

VIII. We are blessed.

Ephesians 1:3 Blessed be the God and Father of our Lord Jesus Christ, who hath blessed us with all spiritual blessings in heavenly places in Christ:

John 20:29 blessed are they that have not seen, and yet have believed.

Matthew 5:3-11 (Please look up these verses in you Bible)

IX. We are content.

Philippians 4:11 for I have learned, in whatsoever state I am, therewith to be content.

X. We are protected.

2 Peter 2:9 The Lord knoweth how to deliver the godly out of temptations,

2 Timothy 4:18 And the Lord shall deliver me from every evil work, and will preserve me unto his heavenly kingdom: to whom be glory for ever and ever. Amen.

Ephesians 6:10-18 (Please check out these scriptures on you own.).

XI. We are comforted.

2 Corinthians 1:3-4 Blessed be God, even the Father of our Lord Jesus Christ, the Father of mercies, and the God of all comfort; Who comforteth us in all our tribulation, that we may be able to comfort them which are in any trouble, by the comfort wherewith we ourselves are comforted of God.

2 Corinthians 7:4 I am filled with comfort, I am exceeding joyful in all our tribulation.

XII. We have power.

Luke 10:19 Behold, I give unto you power to tread on serpents and scorpions, and over all the power of the enemy:

Matthew 9:8 But when the multitude saw it, they marvelled, and glorified God, which had given such power unto men.

Philippians 4:13 I can do all things through Christ which strengtheneth me.

John 1:12 But as many as received him, to them gave he power to become the sons of God, even to them that believe on his name:

Romans 8:37 Nay, in all these things we are more than conquerors through him that loved us.

Acts 1:8 But ye shall receive power, after that the Holy Ghost is come upon you:

XIII. We have eternal life.

John 3:15 That whosoever believeth in him should not perish, but have eternal life.

Romans 6:23 For the wages of sin is death; but the gift of God is eternal life through Jesus Christ our Lord.

XIV. We have everlasting life.

John 3:16 that whosoever believeth in him should not perish, but have everlasting life.

XV. All things are yours.

1 Corinthians 3:21 Therefore let no man glory in men. For all things are yours;

XVI. Nothing is impossible to you.

Mark 9:23 Jesus said unto him, If thou canst believe, all things are possible to him that believeth.

Matthew 17:20 and nothing shall be impossible unto you.

XVII. Our names are written in heaven.

Luke 10:20 Notwithstanding in this rejoice not,

Notes

Notes

that the spirits are subject unto you; but rather rejoice, because your names are written in heaven.

XVIII. We will never die.

<u>John 11:26</u> And whosoever liveth and believeth in me shall never die.

XIX. We will never hunger of thirst.

<u>John 6:35</u> And Jesus said unto them, I am the bread of life: he that cometh to me shall never hunger; and he that believeth on me shall never thirst.

XX. The kingdom of God is within us.

<u>Luke 17:21</u> Neither shall they say, Lo here! or, lo there! for, behold, the kingdom of God is within you.

XXI. God the Father and Jesus Christ are in us.

<u>John 14:20</u> At that day ye shall know that I am in my Father, and ye in me, and I in you.

<u>John 14:23</u> Jesus answered and said unto him, If a man love me, he will keep my words: and my Father will love him, and we will come unto him, and make our abode with him.

XXII. The Holy Spirit is in us.

<u>John 14:1</u>7 Even the Spirit of truth; whom the world cannot receive, because it seeth him not, neither knoweth him: but ye know him; for he dwelleth with you, and shall be in you.

<u>Romans 8:11</u> But if the Spirit of him that raised up Jesus from the dead dwell in you, he that raised up Christ from the dead shall also quicken your mortal bodies by his Spirit that dwelleth in you.

Comment: We, as Christians, can't even boast of the things that we are in

Christ. Why? Because of: <u>**1 Corinthians 15:10**</u> But by the grace of God I am

what I am. Only by the Grace of God, we are what we are.

It would be a blessed condition if all believers realized and accepted who we are in Jesus Christ. If we did, you would never again hear a moan or a groan. You would never again hear a negative confession. There would be no more need for anyone to seek counseling-except what is already provided for in the Bible-God's Word. However, since we have not reached that plateau of complete faith and trust in God and his Word, we feel a work such as this is necessary.

Notes

Notes

PROTECTION

Many believers do not know what protections God has promised us through his Word—as well as their knowing only a few of the 7500+ promises, that God has for us. As believers we can read about the promises, but just knowing them is not enough.. As Christians we must accept them, and stand on them in faith. In this section we hope to show some of the protection God has built around us. When you combine this with the previous section showing who you are in Christ Jesus, we will probably have to anchor you down so that you don't lift off the earth (ahead of schedule, that is). Take it from us, the spiritual lift-off sensation is super! Let's look at some of the protection scriptures:

Psalm 3:3 But thou, O LORD, art a shield for me; my glory, and the lifter up of mine head.

Psalm 23:5 Thou preparest a table before me in the presence of mine enemies: thou anointest my head with oil; my cup runneth over.

Psalm 23:6 Surely goodness and mercy shall follow me all the days of my life: and I will dwell in the house of the LORD for ever.

Psalm 27:1 The LORD is my light and my salvation; whom shall I fear? the LORD is the strength of my life; of whom shall I be afraid?

Proverbs 16:7 When a man's ways please the LORD, he maketh even his enemies to be at peace with him.

Joshua 1:9 Have not I commanded thee? Be strong and of a good courage; be not afraid, neither be thou dismayed: for the LORD thy God is with thee whithersoever thou goest.

Psalm 145:18 The LORD is nigh unto all them that call upon him, to all that call upon him in truth.

1 Samuel 2:10 The adversaries of the LORD shall be broken to pieces; out of heaven shall he thunder upon them: the LORD shall judge the ends of the earth; and he shall give strength unto his king, and exalt the horn of his anointed.

2 Samuel 22:2 And he said, The LORD is my rock, and my fortress, and my deliverer;

2 Samuel 22:3 The God of my rock; in him will

I trust: he is my shield, and the horn of my salvation, my high tower, and my refuge, my saviour; thou savest me from violence.

Psa 18:1 ... I will love thee, O LORD, my strength.

Psa 18:2 The LORD is my rock, and my fortress, and my deliverer; my God, my strength, in whom I will trust; my buckler, and the horn of my salvation, and my high tower.

Psalm 18:3 I will call upon the LORD, who is worthy to be praised: so shall I be saved from mine enemies.

Isaiah 41:10 Fear thou not; for I am with thee: be not dismayed; for I am thy God: I will strengthen thee; yea, I will help thee; yea, I will uphold thee with the right hand of my righteousness.

Isaiah 54:17 No weapon that is formed against thee shall prosper; and every tongue that shall rise against thee in judgment thou shalt condemn. This is the heritage of the servants of the LORD, and their righteousness is of me, saith the LORD.

2 Kings 17:39 But the LORD your God ye shall fear; and he shall deliver you out of the hand of all your enemies.

Psalm 118:6 The LORD is on my side; I will not fear: what can man do unto me?

Nahum 1:7 The LORD is good, a strong hold in the day of trouble; and he knoweth them that trust in him.

Proverbs 30:5 Every word of God is pure: he is a shield unto them that put their trust in him.

Psalm119:105 Thy word is a lamp unto my feet, and a light unto my path.

Psalm 119:114 Thou art my hiding place and my shield: I hope in thy word.

Psalm 91:1 He that dwelleth in the secret place of the most High shall abide under the shadow of the Almighty.

Psalm 91:2 I will say of the LORD, He is my refuge and my fortress: my God; in him will I trust.

Psalm 91:7 A thousand shall fall at thy side, and ten thousand at thy right hand; but it shall not come nigh thee.

Psalm91:10 There shall no evil befall thee, neither shall any plague come nigh thy dwelling.

Notes

Notes

Psalm 91:11 For he shall give his angels charge over thee, to keep thee in all thy ways.

Psalm 91:16 With long life will I satisfy him, and show him my salvation.

Psalm 121:7 The LORD shall preserve thee from all evil: he shall preserve thy soul.

Psalm 121:8 The LORD shall preserve thy going out and thy coming in from this time forth, and even for evermore.

Proverbs 29:25 The fear of man bringeth a snare: but whoso putteth his trust in the LORD shall be safe.

Isaiah 59:19 When the enemy shall come in like a flood, the Spirit of the LORD shall lift up a standard against him.

Here are some New Testament scriptures:

2 Timothy 4:18 And the Lord shall deliver me from every evil work, and will preserve me unto his heavenly kingdom: to whom be glory for ever and ever. Amen.

2 Thessalonians 3:3 But the Lord is faithful, who shall stablish you, and keep you from evil.

Ephesians 6:10 Finally, my brethren, be strong in the Lord, and in the power of his might.

Ephesians 6:11 Put on the whole armour of God, that ye may be able to stand against the wiles of the devil.

Ephesians 6:12 For we wrestle not against flesh and blood, but against principalities, against powers, against the rulers of the darkness of this world, against spiritual wickedness in high places.

Ephesians 6:13 Wherefore take unto you the whole armour of God, that ye may be able to withstand in the evil day, and having done all, to stand.

Ephesians 6:14 Stand therefore, having your loins girt about with truth, and having on the breastplate of righteousness;

Ephesians 6:15 And your feet shod with the preparation of the gospel of peace;

Ephesians 6:16 Above all, taking the shield of faith, wherewith ye shall be able to quench all the fiery darts of the wicked.

Ephesians 6:17 And take the helmet of salvation,

and the sword of the Spirit, which is the word of God:

Ephesians 6:18 Praying always with all prayer and supplication in the Spirit, and watching thereunto with all perseverance and supplication for all saints;

Luke 10:19 Behold, I give unto you power to tread on serpents and scorpions, and over all the power of the enemy: and nothing shall by any means hurt you.

Romans 8:31 What shall we then say to these things? If God be for us, who can be against us?

John 6:35 And Jesus said unto them, I am the bread of life: he that cometh to me shall never hunger; and he that believeth on me shall never thirst.

John 10:28 And I give unto them eternal life; and they shall never perish, neither shall any man pluck them out of my hand.

John 10:29 My Father, which gave them me, is greater than all; and no man is able to pluck them out of my Father's hand.

Matthew 11:28 Come unto me, all ye that labour and are heavy laden, and I will give you rest.

Matthew 11:29 Take my yoke upon you, and learn of me; for I am meek and lowly in heart: and ye shall find rest unto your souls.

Matthew 11:30 For my yoke is easy, and my burden is light.

1 Corinthians 10:13 There hath no temptation taken you but such as is common to man: but God is faithful, who will not suffer you to be tempted above that ye are able; but will with the temptation also make a way to escape, that ye may be able to bear it.

Revelation3:10 Because thou hast kept the word of my patience, I also will keep thee from the hour of temptation, which shall come upon all the world, to try them that dwell upon the earth.

Revelation 3:8 I know thy works: behold, I have set before thee an open door, and no man can shut it: for thou hast a little strength, and hast kept my word, and hast not denied my name.

Revelation 2:26 And he that overcometh, and keepeth my works unto the end, to him will I give power over the nations:

Notes

Notes

<u>**Jude 1:24**</u> Now unto him that is able to keep you from falling, and to present you faultless before the presence of his glory with exceeding joy,

<u>**Jude 1:25**</u> To the only wise God our Saviour, be glory and majesty, dominion and power, both now and for ever. Amen.

<u>**2 Peter 2:9**</u> The Lord knoweth how to deliver the godly out of temptations,

Now dear saints, after being made aware of who you are in Christ Jesus, and after seeing the protection God has designed for you, who believe and trust him-what else is there to expect from him? When we fully realized the wonderful state into which we have been placed by the Lord, we stopped asking him for more favors. We began just to praise and thank him for his mercy and grace-knowing he has given us all things....

<u>**2 Peter 1:3**</u> According as his divine power hath given unto us all things that pertain unto life and godliness, through the knowledge of him that hath called us to glory and virtue:

<u>**1 Corinthians 3:21**</u> For all things are yours;

THE TONGUE

James 3:2 For in many things we offend all. If any man offend not in word, the same is a perfect man, and able also to bridle the whole body.

If (there's that word "if" again) - if someone were to ask me what one of the biggest drawbacks is to a fruitful Christian walk with the Lord, the tongue of man would be the answer. However, the tongue can also be the biggest boon to a believer - the positive tongue, which shares the Word of God can be a blessing to any believer's walk.

Genesis 1:3, 6, 9,,11, 14, 20, 24, 29 all say, "and God said".
Comment: This entire thing was created by God's spoken words - the words of His tongue.

Psalm 39:1 I said, I will take heed to my ways, that I sin not with my tongue: I will keep my mouth with a bridle,
Palm 119:172 My tongue shall speak of thy word: for all thy commandments are righteousness
Psalm 141:3 Set a watch, O LORD, before my mouth; keep the door of my lips.
Psalm 139:4 For there is not a word in my tongue, but, lo, O LORD, thou knowest it altogether.
Proverbs 21:23 Whoso keepeth his mouth and his tongue keepeth his soul from troubles.
Proverbs 18:21 Death and life are in the power of the tongue: and they that love it shall eat the fruit thereof.
Proverbs 12:6 The words of the wicked are to lie in wait for blood: but the mouth of the upright shall deliver them.
Proverbs 13:3 He that keepeth his mouth keepeth his life: but he that openeth wide his lips shall have destruction
Proverbs 6:2 Thou art snared with the words of thy mouth, thou art taken with the words of thy mouth. (Wow, what a dire trap for the wrong words we may speak).
Ecclesiastes 5:6 Suffer not thy mouth to cause

Notes

thy flesh to sin; neither say thou before the angel, that it was an error: wherefore should God be angry at thy voice, and destroy the work of thine hands.

Comment: The above verses are of the Old Testament. We could have commented on every one of them - what is important is how they speak to your spirit. However, they do say, that we should be careful about what we say.

Now for some New Testament: (Under which I now live.)

Matthew 12:34-37 O generation of vipers, how can ye, being evil, speak good things? for out of the abundance of the heart the mouth speaketh.

35 A good man out of the good treasure of the heart bringeth forth good things: and an evil man out of the evil treasure bringeth forth evil things.

36 But I say unto you, That every idle word that men shall speak, they shall give account thereof in the day of judgment.

37 For by thy words thou shalt be justified, and by thy words thou shalt be condemned.

Matthew 15:11 Not that which goeth into the mouth defileth a man; but that which cometh out of the mouth, this defileth a man.

Matthew 15:18-20 But those things which proceed out of the mouth come forth from the heart; and they defile the man.

19 For out of the heart proceed evil thoughts, murders, adulteries, fornications, thefts, false witness, blasphemies:

20 These are the things which defile a man: but to eat with unwashen hands defileth not a man.

Mark 11:23 For verily I say unto you, That whosoever shall say unto this mountain, Be thou removed, and be thou cast into the sea; and shall not doubt in his heart, but shall believe that those things which he saith shall come to pass; he shall have whatsoever he saith.

Luke 6:45 A good man out of the good treasure of his heart bringeth forth that which is good; and an evil man out of the evil treasure of his heart bringeth forth that which is evil: for of the abundance of the heart his mouth speaketh.

Notes

Romans 10:10 For with the heart man believeth unto righteousness; and with the mouth confession is made unto salvation.

1 Peter 3:10 For he that will love life, and see good days, let him refrain his tongue from evil, and his lips that they speak no guile:

1 Peter 4:11 If any man speak, let him speak as the oracles of God

Question: Does the word "oracle" speak to your spirit as it does to mine - that it means Words of God?

1 Peter 1:15 But as he which hath called you is holy, so be ye holy in all manner of conversation;

Ephesians 4:29 Let *no* corrupt communication proceed out of your mouth, but that which is good to the use of edifying, that it may minister grace unto the hearers.

Colossians 3:8 But now ye also put off all these; anger, wrath, malice, blasphemy, filthy communication out of your mouth.

Titus 2:1 But speak thou the things which become sound doctrine.

Philippians 1:27 Only let your conversation be as it becometh the gospel of Christ

Hebrews 13:5 Let your conversation be without covetousness

Colossians 4:6 Let your speech be alway with grace, seasoned with salt, that ye may know how ye ought to answer every man.

James 3:8-12 But the tongue can no man tame; it is an unruly evil, full of deadly poison.

9 Therewith bless we God, even the Father; and therewith curse we men, which are made after the similitude of God.

10 Out of the same mouth proceedeth blessing and cursing. My brethren, these things ought not so to be.

11 Doth a fountain send forth at the same place sweet water and bitter?

12 Can the fig tree, my brethren, bear olive berries? either a vine, figs? so can no fountain both yield salt water and fresh.

Comment: Again, it is not easy to refrain from sharing my understanding of how the power of the tongue fairly leaps at us out of the above scripture

Notes

verses. However, we will be silent, and know that He is God (**Psalm 46:10**.) However, it must be shared, that believers should be lining up their words more with God's Words.

Jeremiah 23:36 for every man's word shall be his burden; for ye have perverted the words of the living God, of the LORD of hosts our God.

How about this gem?

Deuteronomy 4:2 Do not add to what I command you and do not subtract from it, but keep the commands of the LORD your God that I give you.

WHO SHOULD WE BELIEVE?

This question comes up more with the newly saved than with the more " mature" Christians—although even they sometimes misplace their trust. After listening to so many varied and diverse opinions and interpretations of God's Word, one can begin to question who and what to believe—and where one should place trust. **Proverbs 3:5** clearly states: "Trust in the LORD with all thine heart;"

Romans 14:5 Let every man be fully persuaded in his own mind.

Philippians 2:12 work out your own salvation with fear and trembling.

1 Corinthians 2:5 That your faith should not stand in the wisdom of men, but in the power of God.

1 Corinthians 3:21 Therefore let no man glory in men. For all things are yours;

John 5:39 Search the scriptures;

Isaiah 34:16 Seek ye out of the book of the LORD, and read:

Psalm 119:89 For ever, O LORD, thy word is settled in heaven.

Mark 1:15 repent ye, and believe the gospel.

John 6:29 This is the work of God, that ye believe on him whom he hath sent.

John 14:1 ye believe in God, believe also in me.

Acts 16:31 And they said, Believe on the Lord Jesus Christ,

John 14:26 But the Comforter, which is the Holy Ghost, whom the Father will send in my name, he shall teach you all things,

John 16:13 Howbeit when he, the Spirit of truth, is come, he will guide you into all truth:

1 Corinthians 2:13 Which things also we speak, not in the words which man's wisdom teacheth, but which the Holy Ghost teacheth;

1 Peter 4:11 If any man speak, let him speak as the oracles of God;

The above scriptures speak loudly that: we should, ourselves, be responsible for where we are; we must believe in God and his Son Christ Jesus;

Notes

the Holy Ghost is our teacher; all answers are found in God's Word.

1 John 2:27 and ye need not that any man teach you:

John 6:45 And they shall be all taught of God.

Hebrews 8:10 saith the Lord; I will put my laws into their mind, and write them in their hearts:

1 Thessalonians 4:9 for ye yourselves are taught of God to love one another.

LAW (letter) vs. FAITH(spirit)

Introduction: This section was inspired by the understanding that jumped off the pages of my Bible as I was searching the scriptures. These few verses led into the composition of this section:

Matthew 26:28 For this is my blood of the *new testament*, which is shed for many for the remission of sins.

Mark 14:24 And he said unto them, This is my blood of the *new testament*, which is shed for many.

1 Corinthians 11:25 After the same manner also he took the cup, when he had supped, saying, this cup is the *new testament in my blood*: this do ye, as oft as ye drink it, in remembrance of me.

2 Corinthians 3:6 Who also hath made us able ministers of the *new testament*; not of the letter, but of the spirit: for the letter killeth, but the spirit giveth life.

2 Corinthians 3:11 For if that which is done away was glorious, *much more that which remaineth is glorious.*

2 Corinthians 3:14 But their minds were blinded: for until this day remaineth the same vail untaken away in the reading of the old testament; *which vail is done away in Christ*.

Hebrews 8:6 But now hath he obtained a more excellent ministry, by how much also he is the *mediator of a better covenant*, which was established upon better promises.

Hebrews 8:13 In that he saith, *A new covenant*, he hath made the first old. Now that which decayeth and waxeth old is ready to vanish away.

Hebrews 12:24 *And to Jesus the mediator of the new covenant*, and to the blood of sprinkling, that speaketh better things than that of Abel.

LAW (letter) vs. FAITH (Spirit)

1 Timothy 1:9 Knowing this, that the law is not made for a righteous man,

Romans 7:4 Wherefore, my brethren, ye also are become dead to the law by the body of Christ;

Galatians 2:19 For I through the law am dead to

Notes

the law, that I might live unto God.

Romans 6:14 For sin shall not have dominion over you: for ye are not under the law, but under grace.

Comment: This doesn't say that we will not sin-only that sin will not have

dominion over us.

Galatians 2:21 for if righteousness come by the law, then Christ is dead in vain.

Galatians 3:24 Wherefore the law was our schoolmaster to bring us unto Christ, that we might be justified by faith. Gal 3:25 But after that faith is come, we are no longer under a schoolmaster.

Galatians 5:18 But if ye be led of the Spirit, ye are not under the law.

Ephesians 2:15 Having abolished in his flesh the enmity, even the law of commandments contained in ordinances;

Colossians 2:14 Blotting out the handwriting of ordinances that was against us,

Galatians 3:19 Wherefore then serveth the law? It was added because of transgressions, till the seed should come to whom the promise was made;

Romans 7:6 But now we are delivered from the law,

Romans 4:14 For if they which are of the law be heirs, faith is made void, and the promise made of none effect:

Romans 7:6 But now we are delivered from the law,

2 Corinthians 3:6 Who also hath made us able ministers of the *new testament*; not of the letter, but of the spirit: for the letter killeth, but the spirit giveth life.

John 1:17 For the law was given by Moses, but grace and truth came by Jesus Christ.

Romans 3:21 But now the righteousness of God *without the law* is manifested,

Romans 3:28 Therefore we conclude that a man is justified by faith without the deeds of the law.

Galatians 2:16 Knowing that a man is not justified by the works of the law, but by the faith of Jesus Christ, even we have believed in Jesus Christ, that we might be justified by the faith of Christ, and not by the works of the law: for by the works of the law shall no flesh be justified.

Romans 8:2 For the law of the Spirit of life in Christ Jesus hath made me free from the law of sin and death.

Romans10:4 For Christ is the end of the law for righteousness to every one that believeth.

Romans 4:15 Because the law worketh wrath: for where no law is, there is no transgression.

Galatians 3:12 And the law is not of faith:

Galatians 3:13 Christ hath redeemed us from the curse of the law,

Galatians 5:4 Christ is become of no effect unto you, whosoever of you are justified by the law; ye are fallen from grace.

Hebrews 7:19 For the law made nothing perfect, but the bringing in of a better hope did;

Galatians 5:1 Stand fast therefore in the liberty wherewith Christ hath made us free, and be not entangled again with the yoke of bondage.

2 Corinthians 5:17 Therefore if any man be in Christ, he is a new creature: old things are passed away; behold, all things are become new.

Hebrews 8:13 In that he saith, A *new covenant*, he hath made the first old. Now that which decayeth and waxeth old is ready to vanish away.

2 Corinthians 3:14 But their minds were blinded: for until this day remaineth the same veil untaken away in the reading of the old testament; *which veil is done away in Christ*.

Romans 3:20 Therefore by the deeds of the law there shall no flesh be justified in his sight: for by the law is the knowledge of sin.

Galatians 3:10 For as many as are of the works of the law are under the curse:

Galatians 3:11 - Heb 10:38 - Rom 1:17 The just shall live by faith.

Philippians 3:9 And be found in him, not having mine own righteousness, which is of the law, but that which is through the faith of Christ, the righteousness which is of God by faith:

There are many believers, who question the relative credibility of the old vs. the New Testament Some say we should give no place to the old testament-only the new. Those, who believe in God, but

Notes

Notes

stumble at the stumbling stone, believe only in the old testament. It speaks to us that the scriptures cited above plainly state that we are under the New Testament-the new covenant. It also speaks to our spirits that, although we are now under the New Testament-living by faith in Jesus Christ-the old testament (the law) was not erased. Yes, it has been superseded by the New Testament; we admit that the new was built on the old-the old pointed to the new. **1 Timothy 1:8** But we know that the law is good, if a man use it lawfully; How does one use the law lawfully? It can be used lawfully only in the light of the glorious gospel of Jesus Christ. **Romans 7:12** Wherefore the law is holy, and the commandment holy, and just, and good.

We believe that the old testament was an introduction leading us to the coming of Christ Jesus and the new covenant. Although we no longer live under the old testament, we do recognize that it was the basis for the new promise. This point was made when Jesus said:

Matthew 5:17 Think not that I am come to destroy the law, or the prophets: I am not come to destroy, but to fulfill. To fulfill means to complete. When Christ came to complete the old law and the prophets, he made the old and new testaments an entire whole-the complete Word of God. It speaks to us that proof of this is found in the hundreds of references to the old testament in the New Testament. Is it possible, that the New Testament gives us all the OT verses we should consider in our walk with the Lord? Please allow us to offer one example. When Jesus Christ was tempted of the devil in the wilderness in **Matthew 4:1-10**, he answered satan's three temptations by citing **Deuteronomy 8:3, 6:16, and 6:13.** We would also like to cite **Romans 7:7**: What shall we say then? is the law sin? God forbid. Nay, I had not known sin, but by the law: for I had not known lust, except the law had said, Thou shalt not covet.

Some seek to ignore the old testament by standing on **Galatians 3:13**, which says, Christ hath redeemed us from the curse of the law, Christ did redeem us from the curse of the law-not from the law. The OT is not to be ignored - only to be recognized as only the foundation for the New Testament. Although we accept that we are dead to the law; we are not under the law; we are free from the law—none of this says that the law does not exist.

God created us—he created the flesh as well as the spirit. He knows our hearts. **1 Corinthians 15:44** There is a natural body, and there is a spiritual body. Thank God for saying through Paul—**Romans 7:24-25** O wretched man that I am! who shall deliver me from the body of this death? I thank God through Jesus Christ our Lord. So then with the mind I myself serve the law of God; but with the flesh the law of sin.

The following scripture verses link the old and New Testaments:
Matthew1:17Matthew 11:10
Matthew 1:22-23Matthew 12:3-5
Matthew 2:5-6Matthew 12:39-42
Matthew 2:17-18Matthew 12:35
Matthew 3:3Matt hew15-4
Matthew 4:4Matthew 15:7-9
Matthew 4:6Matthew 19:4-5
Matthew 4:10Matthew 21:16
Matthew 4:14-16Matthew 24:43
Matthew 5:31Matthew 24:39-39
Matthew 5:33Matthew 26:24
Matthew 5:38Matthew 26:56
Matthew 5:43

Luke 24:27 And beginning at Moses and all the prophets, he expounded unto them in all the scriptures the things concerning himself.
Note: If he linked the old and New Testaments, it would seem appropriate for us to
be able to do the same-seeing that we are joint-heirs with Jesus Christ.

After citing all of the above verses, please allow the following observations. It speaks heavily to us that spending untold, multiple millions of hours dissecting the old testament verses, and trying to

Notes

equate them to New Testament scriptures, amounts to straining at a gnat and swallowing a camel (**Matthew 23:24**). God told us in: **Luke 9:62** And Jesus said unto him, No man, having put his hand to the plow, and looking back, is fit for the kingdom of God. God placed the old testament in proper perspective, in **Hebrews 8:13**In that he saith, A new covenant, he hath made the first old. Now that which decayeth and waxeth old is ready to vanish away. He also said in **2 Corinthians 3:6** Who also hath made us able ministers of the new testament; not of the letter, but of the spirit: for the letter killeth, but the spirit giveth life.

The old tabernacle is discussed in **Hebrews 9**; in verse 11 the old tabernacle was replaced by the new tabernacle through these words: **Hebrews 9:11** But Christ being come an high priest of good things to come, *by a greater and more perfect tabernacle*, not made with hands, that is to say, not of this building; In light of all this, one has to question why we spend so much delving into and discussing the old tabernacle, the old law, the old testament. Because the old testament is fulfilled, we can refer to it for support—as a house is supported by its foundation. We can cite its scriptures, when we want to show relativity.

However, we can not see why we should taffy-pull its verses. They have been fulfilled, and set aside by the birth, life, ministry, and blood sacrifice of our Savior and Redeemer Jesus Christ of Nazareth.

God said in: **2 Corinthians 5:17** Therefore if any man be in Christ, he is a new creature: old things are passed away; behold, all things are become **new.** If all things have become new, and the old things have passed away-why do we delve into the old? One answer might be that our well-intentioned teachers are trying to increase our understanding. However, even if this happens, we are told not to lean on our own understanding. It seems fair to observe that, if we walked in the promises of the New Testament, we would by too busy to trouble ourselves with the old law.

We offer the following scriptures, which may

shed more light on this subject:

Romans 7:6 But now *we are delivered* from the law, that being dead wherein we were held; that we should serve in newness of spirit, and not in the oldness of the letter.

Romans 8:2-4 For the law of the Spirit of life in Christ Jesus hath made me free from the law of sin and death. For what the law could not do, in that it was weak through the flesh, God sending his own Son in the likeness of sinful flesh, and for sin, condemned sin in the flesh: That the righteousness of the law might be fulfilled in us, who walk not after the flesh, but after the Spirit.

1 Corinthians 2:5 That your faith should not stand in the wisdom of men, but in the power of God.

2 Corinthians 3:5-6 Not that we are sufficient of ourselves to think any thing as of ourselves; but our sufficiency is of God; Who also hath made us able ministers of the new testament; not of the letter, but of the spirit: for the letter killeth, but the spirit giveth life.

Galatians 2:16 Knowing that a man is not justified by the works of the law, but by the faith of Jesus Christ, even we have believed in Jesus Christ, that we might be justified by the faith of Christ, and not by the works of the law: for by the works of the law shall no flesh be justified.

Galatians 3:24-25 Wherefore the law was our schoolmaster to bring us unto Christ, that we might be justified by faith. But after that faith is come, we are *no longer* under a schoolmaster.

Philippians 1:27 Only let your conversation be as it becometh the gospel of Christ:

Phililippians 3:13-14 Brethren, I count not myself to have apprehended: but this one thing I do, forgetting those things which are behind, and reaching forth unto those things which are before, I press toward the mark for the prize of the high calling of God in Christ Jesus.

John 1:17 For the law was given by Moses, but grace and truth came by Jesus Christ.

We cannot imagine how these verses, and this

Notes

entire section, speak to you—that is between you and the Holy Spirit, who opens our understanding. We believe we should thank God in and for all things—including the old testament. We do, however, walk in the Spirit of the New Testament, which replaced the old through the shed blood of Christ Jesus.

Please allow us to offer another illustration that might help bring this discourse into sharper focus. When one builds a house, he must first install a firm foundation—the house is then built upon that foundation. One does not live in the foundation—he lives in the house, which receives its support from the foundation. Let us relate this to our subject. The old testament is the foundation upon which our house, the New Testament was built. We do not live in the foundation, although it is always there—we live in our house-the New Testament.

Many believers come to us expressing frustration over not being able to understand certain scriptures. Others bemoan the fact they don't comprehend what is happening in the world. These brethren race around to this one and that one in order to satisfy their desire for understanding. After agreeing on the thank-you scriptures, we share the following.

Proverbs 3:5 Trust in the LORD with all thine heart; and lean not unto thine own understanding.
Question: Is this telling us not to worry about nor lean on our own understanding? We believe it is. If we place complete trust in the Lord, we will be in a position to accept his understanding as given by the Holy Spirit.
1 John 2:27 But the anointing which ye have received of him abideth in you, and ye need not that any man teach you: but as the same anointing teacheth you of all things, and is truth, and is no lie, and even as it hath taught you, ye shall abide in him.
Psalm 119:104 Through thy precepts I get understanding:
Comment: God's precepts are his Words. If we claim his word, even without understanding, the Holy Spirit will eventually deliver the understanding.

Notes

(<u>John 14:26 &16:13).</u>

<u>Psalm 119:130</u> The entrance of thy words giveth light; it giveth understanding unto the simple.

Question: Is this confirmation, or what?

<u>Luke 24:45</u> Then opened he their understanding, that they might understand the scriptures,

Comment: Jesus Christ opened the understanding).

<u>1 John 5:20</u> And we know that the Son of God is come, and hath given us an understanding,

Question: Do you believe that the Son of God is come? You do? It follows then that he has given you an understanding. The understanding is there as if behind a locked door. The Key to opening the door of our understanding is God's Word. Claiming God's Word releases the power of the Holy Spirit to render an understanding. Remember, the verse says <u>an</u>, not all understanding

<u>Ephesians 1:17</u> That the God of our Lord Jesus Christ, the Father of glory, may give unto you the spirit of wisdom and revelation in the knowledge of him: <u>Ephesians 1:18</u> The eyes of your understanding being enlightened;

We once also felt the frustration of not understanding scripture. It stills happens but when the peace of Jesus Christ was really received, accepted, and practiced , we knew that God's Holy Spirit would open up our understanding. Knowing this, and fully trusting in him, gave us the promised comfort. We may have been short of some understanding, but it didn't bother us anymore—we learned to be content. Once we achieved contentment, it spoke to us that, if we act on what we do understand, we wouldn't have time to worry about what we don't comprehend.

Maybe the parable of the talents, as found in <u>Matthew 25</u>, can shed more light. Verses 21 and 23 are quite similar. Verse 21 says: "Well done, thou good and faithful servant: thou hast been faithful over a few things, I will make thee ruler over many things: enter thou into the joy of thy lord." God didn't create us to have total understanding. He knows what man is—he told us that we will know only in part(<u>1 Corinthians 13:9</u>). We shall know as we are known,

Notes

when he that is perfect is come. God said in **Matthew 17:20** If ye have faith as a grain of mustard seed,...and nothing shall be impossible unto you.

Galatians 5:1 tells us: Stand fast therefore in the liberty wherewith Christ hath made us free, and be not entangled again with the yoke of bondage. Oxen have no choice, when the yoke is placed on them—they must suffer it. That is not so with believers—we have a choice. We can either remain in bondage, or we can stand fast on the promised liberty. You choice to make.

The flesh strives for understanding. The spirit, however, patiently waits for it according to God's Will.

God said in **Proverbs 8:14** - ...I AM UNDER-STANDING...

GIFTS

There is much concern in the Christian community about gifts. In fact, many believers spend much time trying to qualify for God's gifts. There are even some, who believe that if a saved person doesn't overtly display certain gifts, his salvation is in question. The subject of gifts is often raised in Bible studies and fellowship gatherings-one will normally find believers lining up on one side of the issue or the other. In our counseling ministry we are often asked our opinion about God's gifts, and where they fit into God's Will. We again confess we have no "opinion"; all we can offer is what is written in God's Word, and how it speaks to our spirit. If you consider this "opinion"-so be it. No problem.

The gifts we will be considering are found mentioned in **1 Corinthians 12-8-10**. They are the gifts of the word of wisdom, the word of knowledge, faith, healing, working of miracles, prophecy, discerning of spirits, tongues and the interpretation of tongues-nine gifts in all. Let us first define the individual gifts as follows:

1. Word of wisdom - the ability to form a sound judgment concerning a matter.

2. Word of knowledge - the sum of information gathered-the act or state of knowing.

3. Faith - trust and belief in a conviction-whether or not supported by evidence.

4. Healing - the act of restoring health or making sound the body. The act of reconciling or settling differences.

5. Working of Miracles - An act or happening that departs from the laws of nature, or goes beyond what is known concerning these laws.

6. Prophecy - The work, function, or vocation of a prophet. Inspired utterance, interpretation, or declaration of the will or purpose of God.

7. Discerning of spirits - The ability to recognize or distinguish the inner person(spirit).

8. Divers tongues - The Spirit-led ability to speak in another known tongue(language) not known to the speaker-however recognized by a person of that nationality.

Notes

9. Interpretation of tongues - The ability to translate orally the utterance of tongues.

There never seems to be disagreement about the first seven of God's gifts given through the Holy Spirit. The attitude prevails that, "Either you have it (them), or you don't". We rarely find one believer trying to convince another, that he should, or must, exercise one or all of the first seven gifts. This is not so, when it comes to tongues. For some reason the Christian, who has been given the gift of tongues, often wants other believers to also exercise this gift. Many will even pray over someone to receive the gift.

Let us first look at this thing called a gift—just what is a gift? A gift is anything that is given; anything that is voluntarily transferred by one to another without compensation. It is a present freely given. God said in **Romans 8:32** He that spared not his own Son, but delivered him up for us all, how shall he not with him also **freely** give us all things? "Freely" means not determined by anything beyond its nature or being; not necessitated by an external force, cause, or agency; not duly influenced; spontaneous and/or independent. When God says he shall **freely** give us all things, he will give because of his nature-not because of pleadings, prayers, or any other form of external pressure. God said in: 1 Cointhians 2:12 Now we have received, not the spirit of the world, but the spirit which is of God; that we might know the things that are **freely** given to us of God. There is that word, "freely" again. It speaks to us, that we don't have to earn or qualify for the spiritual gifts of God. When God decides, and he has decided, that we are ready for one of his gifts, he will grant it through his Holy Spirit. We need not beg or pray for the gift—it will be **freely** given. God said through his Son in **Mat 10:8** freely ye have received, freely give.

We are going to consider the gift of tongues— we chose this one, because it is the most discussed, and seems to create the most controversy. Almost all of **1 Corinthians 14** is devoted to tongues. The first verse in the love chapter, **1 Corinthians 13**, speaks of the tongues of men and of angels. We have not chosen tongues, because we rank it higher in importance than the other gifts-it is not ranked above the other gifts as far as desirability is concerned. Except for God placing prophecy (which are God's Words) over the speaking in tongues through Paul, no gift is placed over another in importance. All the gifts are of equal importance, because they are specially granted by God through the Holy Spirit—-each gift has its function in God's plan-his Will. We have never heard a believer, who has the gift of knowledge or healing, exhort another believer to go for these gifts. However, we have often run into those with the gift of tongues insist that others should qualify for this gift. Some even claim there is no salvation without the expression of the gift of tongues. Others say, that if a believer does not have the gift of tongues, he does not have the Holy Spirit. (We always thought that, if you could say that Jesus is Lord, you have the Holy Spirit—**1 Corinthians 12:3**). Let us look at some scriptures that many well-meaning Christians cite to support their position:

Acts 2:4 And they were all filled with the Holy Ghost, and began to speak with other tongues, as the Spirit gave them utterance.

Acts 10:44 While Peter yet spake these words, the Holy Ghost fell on all them which heard the word.

Acts 10:45 And they of the circumcision which believed were astonished, as many as came with Peter, because that on the Gentiles also was poured out the gift of the Holy Ghost.

Acts 10:46 For they heard them speak with tongues, and magnify God.

Acts 19:6 And when Paul had laid his hands upon them, the Holy Ghost came on them; and they spake with tongues, and prophesied.

Note: Some prophesied. We wonder if others may have been given one or more of the other gifts. They apparently were not all given the gift of tongues.

If one wanted to connect speaking in tongues with the infilling of the Holy Spirit, the above-cited

Notes

verses would appear to be valid back-up for this posture. One could then say, "If you do not speak in tongues, you haven't the Holy Spirit within you:. However, in order to remain in line with other scriptures concerning this area, it would be more fair to accept that the Holy Ghost-by God's leading- chose to give the gift of tongues to certain individuals in conjunction with entering into their spirits. Some were given the gift of prophecy.

There are many instances cited in scripture where the Holy Ghost was given, and no mention was made about speaking in tongues as a result. **Acts 4:31, Acts 9:17, Acts 11:15, Luke 1:41, Acts 4:8, Acts 7:55, Acts 13:19** and **Acts 13:52** are cases in point. They all mention the entrance of the Holy Spirit—without mention of the gift of tongues following. It is apparent that the gift of tongues can be given in conjunction with the infilling of the Holy Spirit, but it doesn't necessarily follow in all cases. Any of the nine gifts could be a result of the entrance of the Holy Ghost. No one seems to claim, that not having the gift of healing means that the Holy Ghost is not present. Why should anyone say this about tongues? It may be that some believers were in so much bondage before coming to the Lord, that they just cannot accept **Galatians 5:1** Stand fast therefore in the liberty wherewith Christ hath made us free, and be not entangled again with the yoke of bondage. Have we accepted what it truly says to us. **Acts 15:10** Now therefore why tempt ye God, to put a yoke upon the neck of the disciples,

God puts the speaking of tongues in pure perspective in **1 Corinthians 14**. We suggest you read the entire chapter aloud—it will speak more strongly and clearly to your spirit, if you hear the words. We are not going to record all of this chapter here—you can go to your Bible for the reading. We will, however, list some of the salient points made by God:

1. Prophecy is preferred over tongues.
2. Tongues edify self; prophecy edifies the church.
3. The sounds of a strange, unknown tongue

signifies little.

4. We are encouraged to seek the gifts that will edify the church.

5. Though Paul spoke in tongues, he said he would rather speak five words with his

understanding than ten thousand words in an unknown tongue.

6. Tongues are a sign to the unbeliever—prophesying serves the believer.

7. We are told to covet to prophesy, but not to forbid tongues.

Note: **1 Corinthians 12:31** says: But covet earnestly the best gifts: According to chapter 14, tongues does not qualify as one of the best gifts. To covet is to desire possession of, to long for, or to crave.

There are fellowships, churches, if you will, that are so taken with furthering the speaking in tongues, that they sponsor classes in the subject. The aim is to instruct and train believers so that they can experience the gift. We have yet to see any classes offering instructions in the interpretation of tongues. After all, when one speaks in tongues, there is supposed to be an interpreter present. It speaks to us, that teaching the gift of tongues is like teaching a child how to accept and appreciate gifts given to him on his birthday. A child needs no training in this area—except for a little instruction on how to show gratitude. If a child receives seven gifts, he will appreciate them so much, that he won't be concerned about what he did not receive.

The disagreements caused in this area seem to arise from different definitions. The word "unknown", which appears often before the word "tongues" in many verses of scripture is italicized—this means it was inserted at a later time. The word "unknown" can refer to an unknown language, or tongue, that exists in fact in the world It is not known to the speaker, who is speaking in the spirit. However, it is more often used in reference to an oral exercise in utterances, which are not recognized or understood by anyone else. It speaks to us that the speaking in tongues, which is acceptable in

Notes

Notes

God's eyes, are the different known tongues (languages). Some of these are mentioned in <u>**Acts 2:4-11**</u>. We believe that the tongues, that are not acceptable to God, are those criticized by God through Paul in <u>**1 Corinthians 14**</u>. The church was emulating the heathens, who made a practice of chanting gibberish. Their utterances served more to stir up emotions rather than godly edifying. It was this that God, through Paul, was criticizing the church for in <u>**1 Corinthians 14.**</u>

God commanded us to refrain from using "vain repetitions as the heathen do" in <u>**Matthew 6:7.**</u> Do you see the possible connection here? We do! If you re-defined the word "unknown" in your reading, you will find it easier to accept that Spirit-led speaking in tongues involves another *known* language. This is the only understanding that brings all the scriptures in agreement for us. In the light of this belief a further understanding of the following scripture verses was given to us:

<u>**Colossians 3:**</u>8 But now ye also put off all these; anger, wrath, malice, blasphemy, filthy communication out of your mouth.

<u>**1 Peter 4:11**</u> If any man speak, let him speak as the oracles of God;

<u>**Titus 2:1**</u> But speak thou the things which become sound doctrine:

<u>**Ephesians 4:29**</u> Let no corrupt communication proceed out of your mouth, but that which is good to the use of edifying, that it may minister grace unto the hearers.

<u>**Ephesians 4:31**</u> Let all bitterness, and wrath, and anger, and clamour, and evil speaking, be put away from you, with all malice:

<u>**Matthew 12:37**</u> For by thy words thou shalt be justified, and by thy words thou shalt be condemned.

<u>**Romans 12:6**</u> Having then gifts differing according to the grace that is given to us,

<u>**1 Corinthians 12:7**</u> But the manifestation of the Spirit is given to every man to profit withal.

The next three verses do not say that the gifts are

given to all—they say, that the various gifts are distributed to this one and that one. Verse 11 says: "dividing to every man severally as he will", which is also indicated in **Romans 12:6-8**. **1 Corinthians 7:7** But every man hath his proper gift of God, one after this manner, and another after that. **Ephesians 4:7** Ephesians 4:7 But unto every one of us is given grace according to the measure of the gift of Christ. **Question:** Are you getting the picture?

We do not know how all this speaks to you—we can only share our position as regarding God's gifts as given through his Spirit. The gifts are of God—they are **freely** given as God has decided. They are not necessary to salvation—they are a bonus for walking in line with his Will. One doesn't have to ask for, pray for, qualify for or do anything outwardly to receive a gift from God. God has decided who will receive his gifts—if you are on his "gift list" he will deliver the gift (s) in his time. This position has stopped much of the straining at a gnat and swallowing a camel. It has also stopped a lot of idle talk. It is another area in which much of the clutter has been swept out of the path of our Christian walk. We thank God in the name of his Son Jesus Christ for his peace and contentment.

We can all thank God for: **1 Corinthians 13:10** But when that which is perfect is come, then that which is in part shall be done away.

The understanding we have received here has provided another blessing—it has further helped in sweeping away much fleshly emotion out of our Christian walk. PTL!!

Here is another "gem", that came to me recently while searching the scriptures for more input as regards the gift of tongues. It is found in: **Acts 2:11** Cretes and Arabians, we do hear them speak in our tongues the wonderful works of God. Those, who witnessed the speaking in tongues, recognized their own tongues being spoken - not gibberish.

Notes

ANGER

Let us consider the challenge of anger. There are many Christians, who have a problem with anger. They ask for the counsel that will help them control their anger. They ask, "How can I stop myself from getting mad"? One answer obvious—they can't. If we begin thinking that we can accomplish things, we are in opposition to the scripture that clearly states that all things are of God (**2 Corinthians 5:18**). Even Jesus Christ said: **John 5:30** Ican of mine own self do nothing. We begin to stray from the position that all things are in God' Will. Only God can deliver the believer from his anger. God has shown us how to be victorious in his Word. There are many scriptures that show Christians how they can build peace in their spirits in order to put away the anger of the flesh. It is the flesh that entertains anger. The spirit doesn't-if it stands on God's Word. After agreeing aloud on the thank-you scriptures, we cite the following:

Psalm 37:8 Cease from anger, and forsake wrath:

Ephesians 4:26 Be ye angry and sin not: (We deleted the "comma").

Comment: There are some who cite Ephesians 4:26 when they wish to justify "righteous" anger. They understand the verse to say, "Be ye angry— (and sin not)". We understand it to say, "Be ye angry and sin **not**". In other words, don't either sin or be angry. Let us complete **Ephesians 4:26**: "...Let not the sun go down on your wrath". Verse 27 says, "Neither give place to the devil". It speaks to us that anger is not of faith—it is unrighteousness. Therefore, it is sin. To entertain anger would, in fact, be giving place to the devil. As you will see in a later segment entitled, "Satan's Power", we give no place to that deceiving liar.

Eccleasties 7:9 Be not hasty in thy spirit to be angry: for anger resteth in the bosom of fools. **Note**: We are not fools.

Ephesians 4:31 Let **all** bitterness, and wrath,

and **anger,** and clamour, and evil speaking, be put away from you, with all malice:

Colossians 3:8 But now ye also put off all these; anger,

Proverbs 29:22 An angry man stirreth up strife, and a furious man aboundeth in transgression.

Note: **2 Timothy 2:24** And the servant of the Lord must not strive;)

James 1:19 Wherefore, my beloved brethren, let every man be swift to hear, slow to speak, slow to wrath:

1 Timothy 2:8 I will therefore that men pray every where, lifting up holy hands, without wrath and doubting.

It speaks to us that, in light of the above scriptures, we are not to be an angry people.

Philippians4:8 Finally, brethren, whatsoever things are true, whatsoever things are honest, whatsoever things are just, whatsoever things are pure, whatsoever things are lovely, whatsoever things are of good report; if there be any virtue, and if there be any praise, think on these things.

It speaks loudly to us that the only "things" that qualify under all the categories in **Philippians 4:**8 are God's Words. If we think on God's Words, we can not and will not harbor anger. God's Word tells us to be loving, patient, forgiving, long-suffering, forbearing, content, at peace, protected, comforted, free, giving, rejoicing, thankful, etc.. God's Word says that we are blessed, joint-heirs with Christ, saved, chosen eternal, everlasting, etc.. With all this going for us, how can we be an angry people?

We often hear the remark that believers are allowed "righteous anger". We have yet to find this term mentioned in the Bible. However, we have found **Romans 3:10** ...As it is written, There is none righteous, no, not one: **Note:** If "it is written", then it is supposed that none can harbor "righteous anger". How readest thou?

A patient person has God's power over anger. If

Notes

you will peruse the section on PATIENCE, and read those scriptures, you will find more strength to close the door on anger. The chapter entitled, "REJOICE", will also fill your heart with God's Word, which will deliver you from anger. If you believe that anger is not of faith, and that anger is unrighteousness, you must believe that anger is sin. (**Romans 14:23** & **1 John 5:17**). **Psalms 119:11** tells us how to keep from sinning. It says, "Thy word have I hid in mine heart, that I might not sin against thee."

God has given us his answer to any and all of our challenges. His Word has all the answers. All we have to do is claim and stand on them. God's Word will not return to him void - man's words will.

WORRY

With all that is happening in the world, and with what is even happening in the body of Jesus Christ, many believers tend to worry about where it will all end. They seek delivery from worry. The chapters dealing with patience and rejoicing present scriptures that will also help in putting worry away. After sharing aloud the thank-you scriptures, we share the following:

John 14:1 Let not your heart be troubled: ye believe in God, believe also in me.

Question: Do you believe in God? Do you believe in our Lord Jesus Christ? You do? Then let not your heart be troubled.

John 14:27 Peace I leave with you, my peace I give unto you: not as the world giveth, give I unto you. Let not your heart be troubled, neither let it be afraid.

Comment: He has given us his peace, agreed? Have you accepted his peace? You have? Then can that peace leave any room for worry?

Philippians 4:6 Be careful for nothing;

Comment: Here we are commanded not to be anxious or concerned. Does this mean that, if we insist on entertaining worry, we are not walking with God in this area. We think so, but you will have to answer for yourself.

Philippians 4:11 Not that I speak in respect of want: for I have learned, in whatsoever state I am, therewith to be content.

Comment: Is God saying here that we are to be content no matter what? If you say yes, where is there room for worry?

Galatians 6:17 From henceforth let no man trouble me: for I bear in my body the marks of the Lord Jesus.

Comment: Philippians 4:6 & 11 above eliminate worry over things that may affect us. The scripture, **Galatians 6:17**, cancels out worry about how man can affect us.

Luke 12:22 & **Matthew 6:25** ...Take no thought for your life,

Comment: Another area is removed from worry

Notes

- our lives.

Matthew 6:27 Which of you by taking thought can add one cubit unto his stature?

Luke 12:25 And which of you with taking thought can add to his stature one cubit?

Comment: If you agree, that taking thought is worrying, then these two verses clearly state that nothing can be accomplished by worry. So then, why worry? Worry not only fails to add-it actually diminishes It is not in line with God's Word. Again, if you agree that worry is not of faith, and that it is unrighteousness, then worry is sin by God's definition-and we know what the wages of sin is. It is death.

There are many other that tell us not to be doubtful. One definition of "doubtful" is "apprehension" If you believe apprehension is worry, then you must accept, that God is telling us not to worry. If we obey **Philippians.4:8**, and think on whatsoever things are true, honest, just, pure, lovely, of good report - how can we worry?

Are you beginning to get the picture? We, as believers, have to decide for ourselves if a thing is of faith-or is sin. The Word says that whatsoever is not of faith is sin (**Romans 14:23**). If we accept that worrying is sin, how do we rid ourselves of this burden? **Psalm 119:11** says, "Thy word have I hid in mine heart, that I might not sin against thee." We are to fill our hearts with his Word. It is the Word of God that will stand us in good stead, and will see us through. His Word will deliver us no matter what the world throws in our path. After all, Psalm **119:105** says, "Thy word is a lamp unto my feet, and a light unto my path." Let the Word of God, with the leading of the Holy Spirit bear you up. God promised he would not leave us or forsake us (**Hebrews 13:4, Joshua 1:5, Deuteronomy 31:6).** Do you accept his promise? You do? Then rejoice, and walk in that promise - without worry.

Luke 12:29 "...neither be ye of doubtful mind."

Matthew 24:6 "see that ye be not troubled:"

PEOPLE BUG ME

Another area that appears too often in our counseling ministry has to do with believers being troubled and/or bothered by the actions or words of other Christians. These believers are usually perplexed. They seem to know it is not right to react negatively, but these brethren can't seem to help themselves. After sharing aloud the thank-you scriptures, we share the following:

Galatians 6:17 From henceforth let no man trouble me:

Psalm 119:165 Great peace have they which love thy law: and nothing shall offend them.

John 14:1 Let not your heart be troubled:

John 14:27 Let not your heart be troubled, neither let it be afraid.

Question: Once more, how many times must we be told?

1 Corinthians 12:18 But now hath God set the members every one of them in the body, as it hath pleased him.

Comment: It speaks to us here that God has placed everyone in his plan where he wants them to be. Is it possible that when we judge the actions or postures of other believers, we are also questioning God's Will? We think so. It speaks to us that God has not designed his perfect plan to please man, but to please himself. It says in **Revelation 4:11:** "...for thou hast created all things, and for thy pleasure they are and were created." Much idle talk can be nipped in the bud, if when asked to pass an opinion on another born-again person, you tell the questioner that your opinion is **1 Corinthians 12:18**. Then-leave it at that.

1 Corinthians 7:20 Let every man abide in the same calling wherein he was called.

1 Corinthians 7:24 Brethren, let every man, wherein he is called, therein abide with God.

Philippians 4:11 for I have learned, in whatsoever state I am, therewith to be content.

Question: Does this mean that we remain content even when being bugged? We think so.

Notes

Romans 14:5 One man esteemeth one day above another: another esteemeth every day alike. Let every man be fully persuaded in his own mind.

Philippians 4:6 Be careful for nothing; Nothing?? Nothing!!

Matthew 7:1-5; **Matthew 7:1** Judge not, that ye be not judged.

Comment: Look up **Matthew 7:2-5** yourself- they are life unto those that find them (**Proverbs 4:22**).

Psalm 55:22 Cast thy burden upon the LORD, and he shall sustain thee: he shall never suffer the righteous to be moved.

1 Peter 5:7 Casting all your care upon him; for he careth for you.

Hebrews 12:1 let us lay aside *every* weight,

Comment: Lay it aside. Because we say so? No way-God forbid. Lay it aside because God says so.

Hebrews 13:6 So that we may boldly say, The Lord is my helper, and I will not fear what man shall do unto me.

No worldly advice will enable you to stop being bugged by people or events. However, God's Word will do the job. Just find the scriptures above that speak to your spirit, and stand on them. Claim them aloud-God will take care of the problem.

How does this verse strike you? **1 Corinthians 7:17** But as God hath distributed to every man, as the Lord hath called every one, so let him walk. This scripture pairs up beautifully with **1 Corinthians 12:18**, which was cited earlier in this segment. Please refer back to it, and the comments following.

The following scriptures might help in this area:

Proverbs 16:7 When a man's ways please the LORD, he maketh even his enemies to be at peace with him.

Proverbs 25:21 If thine enemy be hungry, give him bread to eat; and if he be thirsty, give him water to drink:

Matthew 5:44 But I say unto you, Love your

Notes

enemies, bless them that curse you, do good to them that hate you, and pray for them which despitefully use you, and persecute you;

Romans 12:14 Bless them which persecute you: bless, and curse not.

Romans 12:20 Therefore if thine enemy hunger, feed him; if he thirst, give him drink:

Does it speak to your spirit that it might boil down to this in the end?

THE CHALLENGE IS NOT IN THAT PEOPLE BUG YOU - IT IS CENTERED ON HOW YOU REACT SCRIPTURALLY TO THE "BUGGING".

Notes

PATIENCE

Many believers ask for relief from impatience. They ask for prayer that will deliver them from this burden. We could quickly cite **Hebrews 12:1** which tells us to lay aside every weight, but we know that's too much to expect from the believer, who is used to praying about everything. So we agree on the thank-you scriptures and share the following:

James 5:7 Be patient therefore, brethren, unto the coming of the Lord.

James 5:8 Be ye also patient; stablish your hearts: for the coming of the Lord draweth nigh.

Psalm 37:7 Rest in the LORD, and wait patiently for him:

1 Tim 6:11 But thou, O man of God, flee these things; and follow after righteousness, godliness, faith, love, *patience*, meekness.

Luke 21:19 In your patience possess ye your souls.

2 Corinthians 6:4 But in all things approving ourselves as the ministers of God, in much *patience,*

Luke 8:15 having heard the word, keep it, and bring forth fruit with patience.

James 1:3 Knowing this, that the trying of your faith worketh patience.

James 1:4 But let patience have her perfect work, that ye may be perfect and entire, wanting nothing.

Romans 5:3-4 And not only so, but we glory in tribulations also: knowing that *tribulation worketh patience;* And patience, experience; and experience, hope:

Romans 8:25 But if we hope for that we see not, then do we with patience wait for it.

Hebrews 6:15 And so, *after he had patiently endured*, he obtained the promise.

1 Peter 2:20 but if, when ye do well, and suffer for it, ye take it patiently, this is acceptable with God.

Colossians 1:11 Strengthened with all might, according to his glorious power, unto all patience and longsuffering with joyfulness;

Romans 15:4 For whatsoever things were written aforetime were written for our learning, that we

Notes

through patience and comfort of the scriptures might have hope.

1 Thessalonians 5:14 ...be patient toward *all* men.

Revelation 3:10 Because thou hast kept the word of my patience, I also will keep thee from the hour of temptation, which shall come upon all the world, to try them that dwell upon the earth.

It is confession time again. One of my most glaring faults in my old life was this bane of impatience. After being saved, I started an all-out war against this condition. I prayed, I sought prayer, I fasted, I did everything I knew how to do. Finally, a wonderful spirit-filled brother suggested that, maybe I should stop trying to do it myself, and let God do it. (In other words, take the "I" out of the mix). He suggested I find scriptures that address the problem, claim them, and stand fast on them. Since nothing was working anyway, it was easy for me to give this new tack a try. The scriptures dealing with patience were beautiful, and deliverance fairly leaped off the pages of my Bible. Please understand that I have not yet made it all the way. With God's Word as my weapon against this challenge, I thank Him in the Name of Jesus Christ for the distance I have come.

Now maybe you and I, maybe all of us, can claim and stand on: **Hebrews 12:1** ...let us lay aside every weight, (Also, please look up **Hebrews 10:36**).

Notes

LUST

Many believers, young and old, bemoan the fact that they just can't seem to stop thinking about lustful things. They come to us seeking prayer that will deliver them from this state.

The lustful thought is as sinful as the act. **Proverbs 23:7** says: "For as he thinketh in his heart, so is he:" In **Matthew 5:28** we find: "But I say unto you, That whosoever looketh on a woman to lust after her hath committed adultery with her already in his heart." Lust covers inordinate desire expressed in many areas. How do we rid ourselves of this cancer- this evil thinking and desiring? First let us accept the fact that God created all things (**Revelation 4:11**, **2 Corinthians 5:18**, and **Isaiah 45:7**).

God knows what man is-he knows our hearts. He gave us his Word so that we would have the eternal answer to our fleshly and temporal weaknesses. After sharing aloud the thank-you scriptures, we share the following:

Psalm119:11 Thy word have I hid in mine heart, that I might not sin against thee.

Comment: God's Word and sin are like oil and water-they can't mix together, and can't occupy the same space. If we keep claiming God's Word, his Word **will** displace sin. At first, we thought we had to memorize the Word in order to hide it in our hearts. Later, we were given an understanding that we had only to read the Word aloud, because "out of the abundance of the heart the mouth speaketh". Not only do our words indicate what is in our hearts, but the reverse is also true. We can actually fill our hearts with spiritual abundance just by speaking aloud God's Words. It is pretty much a matter of stopping ourselves from trying to do it, and allow God's Word to "do it."

Galatians 6:7-8 Be not deceived; God is not mocked: for whatsoever a man soweth, that shall he also reap. For he that soweth to his flesh shall of the flesh reap corruption; but he that soweth to the Spirit shall of the Spirit reap life everlasting.

Notes

Comment: Do you believe this? It's your choice. What will you sow? If you sow to the flesh, you shall reap the corruption of the flesh-it is promised. Thank God it is also promised, that we will enjoy the everlasting joy of the Spirit, if we sow to the Spirit.

2 Corinthians 10:5 Casting down imaginations,

Comment: Imaginations are mental images. The only way to cast down he mental images of the flesh is to build up the store of God's Words in your heart.

Hebrews 2:18 For in that he himself hath suffered being tempted, he is able to succour them that are tempted.

Question: How does he succor them that are tempted? Right-by His Word.

Romans 8:1 There is therefore now no condemnation to them which are in Christ Jesus, who walk not after the flesh, but after the Spirit.

Comment: Many believers excuse sin under the umbrella provided by the first part of this verse. They conveniently slide by the last part, "who walk not after the flesh, but after the Spirit." How do we walk after the Spirit? Right again, by claiming God's Words through which the Holy Spirit can move. God's Word will work against the machinations of the flesh.

John 6:63 It is the spirit that quickeneth; the flesh profiteth nothing:

Comment: The world has a saying: "The forbidden fruit rots quickly". **Hebrews 11:25** says: "Choosing rather to suffer affliction with the people of God, than to enjoy the pleasures of sin for a season;" Sin gives pleasure only for a season, a short while. However, the spirit gives joy and life eternal through God's Word.

Titus 2:12 Teaching us that, denying ungodliness and worldly lusts, we should live soberly, righteously, and godly, in this present world;

Romans 13:14 But put ye on the Lord Jesus Christ, and make not provision for the flesh, to fulfil the lusts thereof.

Comment: There is a direct ratio between how much we provide for the flesh, and how much we put on the Lord. The more we put on the Lord Jesus Christ, the less we we make provision for the flesh.

Notes

Since Jesus Christ is the Word, we put him on through his Word. **Psalms 119:11** will handle the rest. **Philippians 4:8** tells us what things to think about, remember? If we think on these things, God's Words, we will find it difficult to fulfill the lusts of the flesh.

2 Timothy 2:22 Flee also youthful lusts: but follow righteousness, faith, charity, peace, with them that call on the Lord out of a pure heart.

Question: Is God encouraging us to fellowship with the saints? God is not telling us to hang around lust, or even to pray about it. He tells us to "flee". We flee by standing on his Word-especially **Psalms 119:11**.

2 Peter 1:4 Whereby are given unto us exceeding great and precious promises: that by these ye might be partakers of the divine nature, having escaped the corruption that is in the world through lust.

Comment: We have been given the promises-it's a fact-it is finished. By these we can escape corruption. Now, if you refuse the promises and slip into lust, it is your choice to make. **James 1:14** says: But every man is tempted, when he is drawn away of his own lust, and enticed. Only his promises, his Words, will again deliver you.

Hebrews 12:1 let us lay aside every weight, and the sin which doth so easily beset us,

Matthew 8:16 and he cast out the spirits with his word,

Comment: Since we are joint heirs with Christ, we also can cast out spirits with his Word. It worked for Christ, and will also work for us.

Galatians 5:16 This I say then, Walk in the Spirit, and ye shall not fulfil the lust of the flesh.

Question: How do we walk in the Spirit? By George, you have it-*through his Word.*

1 Peter 2:11 Dearly beloved, I beseech you as strangers and pilgrims, abstain from fleshly lusts,

1 Corinthians 10:6 Now these things were our examples, to the intent we should not lust after evil things,

We are often asked, "How do I know for sure if what I am thinking or doing is sinful? **Romans 14:23** defines sin as follows: for whatsoever is not

Notes

of faith is sin. **1 John 5:17** says, "All righteousness is sin".

Question: Is what you are thinking or doing of faith? Is it unrighteousness? You

will have to answer, and act accordingly.

"When you actually accept this next scripture as God's Truth, his promise, you will have to put lust away from you.

James 1:15 Then when lust hath conceived, it bringeth forth sin: and sin, when it is finished, bringeth forth death.

Then we always have **1 Corinthians 10:13**, There hath no temptation taken you but such as is common to man: but God is faithful, who will not suffer you to be tempted above that ye are able; but will with the temptation also make a way to escape, that ye may be able to bear it.

Ephesians 2
¹ And you hath he quickened, who were dead in trespasses and sins;
² Wherein in time past ye walked according to the course of this world, according to the prince of the power of the air, the spirit that now worketh in the children of disobedience:
³ Among whom also we all had our conversation in times past in the lusts of our flesh, fulfilling the desires of the flesh and of the mind; and were by nature the children of wrath, even as others.
⁴ But God, who is rich in mercy, for his great love wherewith he loved us,
⁵ Even when we were dead in sins, hath quickened us together with Christ, (by grace ye are saved;)
⁶ And hath raised us up together, and made us sit together in heavenly places in Christ Jesus:

THANK YOU FATHER IN THE NAME OF CHRIST JESUS!

Notes

HEALING

This area is one or the most popular with believers seeking relief. The desire for healing usually leads a believer into seeking someone to pray over him, in order to invoke God's blessing and grace in the healing process. It takes a while before many Christians key into **Ephesians 1:3**, Blessed be the God and Father of our Lord Jesus Christ, who hath blessed us with *all spiritual blessings* in heavenly places in Christ: If we accept the truth of **Matthew 6:10**- Thy will *be* done in earth, as it is in heaven-we know the blessings also apply to us here on earth. Believers seek healing in the traditional ways, because of the results-oriented mode of the usual Christian walk. The believer needs something, anything, prays for delivery, and then stands by for quick results. This happens because we expect God to do more than he has already done-in other words, his work is not yet finished. We will address the "it is finished" truth in a later chapter. For now, please let us share with you our belief that God has done all he is going to do. All we have to do now is walk in, and stand fast on, His promises-His Word.

Our counsel is based on the premise that God has done all he is going to do. All we have a to do is claim his promises in the name of his Son Jesus Christ-then stand fast in faith on those promises. First we share the thank-you scriptures, which puts us in line with God's Will-we are now walking with him. When we walk with him, we can claim things according to his will, and not fall contrary to **James 4:3** - Ye ask, and receive not, because ye ask amiss, that ye may consume it upon your lusts. When we ask according to the Will of God, God will honor his promise-he is Truth. This is what makes the Holy Spirit such a wonderful and powerful prayer intercessor. Not only does God know the Spirit's mind, but the Spirit intercedes for us according to the Will of God (**Romans 8:27**). When we pray for deliverances, are our eyes on the Lord, or on our problem?

Isaiah 53:5 But he was wounded for our transgressions, he was bruised for our iniquities: the chastisement of our peace was upon him; and with his stripes we *are* healed.

Comment: The word, "are" does not denote a future happening. It means it *is* done-along with "is" and "be". These words indicate that it has a place in fact-it exists now. If you believe he suffered stripes, then you are healed. Claim it and stand fast.

1 Peter 2:24 Who his own self bare our sins in his own body on the tree, that we, being dead to sins, should live unto righteousness: by whose stripes ye were healed.

Question: Do you believe he bare our sins? You do? Then you were healed. It is finished.

Jeremiah 17:14 Heal me, O LORD, and I shall be healed;

Malachi 4:2 But unto you that fear my name shall the Sun of righteousness arise with healing in his wings;

Exodus 23:25 And ye shall serve the LORD your God, and he shall bless thy bread, and thy water; and I will take sickness away from the midst of thee.

Question: Do you serve the Lord? You do? Then healing is yours. If you are not enjoying God's healing promises, check your serving. Remember that God is not mocked, for whatsoever a man soweth, that shall he also reap. (**Galatians 6:7**)

Exodus 15:26 for I am the LORD that healeth thee.

Comment: There are conditions. Please refer to the complete verse in your Bible, and acquaint yourself with the conditions.

Matthew 8:17 Himself took our infirmities, and bare our sicknesses.

Question: He took and bore; why do we insist on hanging on to our infirmities and sicknesses?

Jeremiah 30:17 For I will restore health unto thee, and I will heal thee of thy wounds, saith the LORD;

Acts 3:16 And his name through faith in his name hath made this man strong, whom ye see and know: yea, the faith which is by him hath given him this perfect soundness in the presence of you all.

Comment: It was the man's faith that made him strong. His faith delivered the soundness. It is written,

Notes

Romans 10:17 So then faith cometh by hearing, and hearing by the Word of God. The faith that delivers the healing comes from the Word of God.

The Word is the only answer.

Proverbs 4:22 For they are life unto those that find them, and health to all their flesh.

Question: What are the "they" referred to here? "They" are the Words of God. God's Words <u>are</u> healing; God's Words <u>are</u> eternal.

Let us look at the words of Our Lord Jesus (God's own Words) as regards healing:

Matthew 8:13 and as thou hast believed, so be it done unto thee.

Matthew 9:22 be of good comfort; thy faith hath made thee whole.

Matthew 9:29 According to your faith be it unto you.

Matthew 21:22 And all things, whatsoever ye shall ask in prayer, believing, ye shall receive.

Mark 10:52 Go thy way; thy faith hath made thee whole.

Luke 8:48 thy faith hath made thee whole; go in peace.

Luke 5:20 And when he saw their faith, he said unto him, Man, thy sins are forgiven thee.

Comment: Are you getting the message that the above scriptures are screaming out at us? It is written that faith gets the job done. We believe it. Do you? It all speaks that the answers all come by faith, including healing.. How do we build faith? We don't, of our own selves. It is written: **Romans 10:17** So then faith cometh by hearing, and hearing by the word of God. The entrance of God's Word builds faith.

Galatians 3:13 Christ hath redeemed us from the curse of the law, being made a curse for us:

Question: What curse is referred to here? From what are we redeemed?

Revelation 22:3 says: And there shall be no more curse: What are the curses from which we have been redeemed through Christ? They are listed in **Deuteronomy 28:21, 22, 27, 28, 34, 35, 59, and 60** (Please refer to these scriptures). The curses not covered in these verses are covered in blanked fashion by **Deuteronomy 28:61** Also *every* sickness, and *every* plague, which is not written in the book of this law, them will the LORD bring upon thee, until thou be destroyed.

Question: Do you accept that Christ has redeemed us from the curse of the law?

We do-and we stand fast and firmly on his redemption. He delivered us once-we do not ask him to do it again. We do not pretend to crucify our Savior afresh.

Ephesians 6:13 and having done all, to stand.

Galatians 5:1 Stand fast therefore in the liberty wherewith Christ hath made us free, and be not entangled again with the yoke of bondage.

When encouraging Christians to stand on God's Word for their deliverance (s), some cite **James 5:14** Is any sick among you? let him call for the elders of the church; and let them pray over him, anointing him with oil in the name of the Lord: This verse is God's Word. How does it agree with our exhorting to stand on the other healing scriptures? There is no conflict here, because God's Word is perfect. It appears that God provided **James 5:14** to cover the believer, who does not have the spiritual leading or maturity to stand on the healing scriptures alone He knows man. It is hoped that the elders will pray a prayer *of faith* over him, which is the Word of God. It speaks to us that God, in his infinite wisdom and mercy, included the anointing with oil, because he knew, that man might possibly need an outward sign to "assist" his faith. The verse does not say that the anointing with oil heals. Verse 15 says that the prayer of faith will save the sick.. What is the prayer of faith? Right-it is the Word of God.

Note: Take a look at these verses-they may give you another understanding:

2 Corinthians 4:16 For which cause we faint not; but though our outward man perish, yet the inward man is renewed day by day.

2 Corinthians 4:17 For our light affliction, which is but for a moment, worketh for us a far more exceeding and eternal weight of glory;

Notes

2 Corinthians 4:18 While we look not at the things which are seen, but at the things which are not seen: for the things which are seen are temporal; but the things which are not seen are eternal.

A dear Canadian brother caused the addition of the following:
Psalm 103:3 Who forgiveth all thine iniquities; who healeth all thy diseases;
Proverbs 4:20 My son, attend to my words; incline thine ear unto my sayings.
Proverbs 4:21 Let them not depart from thine eyes; keep them in the midst of thine heart.
Proverbs 4:22 For they are life unto those that find them, and health to all their flesh.
3 John 1:2 Beloved, I wish above all things that thou mayest prosper and be in health, even as thy soul prospereth.

Problems are part and parcel of our walk with the Lord. God has told Paul (and us) how to "handle" all of the challenges we could possibly encounter here on earth. He did so in
2 Corinthians 12:9-10 And he said unto me, My grace is sufficient for thee: for my ength is made perfect in weakness. Most gladly therefore will I rather *glory in* my infirmities, that the power of Christ may rest upon me. Therefore I *take pleasure in* infirmities, in reproaches, in necessities, in persecutions, in distresses for Christ's sake: for when I am weak, then am I strong. There is no room for moaning, groaning, and/or praying for deliverances - just glorying and taking pleasure in all things.

WHAT GOD HAS WRITTEN - HE HAS WRITTEN! AMEN!

DEATH

The believers, who seek counsel in this area are not the ones who suffer a loss, mourn for a period of time, and then are comforted. These Christians know and accept **Matt 5:4** - Blessed are they that mourn: for they shall be comforted. We normally hear from those, who make a project out of missing and mourning. They almost turn mourning into a ritual. These are the believers, who must refocus on God's Word, and accept the deliverance he promises. Their usual cry is, "How can we live with the sorrow"? The answer is, that we do not live with the sorrow, because then we would be going against all the scriptures that tell us to rejoice. We live with the rejoicing, and with the thank-you scriptures. We also find spiritual blessings in the following scripture verses:

John 3:16 that whosoever believeth in him should not perish, but have everlasting life.
Comment: The believer has eternal life-he doesn't die.
Romans 8:2 For the law of the Spirit of life in Christ Jesus hath made me free from the law of sin and death.
John 8:51 Verily, verily, I say unto you, If a man keep my saying, he shall never see death.
John 5:24 Verily, verily, I say unto you, He that heareth my word, and believeth on him that sent me, hath everlasting life, and shall not come into condemnation; but is passed from death unto life.
1 John 3:14 We know that we have passed from death unto life,
1 Corinthians 15:54 Death is swallowed up in victory.
Revelation 2:10 be thou faithful unto death, and I will give thee a crown of life.
2 Timothy 1:10 But is now made manifest by the appearing of our Saviour Jesus Christ, who hath abolished death, and hath brought life and immortality to light through the gospel:
1 Thessalonians 4:16 and the dead in Christ shall rise first: (WOW-what a promise)!!
Philippians 1:21 For to me to live is Christ, and

Notes

to die is gain.

James 4:14 Whereas ye know not what shall be on the morrow. For what is your life? It is even a vapour, that appeareth for a little time, and then vanisheth away.

Psalm 144:4 Man is like to vanity: his days are as a shadow that passeth away.

Comment: These two scriptures immediately above state, that the life of the flesh is short and wispy.

(The flesh concerns itself with the life on earth-the spirit sees eternal life with Him).

Those, who wish to justify prolonged periods of mourning, usually ask about **Matthew 5:4,** which says: Blessed are they that mourn: for they shall be comforted. They claim that they will receive multiple blessings if they continue in mourning past the comforted stage. We agree that mourning is scriptural and proper-however, we also stress the acceptance of comfort. Yes, we are to mourn-then we are to accept God's comfort through His Word.

As for me, I agree and stand on God's Word as spoken through Paul in **Philippians. 1:21**: For to me to live is Christ, and to die is gain.

AFTER DEATH

We have heard many believers say of a loved one, who has passed away, "She died and went to heaven". Or, "He's in heaven with his parents". We are asked, "Do saved people go to heaven when they die". "What happens to born-again folks upon their deaths"? When these questions are put to us, we answer them with the Word of God. However, generally speaking; my eternal life will be spent in the Holy City New Jerusalem. According to **Revelation 22:3** this city is where God, His throne and Jesus Christ will be found. Why would I want to spend my eternal life anywhere else?

Please know, that I am fully aware of the fact, that the traditional Christians do not agree with my position and posture here. However, we all have the command to be fully persuaded in our own minds.

1 Thessalonians 4:16 For the Lord himself shall descend from heaven with a shout, with the voice of the archangel, and with the trump of God: and the dead in Christ shall rise first:
Question: If the dead in Christ shall rise first, from where are the rising? It would seem that if they were already in heaven, there would be no reason for the rising as referred to here. Then the question becomes pointed-from where are they rising?
John 5:28 Marvel not at this: for the hour is coming, in the which all that are in the graves shall hear his voice, John 5:29 And shall come forth; they that have done good, unto the resurrection of life; and they that have done evil, unto the resurrection of damnation.
Comment: The Word says, all in the graves shall hear his voice, Where are these graves? Are they in heaven? We find no reference in the Bible about there being graves in heaven. They must be here on earth, filled with expectant believers, who are waiting of the second coming of our Lord Jesus Christ. The Word says they shall come forth. Will it be like the coming forth of Lazarus, when he came forth out of his tomb? (Which was here on earth)?
John 6:39 And this is the Father's will which

Notes

hath sent me, that of all which he hath given me I should lose nothing, but should raise it up again at the last day.

Comment: This says to us again that there will be a raising up. Again we have to ask from where will he raise it up again the last day?

John 6:40 and I will raise him up at the last day.

1 Corinthians 15:52 and the dead shall be raised incorruptible, and we shall be changed.

Ephesians5:14 Wherefore he saith, Awake thou that sleepest, and arise from the dead, and Christ shall give thee light.

John 5:25 Verily, verily, I say unto you, The hour is coming, and now is, when the dead shall hear the voice of the Son of God: and they that hear shall live.

Daniel 12:2 And many of them that *sleep in the dust of the earth* shall awake, some to everlasting life, and some to shame and everlasting contempt.

Comment: Hmmm! "Sleep in the dust of the earth"! Hmmm!

1 Thessalonians 4:15 For this we say unto you by the word of the Lord, that we which are alive and remain unto the coming of the Lord shall not prevent them which are asleep.

Comment: If we which are alive and remain shall not prevent them which are asleep, them which are asleep must not be in heaven-they must be in reach of them which will not prevent them.

Colossians 3:3-4 For ye are dead, and your life is hid with Christ in God. When Christ, who is our life, shall appear, then shall ye also appear with him in glory.

Matthew 27:52 And the graves were opened; and many bodies of the saints which slept arose,

Matthew 27:53 And came out of the graves after his resurrection, and went into the holy city, and appeared unto many.

Comment: We know that we are not to add or detract from God's Word. Allow us to make an observation in order to make a point. If the graves were opened after his resurrection, maybe they'll be opened again after his second coming. Then the saints will be able to follow God's Will as stated in:**1 Thessalonians 4:16** For the Lord himself shall descend from heaven with a shout, with the voice of the archangel, and with the trump of God: and the dead in Christ shall rise first: Possible? We believe so. With God *all* things are possible.

John 6:54 Whoso eateth my flesh, and drinketh my blood, hath eternal life; and I will raise him up at the last day.

John 11:24 Martha saith unto him, I know that he shall rise again in the resurrection at the last day.

1 Corinthians 15:42-44 So also is the resurrection of the dead. It is sown in corruption; it is raised in incorruption: It is sown in dishonour; it is raised in glory: it is sown in weakness; it is raised in power: It is sown a natural body; it is raised a spiritual body. There is a natural body, and there is a spiritual body.

Comment: It speaks to here that we are placed in our graves as natural bodies. When Jesus honors us with his coming our spiritual bodies will be raised to join him.

Our spirit is content with what the above scriptures are telling us. Let me state my belief by using my Dad as an example. Dad passed away in 1973 at the age of 71. He was chosen by God, and saved a month and a half before passing on. It is my belief that we interred his natural body. It is also my belief that he is in a sort of holding pattern, awaiting the second coming of Jesus. He won't have long to wait because of: **2 Peter 3:8** But, beloved, be not ignorant of this one thing, that one day is with the Lord as a thousand years, and a thousand years as one day.

1 Corinthians 15:49 And as we have borne the image of the earthy, we shall also bear the image of the heavenly.

1 Peter 1:4 To an inheritance incorruptible, and undefiled, and that fadeth not away, reserved in heaven for you,

1 Peter 1:5 Who are kept by the power of God through faith unto salvation ready to be revealed in the last time.

How about this pearl of great price?

1 Corinthians 15:20-23 But now is Christ risen from the dead, and become the firstfruits of them that

Notes

slept. For since by man came death, by man came also the resurrection of the dead. For as in Adam all die, even so in Christ shall all be made alive. But every man in his own order: Christ the firstfruits; afterward they that are Christ's at his coming.

Question: Is this saying that we shall be made alive when he comes the second time? Since he will come down here, aren't we going to have to be here also. How readest thou?

Your view is asked for, because many of my Christian brethren have taken me to task for my position in this matter. They insist on standing on the traditional teachings that say the believers go to heaven, when they pass away. The Bible, God's Word, says that we all must be fully persuaded in our own minds, and that the scriptures are of no private interpretation. In case some of you are wavering on this issue, please allow me to throw some more logs on the fire of understanding.

Matthew 5:18 & **Luke 16:17** mention the passing away of heaven. **Matthew 24:35** says, "Heaven and earth shall pass away". This is repeated in **Mark 13:31** & **Luke 21:33. Hebrews 1:10-12** also supports the fact that heaven will pass away.

Comment: I don't know about you-but I have no intention of going to a place that will pass away. In **Revelation 21:1-2**, God talks about seeing a new heaven-the Holy City New Jerusalem-which will be lowered to earth. That City is my destination.

John 3:13 And *no man* hath ascended up to heaven, but he that came down from heaven, even the Son of man which is in heaven.

Hebrews 12:22 But ye are come unto mount Zion, and unto the city of the living God, the heavenly Jerusalem,

Note: Since Mt. Zion is here on earth, it follows that the "heavenly Jerusalem"-the Holy City- also must be here on earth; or in place of the earth, that shall pass away.

All of **Revelation 21**, and the first five verses of **Revelation 22**, make it clear that believers will join God, and Christ Jesus in the Holy City-New

Jerusalem. Search the scriptures for yourself. As Jesus answered the lawyer in **Luke 10:26** What is written in the law? how readest thou? "Search the scriptures"

Now, if you wish to continue in the belief that you will go to heaven after the death of your physical body, so be it. Praise the Lord! But, as for me, and my house we will see you in New Jerusalem-where we will spend eternity worshipping, praising, adoring, and exalting our Father God.

It was my thought that this discussion ended with the above paragraph, but I was wrong. Another understanding has been opened to me by the Holy Spirit through God's Word. God said in **John 14:2-3** In my Father's house are many mansions: if it were not so, I would have told you. I go to prepare a place for you. And if I go and prepare a place for you, I will come again, and receive you unto myself; that where I am, there ye may be also.

Comment: Many claim, that the mansions in heaven are their eternal destinations. It speaks to my spirit, the place Jesus referred to as being prepared for us is the Holy City New Jerusalem. The Holy City, New Jerusalem, will be twelve thousands furlongs in length, width, and height. This amounts to thirteen hundred miles in all directions. There will be ample room here for all past, present, and future believers. It is in New Jerusalem where Jesus will prepare a place for us. He said, "I will come again". To where will he come? Here, of course, where he will receive us unto himself. Where will he be, that we may be with him also? Here of course in New Jerusalem, and since New Jerusalem will be lowered to the earth-here is where we will be. These facts are supported by God's Word-they have caused me to be fully persuaded as to where I will spend eternity. I will be in New Jerusalem-I am content. How about you?

As you know, a soaring eagle does not have a quenched spirit. **Isaiah 40:31** says, "But they that wait upon the LORD shall renew their strength; they shall mount up with wings as eagles;" Does this

Notes

mean that if we are entertaining a quenched spirit we are not waiting on the Lord? Gives one pause to think, doesn't it?

Jesus apparently confirmed that John will die, but will tarry until he comes again. Tarry where? It speaks to my spirit that John's spirit will tarry here on earth until Jesus comes back to claim his church. Then shall **1 Thessalonians 4:16-17** come to pass. (Search the scriptures).

Here is another gem for your collection:
John 6:44 No man can come to me, except the Father which hath sent me draw him: **and** I will raise him up at the last day.
Question: >From where will Jesus raise him up? Won't it be from here, when he returns?

Note: When I have stood fast on my understanding, that believers will inhabit the Holy City New Jerusalem for eternity, I have cited the scripture verses telling us that heaven and earth will pass away. They have answered with the verse, that says there will be a new heaven and a new earth. I have answered, that, for the sake of agreement, the new heaven and earth will be incorporated in the New City New Jerusalem - this was offered before I received the understanding I have now. I had no spiritual back-up for my position then. The "back-up" has jumped off the pages of my Bible as I did my daily reading recently: **2 Peter 3:13** Nevertheless we, according to his promise, look for new heavens and a new earth, wherein dwelleth righteousness

The Bible says, that God's throne will be in the Holy City New Jerusalem, and He **is** righteousness. Since God is righteousness, this places the new heaven and earth as an integral part of the Holy City New Jerusalem. I am content.

AFTER DEATH ADDENDUM - (The Kingdom of God - NEW JERUSALEM)

The throne of God is now located somewhere in the heavens-He sits on that throne in the company of his Son Jesus Christ, and is surrounded by angels—**Revelation 5:11** and the number of them was ten thousand times ten thousand, and thousands of thousands;". The scriptures tell us that one day the Holy City, New Jerusalem, will come down from God out of heaven prepared for us. Our Lord God, and the Lamb Christ Jesus, will dwell in that Holy City. It is my belief I will enter through one of the city's twelve gates, and abide with them for all eternity.

The Bible repeatedly refers to the "kingdom of heaven". Christians have been taught and led to believe that this kingdom is somewhere "up there" in the heavens. God's Word does not say that this is so. The Bible says: **Matthew 3:2** for the kingdom of heaven *is at hand.* **Matthew 4:17** for the kingdom of heaven is at hand. **Matthew 10:7** The kingdom of heaven *is at hand*. Now, if the kingdom of heaven is at hand, where do you think it will be located? Do you believe it will be found out of reach? The Bible clearly states that God's Kingdom *is at hand*. The Bible also states that "heaven and earth shall pass away", and that there will be a new heaven and a new earth (**Revelation 21:1**). In fact, the Word commands us to-" look for new heavens and a new earth, wherein dwelleth righteousness."(**2 Peter 3:13**). Can this possibly mean that there will be a complete remodeling (if you will) of God's first creation? No, it is accepted that this was all part of God's creation from the beginning.

The Bible says that no man has ascended up to heaven, except for Jesus Christ-who came down from heaven (**John 3:1**3). It also says that even David, who had a special place in God's heart, did not ascend into the heavens (**Acts 2:34**). Could this also mean that Abraham, and Isaac, and Jacob did not ascend into heaven? **Matthew 8:11** And I say

Notes

unto you, That many shall come from the east and west, and shall sit down with Abraham, and Isaac, and Jacob, in the kingdom of heaven. Could it be that the many, who will come from the east and the west will sit down with the three in the Holy City New Jerusalem - which will be the kingdom of heaven here on this new earth? You will have to answer for yourself-I am fully persuaded and content. May I humbly make a suggestion? Forget what you have heard or been taught-concentrate on the scriptures-through which the Holy Spirit can work, and deliver understanding (as promised in **1 John 5:20**). Give it a try; you can always go back to where you were. It is that understanding that will endure forever, because the Word of God endureth forever.-it will not pass away. It is God's Word that will not return to him void-not men's words (no matter how well-intentioned).

Please allow me to cite some more scripture verses, that may help you get started on your quest for the truth:

Matthew 3:2 And saying, Repent ye: for the kingdom of heaven *is at hand.*

Matthew 4:17 From that time Jesus began to preach, and to say, Repent: for the kingdom of heaven *is at hand.*

Matthew 5:3 Blessed are the poor in spirit: for theirs is the kingdom of heaven.

Matthew 5:10 Blessed are they which are persecuted for righteousness' sake: for theirs is the kingdom of heaven.

Matthew 5:20 For I say unto you, That except your righteousness shall exceed the righteousness of the scribes and Pharisees, ye shall in no case enter into the kingdom of heaven.

Matthew 7:21 Not every one that saith unto me, Lord, Lord, shall enter into the kingdom of heaven; but he that doeth the will of my Father which is in heaven.

Matthew 8:11 And I say unto you, That many shall come from the east and west, and shall sit down with Abraham, and Isaac, and Jacob, in the kingdom of heaven.

Matthew 10:7 And as ye go, preach, saying,

The kingdom of heaven *is at hand*.

Matthew 13:11 He answered and said unto them, Because it is given unto you to know the mysteries of the kingdom of heaven, but to them it is not given.

Matthew 16:19 And I will give unto thee the keys of the kingdom of heaven:

Question: Could those keys be God's Words, which tell us about the New City New Jerusalem?

Matthew 18:3 And said, Verily I say unto you, Except ye be converted, and become as little children, ye shall not enter into the kingdom of heaven.

Matthew 18:4 Whosoever therefore shall humble himself as this little child, the same is greatest in the kingdom of heaven.

Matthew 19:14 But Jesus said, Suffer little children, and forbid them not, to come unto me: for of such is the kingdom of heaven.

Matthew 19:23 Then said Jesus unto his disciples, Verily I say unto you, That a rich man shall hardly enter into the kingdom of heaven.

Acts 2:34 For David is not ascended into the heavens:

Matthew 24:35, **Mark 13:31**, and **Luke 21:33**: Heaven and earth shall pass away, but my words shall not pass away.

Question: Do you look forward to going to a place, that will pass away?

2 Peter 3:13 Nevertheless we, according to his promise, look for new heavens and a new earth, wherein dwelleth righteousness.

Revelation 3:12 Him that overcometh will I make a pillar in the temple of my God, and he shall go no more out: and I will write upon him the name of my God, and the name of the city of my God, *which is new Jerusalem*, which cometh down out of heaven from my God: and I will write upon him my new name.

Revelation 21

¹ And I saw a new heaven and a new earth: for the first heaven and the first earth were passed away; and there was no more sea.

² And I John saw the holy city, new Jerusalem, coming down from God out of heaven, prepared as a

Notes

Notes

bride adorned for her husband.

3 And I heard a great voice out of heaven saying, Behold, the tabernacle of God is with men, and he will dwell with them, and they shall be his people, and God himself shall be with them, and be their God.

4 And God shall wipe away all tears from their eyes; and there shall be no more death, neither sorrow, nor crying, neither shall there be any more pain: for the former things are passed away.

5 And he that sat upon the throne said, Behold, I make all things new. And he said unto me, Write: for these words are true and faithful.

6 And he said unto me, It is done. I am Alpha and Omega, the beginning and the end. I will give unto him that is athirst of the fountain of the water of life freely.

7 He that overcometh shall inherit all things; and I will be his God, and he shall be my son.

8 But the fearful, and unbelieving, and the abominable, and murderers, and whoremongers, and sorcerers, and idolaters, and all liars, shall have their part in the lake which burneth with fire and brimstone: which is the second death.

9 And there came unto me one of the seven angels which had the seven vials full of the seven last plagues, and talked with me, saying, Come hither, I will shew thee the bride, the Lamb's wife.

10 And he carried me away in the spirit to a great and high mountain, and shewed me that great city, the holy Jerusalem, descending out of heaven from God,

11 Having the glory of God: and her light was like unto a stone most precious, even like a jasper stone, clear as crystal;

12 And had a wall great and high, and had twelve gates, and at the gates twelve angels, and names written thereon, which are the names of the twelve tribes of the children of Israel:

13 On the east three gates; on the north three gates; on the south three gates; and on the west three gates.

14 And the wall of the city had twelve foundations, and in them the names of the twelve apostles of the Lamb.

Notes

15 And he that talked with me had a golden reed to measure the city, and the gates thereof, and the wall thereof.

16 And the city lieth foursquare, and the length is as large as the breadth: and he measured the city with the reed, twelve thousand furlongs. The length and the breadth and the height of it are equal.

17 And he measured the wall thereof, an hundred and forty and four cubits, according to the measure of a man, that is, of the angel.

18 And the building of the wall of it was of jasper: and the city was pure gold, like unto clear glass.

19 And the foundations of the wall of the city were garnished with all manner of precious stones. The first foundation was jasper; the second, sapphire; the third, a chalcedony; the fourth, an emerald;

20 The fifth, sardonyx; the sixth, sardius; the seventh, chrysolyte; the eighth, beryl; the ninth, a topaz; the tenth, a chrysoprasus; the eleventh, a jacinth; the twelfth, an amethyst.

21 And the twelve gates were twelve pearls: every several gate was of one pearl: and the street of the city was pure gold, as it were transparent glass.

22 And I saw no temple therein: for the Lord God Almighty and the Lamb are the temple of it.

23 And the city had no need of the sun, neither of the moon, to shine in it: for the glory of God did lighten it, and the Lamb is the light thereof.

24 And the nations of them which are saved shall walk in the light of it: and the kings of the earth do bring their glory and honour into it.

25 And the gates of it shall not be shut at all by day: for there shall be no night there.

26 And they shall bring the glory and honour of the nations into it.

27 And there shall in no wise enter into it any thing that defileth, neither whatsoever worketh abomination, or maketh a lie: but they which are written in the Lamb's book of life.

Revelation 22

1 And he shewed me a pure river of water of life, clear as crystal, proceeding out of the throne of God

Notes

and of the Lamb.

² In the midst of the street of it, and on either side of the river, was there the tree of life, which bare twelve manner of fruits, and yielded her fruit every month: and the leaves of the tree were for the healing of the nations.

³ And there shall be no more curse: *but the throne of God and of the Lamb shall be in it;* and his servants shall serve him:

⁴ And they shall see his face; and his name shall be in their foreheads.

⁵ And there shall be no night there; and they need no candle, neither light of the sun; for the Lord God giveth them light: and they shall reign for ever and ever.

Revelation 22:19 And if any man shall take away from the words of the book of this prophecy, God shall take away his part out of the book of life, and out of the holy city, and from the things which are written in this book.

2 Cointhians 1:2 Grace be to you and peace from God our Father, and from the Lord Jesus Christ.

2 Corinthians 13:14 The grace of the Lord Jesus Christ, and the love of God, and the communion of the Holy Ghost, be with you all. Amen.

Revelation 22:21 The grace of our Lord Jesus Christ be with you all. Amen.

NONE LOST??

There are many believers who stand on the premise that all the world (all of mankind) will be saved - "none will be lost". They say, that our wonderful, loving, merciful, forgiving and grace-full God would not "allow" the loss of any of the people He created. This may sound pleasing to the flesh, but the Word of God speaks otherwise to my spirit. The proponents of the "all-saved, none lost" position cite mainly two scripture verses - upon which they verify their position: **2 Peter 3:9** The Lord is not slack concerning his promise, as some men count slackness; but is longsuffering to us-ward, not willing that any should perish, but that all should come to repentance; and, **1 Timothy 2:4** Who will have all men to be saved, and to come unto the knowledge of the truth. (It speaks to my spirit, that the "any" and "all" refer to any and all, *who are saved.* If it is your persuasion to remain rested on these verses to promote the "none lost" posture - so be it. We will not argue the point - only share with you how scripture speaks to our spirits. Let us look at the obverse side of this coin - which believers have been tossing around for centuries.

We will offer scripture verses, that "sing" a different "tune" to be considered. We look at definitions of words, and the applicable scripture verses.

Damnation: hopeless; disaster-prone; ruined; done for; ill-fated.

Matthew 23:14 therefore ye shall receive the greater *damnation.*

Matthew 23:33 Ye serpents, ye generation of vipers, how can ye escape the *damnation of hell?*

Mark 12:40 these shall receive greater *damnation.*

Luke 20:47 the same shall receive greater **damnation.**

John 5:29 And shall come forth; they that have done good, unto the resurrection of life

and they that have done evil, unto the resurrection of *damnation*

Romans 13:2 and they that resist shall receive

Notes

to themselves damnation

1 Timothy 5:12 Having *damnation*, because they have cast off their first faith.

2 Peter 2:3 whose judgment now of a long time lingereth not, and their *damnation* slumbereth not.

Question: Isn't it apparent, that there will be a damnation to to be reckoned with by many?

Destruction: obliteration; devastation; demolition; ruin.

Matthew 7:13 and broad is the way, that leadeth to *destruction*, and many there be

which go in thereat:

Romans 3:16 *Destruction* and misery are in their ways:

Romans 9:22 What if God, willing to shew his wrath, and to make his power known, endured with much longsuffering the vessels of wrath fitted to *destruction*

Philippians 3:19 Whose end is *destruction*, whose God is their belly, and whose glory is in their shame, who mind earthly things.)

2 Thessalonians 1:9 Who shall be punished with *everlasting destruction* from the presence of the Lord, and from the glory of his power;

2 Peter 2:1 and bring upon themselves swift *destruction*.

2 Peter 3:16 which they that are unlearned and unstable wrest, as they do also the other scriptures, unto their own *destruction*.

Question: Do these verses say, that destruction of some is also part of God's ultimate plan?

Everlasting Fire: eternal; endless; ceaseless; never-ending; perpetual; unending.

Matthew 18:8 rather than having two hands or two feet to be cast into *everlasting fire*.

Matthew 25:41 Depart from me, ye cursed, into *everlasting fire*,

Comment: It appears there is an *everlasting fire*, with which some will have to deal.

Condemnation: blame; disapproval; denunciation; censure; scorn.

Luke 23:40 Dost not thou fear God, seeing thou

art in the same *condemnation?*

John 5:24 Verily, verily, I say unto you, He that heareth my word, and believeth on him that sent me, hath everlasting life, and shall not come into *condemnation*

Romans 5:16 And not as it was by one that sinned, so is the gift: for the judgment was by one to *condemnation*, but the free gift is of many offences unto justification.

1 Corinthians 11:34 that ye come not together unto *condemnation*.

1 Timothy 3:6 Not a novice, lest being lifted up with pride he fall into the *condemnation* of the devil.

James 5:12 but let your yea be yea; and your nay, nay; lest ye fall into *condemnation.*

Jude 1:4 For there are certain men crept in unawares, who were before of old ordained to this *condemnation,* ungodly men, turning the grace of our God into lasciviousness, and denying the only Lord God, and our Lord Jesus Christ.

Comment: Would you not agree, that *condemnation* for some is in God's Will?

Lake of Fire: (Into which both death and hell shall be thrown.)

Revelation 19:20 These both were cast alive into a *lake of fire* burning with brimstone.

Revelation 20:10 And the devil that deceived them was cast into the *lake of fire* and brimstone, where the beast and the false prophet are, and shall be tormented day and night for ever and ever.

Revelation 20:14 And death and hell were cast into the *lake of fire*. This is the second death

Revelation 20:15 And whosoever was not found written in the book of life was cast into the *lake of fire*.

Revelation 21:8 shall have their part in the *lake which burneth with fire* and brimstone: which is the second death.

Question: Do not these verses state, that many will end up in the eternal, ever-burning *lake of fire?*

In the first paragraph above, we cited **2 Peter 3:9** where it mentions that the Lord is not willing

Notes

that any man should perish. Please note the verse says, "should" - not "shall". "Shall" denotes an imperative sense, it means it has futurity - whatever is covered by this word will happen. "Should", on the other hand, means that something ought to be - or is supposed to be - not positively meant to be. Let us look at verses that deal with "perish":

Perish: expire; die; pass away.
__Luke 13:3__ I tell you, Nay: but, except ye repent, *ye shall all likewise perish*
__Luke 13:5__ I tell you, Nay: but, except ye repent, *ye shall all likewise perish*
__John 3:15-16__ That whosoever believeth in him *should not perish*, but have eternal life.

For God so loved the world, that he gave his only begotten Son, that whosoever believeth in him *should not perish*, but have everlasting life.
__John 10:27-28__ My sheep hear my voice, and I know them, and they follow me: And I give unto them eternal life; and they shall never *perish*, neither shall any man pluck them out of my hand.
__Acts 13:41__ Behold, ye despisers, and wonder, *and perish*
__Romans 2:12__ For as many as have sinned without law *shall also perish* without law
__1 Corinthians 1:18__ For the preaching of the cross is to *them that perish* foolishness; but unto us which are saved it is the power of God.
__2 Thessalonians 2:10__ And with all deceivableness of unrighteousness *in them that perish*; because they received not the love of the truth, that they might be saved
__2 Peter 2:12__ But these, as natural brute beasts, made to be taken and destroyed, speak evil of the things that they understand not; and *shall utterly perish* in their own corruption;
Question: Will some be saved, and others perish? Sure looks like it, doesn't it?

Damned:
__Mark 16:6__ He that believeth and is baptized shall be saved; but he that believeth not *shall be damned.*
Comment: Looks as if some will be damned, doesn't it?

It speaks to my spirit, that the scriptures say what they mean, and mean what they say. There is a large group of believers, that say that scripture verses can be "taken out of context" - in my opinion the use of the "context" argument is only a way to negate and/or skirt around any verse's true meaning. They apply that reasoning to the many scripture verses cited above - they "feel", that they are out of context when looking at **2 Peter 3:9** and **1 Timothy 2:4** (to me the "out of context" theory is a weapon of the flesh, while God's Word is the sword of the Spirit.) Sometimes, they even look at one verse negating and/or changing the meaning of another. It settled in my spirit long ago to accept God's Word, as presented in the Bible, as His inspired Word - perfect in all its content. This delivered me from the propensity to try to slide around God's Will and Plan for my life. In other words, as an old saying goes, "I take Him at His Word". Let's look at some other verses, that may re-direct the beliefs of many, who still believe that none shall perish.

Matthew 20:16 So the last shall be first, and the first last: for many be called, ***but few chosen.***

Matthew 22:14 For many are called, ***but few are chosen***.

1 Timothy 6:12 Fight the good fight of faith, lay hold on eternal life, whereunto thou art also called

Matthew 7:13 Enter ye in at the strait gate: for wide is the gate, and broad is the way, that leadeth to destruction, and many there be which go in thereat:

Luke 13:24 Strive to enter in at the strait gate: for many, I say unto you, will seek to enter in, ***and shall not be able.***

Now let us look at how all of these verses cited can be brought into line with **2 Peter 3:9** and **1 Timothy 2:4**. After all, God would not have given us an imperfect Word with which to conduct our walk with Him, would He? In order to establish the perfection of God's Word, the "any should perish" and the "all men to be saved" must refer only those, who are saved. The rest will suffer all the other scripture verses cited.

Notes

WITNESSING

Many believers confess that they have a hard time witnessing to unbelievers. They find it hart to tell someone about Jesus Christ, and being born again. They often ask for prayer that will deliver them from this dilemma, and make their witnessing easier to come by. The main reason believers have trouble in this area is that they feel they are responsible for getting people saved (wonder where they heard that?). They are not-the Bible clearly states that God chooses us; we don't choose him. Yes, God gives us the ability to accept or reject, which is already fulfilled in his will. He gives us the choice-the element of choice appears only after he has chosen us. It speaks to our spirit that all God expects from us is to tell people about his son Jesus Christ.

We don't even have to worry about the words to use in our witnessing-God has already given us the words, His Words. To begin with, believers have an automatic and natural way to identify themselves as Christians to someone they have just met. Upon greeting someone we usually say, "Hello, how are you"? The normal response is, "Fine, thanks, and you"? How many of us answer, "Saved, thanks-born again"! The words "saved" and "born again" are God's Words-you can find them in your Bible. What have we accomplished here? We have shared the Word of God, while sharing with someone that we are Christians. After answering thusly, we have been asked, "What does that mean"? We answer simply, "It just means that we are Christians-followers of Jesus Christ". If the conversation goes no further, we have witnessed Christ, and have rightly divided God's Word. In this busy world we often get no further in the effort. However, sometimes we do-when that happens, we share the the scriptures that refer to being born again or being saved. We suggest you memorize the verses that speak to you, and practice saying them aloud. You will be blessed by what you hear, and you'll get used to hearing your own voice saying the wonderful Words of God. Please allot us to cite some scriptures from which you may

Notes

want to make a choice for your witnessing effort.

Acts 16:31 And they said, Believe on the Lord Jesus Christ, and thou shalt be saved, and thy house.

John 6:47 Verily, verily, I say unto you, He that believeth on me hath everlasting life.

John 3:15 That whosoever believeth in him should not perish, but have eternal life.

John 3:16 For God so loved the world, that he gave his only begotten Son, that whosoever believeth in him should not perish, but have everlasting life.

These verses are short, and should be familiar to most believers. Pick the one you are most comfortable with, and memorize it in preparation for sharing it with an unbeliever. They are so short you may want to memorize them all-more ammunition for your spiritual "gun". If you spark and interest with your first verse, you may want others as back-up and confirmation. If the witness is cut short by the unbeliever, be thankful and offer up the thank-you scriptures in praise. You have done all, and can stand fast-Rejoice. If the unbeliever continues showing interest, you may want one or more of the following verses as support:

1 John 5:18 but he that is begotten of God keepeth himself, and that wicked one toucheth him not.

1 John 5:1 Whosoever believeth that Jesus is the Christ is born of God: and every one that loveth him that begat loveth him also that is begotten of him.

Ephesians 2:5 Even when we were dead in sins, hath quickened us together with Christ, (by grace ye are saved;)

2 Corinthians 5:17 Therefore if any man be in Christ, he is a new creature: old things are passed away; behold, all things are become new.

Acts 3:19 Repent ye therefore, and be converted, that your sins may be blotted out,

1 Peter 1:23 Being born again, not of corruptible seed, but of incorruptible, by the word of God, which liveth and abideth for ever.

Romans 5:6 For when we were yet without strength, in due time Christ died for the ungodly.

Notes

Romans 5:7 For scarcely for a righteous man will one die: yet peradventure for a good man some would even dare to die.

Romans 5:8 But God commendeth his love toward us, in that, while we were yet sinners, Christ died for us.

Romans 5:9 Much more then, being now justified by his blood, we shall be saved from wrath through him.

There are many other scripture verses you could share. We'll leave it up to you to search the scriptures, and find them. If the unbeliever is really being worked on by the Holy Spirit, you could share:

John 3:3 Jesus answered and said unto him, Verily, verily, I say unto thee, Except a man be born again, he cannot see the kingdom of God.

John 3:4 Nicodemus saith unto him, How can a man be born when he is old? can he enter the second time into his mother's womb, and be born?

John 3:5 Jesus answered, Verily, verily, I say unto thee, Except a man be born of water and of the Spirit, he cannot enter into the kingdom of God.

John 3:6 That which is born of the flesh is flesh; and that which is born of the Spirit is spirit.

John 3:7 Marvel not that I said unto thee, Ye must be born again.

Regardless of how the witness turns out, rejoice and be glad. Give thanks unto the Lord. Be content and at peace with the peace that Jesus Christ gave us, and left us. Let no one trouble you, and be careful for nothing. (All scriptural encouragements-not ours).

It shouts to me that the unbelieving spouse is covered, and can thank God for being married to a believer(although they seldom do-no matter). The believing spouse can be at peace, and not try to force his or her belief on the unbeliever. Place that burden upon the Lord. (**Psalm 55:22** Cast thy burden upon the LORD, and he shall sustain thee:)

God said: **Ecclesiastes 12:13** Let us hear the conclusion of the whole matter:

Please allow us to offer our conclusion of this particular matter.

It is a great temptation for the believing spouse to argue the right of wrong of the respective positions taken here. Since the unbeliever is not under the blood, he or she is not bound by God's Words, which tell the Christian to be patient, long-suffering, not to strive, forbearing, and to think on the things listed in: **Philippians 4:8** Finally, brethren, whatsoever things are true, whatsoever things are honest, whatsoever things are just, whatsoever things are pure, whatsoever things are lovely, whatsoever things are of good report; if there be any virtue, and if there be any praise, think on these things. (**Note:** All of "these things' are God's Words-we are told to "think" on these things, and not told to argue about them). Alas, the unbeliever is not covered by the umbrella of God's Word. However, the believer is. The believer has to decide whether any disputes involved here are of the Spirit or of the flesh.

COMMENT: The Christian would ultimately have to decide if the arguing and striving in this area is of the Spirit, or of the flesh. May you have a joyous deciding experience.

WITNESS RESISTANCE

Many Christians have sought my counsel concerning the witnessing to an unbeliever, who says, "Since I am not a believer, your scripture citings are a waste of time and effort". Admittedly, it was my policy early on to forge ahead-no matter what. It has since spoken to my spirit that:

1. God does the choosing (**Ephesians 1:4, John 15:16 & 19).**

2. Saving someone is not my responsibility.

3. It is my duty and charge from God only to share the message of salvation.

The following is what I now share with the resisting unbeliever:

You are right, but please allow me to share this story. If a totally blind person enters a brilliantly-lighted room, he doesn't see the light. This doesn't

Notes

mean the light is not present-he just doesn't see it. It **is** there, regardless of his inability to see it. We Christians feel somewhat the same way, when an unbeliever doesn't "see" Jesus-who we know is the Light of the World. To us, the unbeliever is in a form of spiritual darkness. Not seeing him does not mean he is not present-he is there. He is not seen because of the spiritual darkness that prevails(the Bible refers to darkness as a veil).

You do not see our Light of the World-fine! It is still our duty to share Jesus with all. It has been a blessing talking with you".

What has been accomplished here?

1. By saying, "You are right", we set the unbeliever at ease. He will relax a little.
2. Since stories are usually welcome, he may give a listen.
3. He has been witnessed to without being really aware of it.

MARRIAGE

We get a lot of action on this one. Believers are either seeking advice upon going into a marriage, or are asking how to better their marriage situations. In counseling, we can either make people "feel better" about marriage with the usual candy-coated advice given by most, or we can share scriptures upon which marriages should be based. We know that Jesus Christ is our rock and our foundation-we know that Jesus Christ is the Word. Where better to build than upon him?

Genesis 2:18 And the LORD God said, It is not good that the man should be alone; I will make him an help meet for him.

Proverbs 5:18 Let thy fountain be blessed: and rejoice with the wife of thy youth.

Ephesians 5:33 Nevertheless let every one of you in particular so love his wife even as himself; and the wife see that she reverence her husband.

John 13:34 A new commandment I give unto you, That ye love one another;

John 15:12 This is my commandment, That ye love one another, as I have loved you.

Hebrews 10:24 And let us consider one another to provoke unto love and to good works:

1 Pet 4:8 And above all things have fervent charity among yourselves: for charity shall cover the multitude of sins.

Ephesians 5:21 Submitting yourselves one to another in the fear of God.

Ephesians 5:22 Wives, submit yourselves unto your own husbands, as unto the Lord.

Ephesians5:23 For the husband is the head of the wife, even as Christ is the head of the church: and he is the Saviour of the body.

Ephesians 5:25 Husbands, love your wives, even as Christ also loved the church, and gave himself for it;

Romans 15:7 Wherefore receive ye one another, as Christ also received us to the glory of God.

1 Peter 1:15 But as he which hath called you is holy, so be ye holy in all manner of conversation;

Notes

Philippians 2:3 Let nothing be done through strife or vainglory; but in lowliness of mind let each esteem other better than themselves.

1 Peter 3:8 Finally, be ye all of one mind, having compassion one of another, love as brethren, be pitiful, be courteous:

1 Peter 3:9 Not rendering evil for evil, or railing for railing: but contrariwise blessing; knowing that ye are thereunto called, that ye should inherit a blessing.

Philippians 2:2 Fulfil ye my joy, that ye be likeminded, having the same love, being of one accord, of one mind.

Philippians 2:14 Do all things without murmurings and disputings:

Ephesians 4:29-32 Let no corrupt communication proceed out of your mouth, but that which is good to the use of edifying, that it may minister grace unto the hearers And grieve not the holy Spirit of God, whereby ye are sealed unto the day of redemption. Let all bitterness, and wrath, and anger, and clamour, and evil speaking, be put away from you, with all malice: And be ye kind one to another, tenderhearted, forgiving one another, even as God for Christ's sake hath forgiven you.

Colossians 3:12-15 Put on therefore, as the elect of God, holy and beloved, bowels of mercies, kindness, humbleness of mind, meekness, longsuffering; Forbearing one another, and forgiving one another, if any man have a quarrel against any: even as Christ forgave you, so also do ye, And above all these things put on charity, which is the bond of perfectness. And let the peace of God rule in your hearts, to the which also ye are called in one body; and be ye thankful.

Colossians 3:9 Lie not one to another, seeing that ye have put off the old man with his deeds;

In answering requests for counseling in this area we advise couples to read aloud whichever of the above scriptures speaks to them particularly. They may want to read aloud in unison. This will only take a few minutes, but it will invoke the promises of the Word of God that endureth forever. A marriage cannot help but be blessed, if these scriptures speak out from the heart-so that the Holy Spirit can deliver the understanding. Now if anyone has questions or arguments with the scriptures, please take up your case with the Author and Finisher. Please read aloud again **Ephesians 4:29-32**. Listen and heed what it says. If we did only what these four verses command us to do, can you picture what would happen in the world? Do you agree that the entire world would flip over? Do you agree that any relationship, based on these Words, would flourish? You know it. (By the way, God's Words are not just pretty words-they are commands, and *not* only suggestions)! Many have commented that it is not possible to measure up to the standards set up by God in His Word. We reply by asking, "Do you believe that our Father God, who loves us, would direct us to do things, and not give us the ability to carry them out? After all, God promised that we could do all things through Christ which strengtheneth us (**Philippians 4:13**).

There are as many divorces in Christian marriages as there are in the world's marriages - over 50%. Is it possible, that, it is because we have followed the world's practice of making these vows at the marriage altar: "till death do us part"; in sickness or in health; for better or for worse, etc.? The Bible commands us not to make oaths or vows - it says, "Swear not all". Is it possible, that in making these vows, we are going against God's Word? Would it be better if the wedding couple would confess to each other at the altar the instructions which God has given us in His Word concerning how man and wife should treat each other as they wend their way through the challenges we face as man and wife? Seeing the results we suffer - it couldn't hurt, and is worth a shot, at least. Couldn't hurt!

WHEN ONE IS - AND THE OTHER ISN'T
(Saved, that is)

In this situation, the believer can relax, and praise the Lord in and for all things - as we are commanded to do, anyway. God has this covered.

Notes

1 Corinthians 7:14 For the unbelieving husband is sanctified by the wife, and the unbelieving wife is sanctified by the husband: else were your children unclean; but now are they holy.

Comment: There are many well-intentioned (but misguided) believers, who worry and fret about their spouses being unsaved. The believer should, and can, scripturally relax - God has it covered. **1 Corinthians 7:14** clearly states, that the unbelieving spouse is "sanctified" by the believer spouse. "Sanctified" means made holy, and/or set aside. God's grace also covers the children - Praise the Lord.

We find in **Hebrews 10:14** For by one offering he hath perfected for ever them that are sanctified.

Question: Is this verse saying, that the sanctified spouse has been made perfect? Seems so to my spirit. Looks as if all the believer has to do is await God's perfect timing (**James 5:8** Be ye also patient.) We find in **Hebrews 2:11** For both he that sanctifieth and they who are sanctified are all of one: for which cause he is not ashamed to call them brethren, **Question**: Is this saying, that God and the sanctified ones are made one in His Eyes? Sure looks like it to me. How readest thou? Also, is God saying here, that He calls the sanctified ones "brethren"? Again, looks like it to me.

Here are a few more pertinent verses:
Acts 20:32 And now, brethren, I commend you to God, and to the word of his grace, which is able to build you up, and to give you an inheritance among all them *which are sanctified.*

Acts 26:18 To open their eyes, and to turn them from darkness to light, and from the power of Satan unto God, that they may receive forgiveness of sins, and inheritance among them *which are sanctified by faith* that is in me.

Jude 1:1-2 Jude, the servant of Jesus Christ, and brother of James, to them *that are sanctified by God the Father*, and preserved in Jesus Christ, and called:. 2 Mercy unto you, and peace, and love, be multiplied.

This all speaks to my spirit, that the unbelieving spouse is covered. Many Christians (most, that is) disagree with my posture and position here, and that is fine - we all have the right to be fully persuaded in our own minds as God has stated in **Romans15:5**. However, it shouts to my spirit, that the unbelieving spouse is indeed "covered" by God's Grace and Mercy. The unbelieving spouse can thank God for being led into marrying a believer - or who became a believer after the wedding (as was in my case, by the way.)

It often happens, that an unbelieving spouse, who disagrees with my persuasion here, will continue an active crusade to get his/her spouse saved -that's fine. We are commanded by God to be patient, forbearing, not to strive, to be long-suffering, etc.. We are also commanded to cast our burdens upon the Lord (including the "burden" of having an unbelieving spouse.) In my case, I am blessed in being married to the perfect portrait of the **Proverbs 31:10-12** wife, who, by the way is not saved. We are told to trust in the Lord, and I do. This is no longer a burden to my spirit - it has been cast unto the Lord.

God does the choosing - not us.

Notes

Notes

DIVORCE

This area is another "hot potato"; much of the world has entered into the Christian true scriptural view of this subject, and has been accepted, in many Christian walks. Much that passes for Christian counseling in the area of divorce serves the flesh and not the spirit of man. All we ask is that you allow the Word of God to speak to your spirit- we will be happy to let the Holy Spirit deliver an understanding. Please refer to, and read aloud, **Ephesians 5:20**, **Colossians 3:17**, and **1 Thessalonians 5:18** - these are the thank-you scripture verses. Then, please share the following scripture verses aloud with us.

Matthew 19:3-9 The Pharisees also came unto him, tempting him, and saying unto him, Is it lawful for a man to put away his wife for every cause?

And he answered and said unto them, Have ye not read, that he which made them at the beginning made them male and female,

And said, For this cause shall a man leave father and mother, and shall cleave to his wife: and they twain shall be one flesh?

Wherefore they are no more twain, but one flesh. What therefore God hath joined together, let not man put asunder.

They say unto him, Why did Moses then command to give a writing of divorcement, and to put her away?

He saith unto them, Moses because of the hardness of your hearts suffered you to put away your wives: but from the beginning it was not so.

And I say unto you, Whosoever shall put away his wife, except it be for fornication, and shall marry another, committeth adultery: and whoso marrieth her which is put away doth commit adultery.

Comment: The words "put away" underlined above are treated in **Malachi 2:16** For the LORD, the God of Israel, saith that he *hateth putting away*: God hates the putting away. The Word also says they are one flesh. How does one separate one flesh? The Word says, "let not man put asunder". These pieces of paper called, "divorce decrees", are they of God or man? The proceedings are of men's efforts, the court actions are of man, the verdicts are of man, the papers of divorcement are of man. These papers never cite what God has proclaimed to be the truth-His Truth. Since God said, "Let not put asunder", does this mean that divorces decided by man are not valid in God's eyes. See what is meant by, "hot potato"? The answer is clear to me. What is your answer?

God has said pretty much the same as cited above in **Matthew 5:32**, **Mark 10:2-12**, **Luke 16:18, 1 Corinthians 7:10-11, Romans 7:1-3 and 1 Corinthians 7:39**. Please "search the scriptures", and allow the agreement speak to your hearts. Read them aloud. Remember that these are God's Words-not mine. If you find yourself resisting them, are you reacting out of your spirit-or out of your flesh?

Malachi 2:14 Yet ye say, Wherefore? Because the LORD hath been witness between thee and the wife of thy youth, against whom thou hast dealt treacherously: yet is she thy companion, and the wife of thy covenant. **Malachi 2:15** And did not he make one? Yet had he the residue of the spirit. And wherefore one? That he might seek a godly seed. Therefore take heed to your spirit, and let none deal treacherously against the wife of his youth.

Comment: It would appear from these scriptures that God has made marriage a holy state (as voiced so often in marriage ceremonies). God made the two marriage partners, man and women, *as one*. He commanded man not to put them asunder. Man has conveniently skirted this condition of "oneness", and approved divorce by citing the following verses:

Matthew 5:32 But I say unto you, That whoso-ever shall put away his wife, **saving for the cause of fornication,**

Matthew 19:9 And I say unto you, Whosoever shall put away his wife, **except it be for fornication,**

In other scriptures divorce is not allowed under any circumstances:

Mark 10:9 What therefore God hath joined together, *let not man put asunder.*

1 Corinthians 7:10 And unto the married I

Notes

command, yet not I, but the Lord, Let not the wife depart from her husband:

1 Corinthians 7:11 But and if she depart, let her remain unmarried, or be reconciled to her husband: and let not the husband put away his wife.

Comment: This allows separation, but doesn't not approve divorce.

Romans 7:2 For the woman which hath an husband is bound by the law to her husband so long as he liveth;

Matthew 19:6 Wherefore they are no more twain, *but one flesh*. What therefore God hath joined together, *let not man put asunder*.

Now, the question of agreement of the scripture arises. It would seem that there is conflict here. The seeming conflict is caused by two phrases-"saving for the cause of fornication", and "except it be for fornication". The act of fornication is generally accepted by the world as being an illicit sexual act committed by an unmarried person. Adultery, on the other hand, is generally accepted as being an illicit sexual act performed by a married person. The two scriptural phrases in question seem to provide and "out" for believers, who want to divorce their spouses. Now if you are of this persuasion, and wish to remain so, Praise the Lord. This will keep the divorce rate in the Christian world even with the world's percentage, which is over 50% at the moment.

We confess that we are not sure how the scriptures find agreement in this area. We can, however, offer one understanding that might bring all the scriptures in line with each other. What if the word "fornication", as used in the above verses, refers to sexual activity between husband and wife-as well as the illicit connotation? If one accepts this position, it could mean that husband and wife must remain together without the element of sexual relations. The husband would make himself a eunuch. In this situation a man would not be putting away his wife, except in the area of sexual relations. He would not be putting them asunder. We admit that we may be reaching here. If you have a better, or different

Notes

understanding of how these scriptures can be brought into agreement, please share it with us. Hot Potato? Sure is!

The usual rationalization given by those, who skirt God's Word in this area is, "But God wouldn't want us to go through life being lonely". Where does it say this in the Bible? If you believe that God's Will is finished, as we do, the only thing left for the believer is obedience to his Word. Loneliness is a condition of the flesh, not of the spirit of man. Loneliness in not addressed in the Word of God, but patience, obedience, love, rejoicing, thankfulness and obedience are. (Besides, how can one be lonely, when God said he would not leave us or forsake us)?

You may find an understanding in **Matthew 19:11-12**, "But he said unto them, All men cannot receive this saying, save they to whom it is given. For there are some eunuchs, which were so born from their mother's womb: and there are some eunuchs, which were made eunuchs of men: and there be eunuchs, which have made themselves eunuchs for the kingdom of heaven's sake. He that is able to receive it, let him receive it".

When we share how the Spirit speaks to us concerning divorce, we usually get comments as follows:
1. "You don't know the circumstances".
2. "You have no idea what she did to me".
3. "She treated me shamefully, and made my life miserable".
4. "She was unfaithful to me".
5. "I just couldn't take it any more".

You have probably heard these, and many more. It would seem that only way "out" is divorce. We agree that the only "easy" way out is divorce. However, God says:
Matthew 5:44 But I say unto you, Love your enemies, bless them that curse you, do good to them that hate you, and pray for them which despitefully use you, and persecute you;
Matthew 5:39 But I say unto you, That ye resist

Notes

not evil: but whosoever shall smite thee on thy right cheek, turn to him the other also.

Luke 6:27 But I say unto you which hear, Love your enemies, do good to them which hate you,

Luke 6:28 Bless them that curse you, and pray for them which despitefully use you.

Luke 6:29 And unto him that smiteth thee on the one cheek offer also the other; and him that taketh away thy cloak forbid not to take thy coat also.

Comment: You may want to check out the FORGIVENESS section of this Manual.

My Bible indicates no exceptions to the above scriptures. It speaks to us that even the "Yeah, But" sect has no leg to stand on here (but they will probably try). It seems that the only real challenge is being obedient to God's Word. Everything lies in the ability to *love and forgive.* The flesh wants out - the spirit forgives, forgets and endures. **1 Corinthians 13:7** says: *Beareth* all things, believeth all things, hopeth all things, *endureth* all things. Of course, the scripture is talking about charity, or love. God orders us to love one another, so we come under this verse. God would not have said, "Let not man put asunder" without giving us the strength and spiritual insight to endure whatever manifests itself in our lives. After all, we are joint-heirs with Christ. Do you remember: **Philippians 4:13** I can do all things through Christ which strengtheneth me.?

1 Corinthians 7:27 Art thou bound unto a wife? *seek not to be loosed.*

Exodus 20:14 Thou shalt not commit adultery.

Deuteronomy 5:18 Neither shalt thou commit adultery.

Matthew 5:32 and whosoever shall marry her that is divorced committeth adultery.

Question: Are we forbidden to marry a divorced person? We think so. (We know so).

Two verses have now spoken to me as regards the reconciling of the questions posed by the two phrases cited earlier: "saving for the cause of forni-cation" and "except for the cause of fornication".

Mark 10:11 And he saith unto them, Whosoever shall put away his wife, and marry another, committeth adultery against her.

Mark 10:12 And if a woman shall put away her husband, and be married to another, she committeth adultery.

Comment: Notice that no provision (escape clause) for the "fornication" posture is mentioned in these two verses. These verses state simply that if anyone, who re-marries after being divorced, is committing adultery. Admittedly, this can be a bitter pill to swallow in the flesh; but, in the spirit, it is the truth as it speaks to my spirit. Again, since every man must be fully persuaded in his own mind, your spirit must determine your own posture in this matter. Is it possible, that God's Perfect Plan does not allow divorce so as to stop the possibility of committing adultery in a re-marriage situation—thereby stopping the possibility of two sins being committed?

(DIVORCE ADDENDUM)

DIVORCE AND *RE*-MARRIAGE

WHAT DOES GOD'S WORD SAY?

Matthew 19:6 "What therefore God hath joined together, let not man put asunder,"

It is being taught by many, that our Lord "allows a putting-away and re-marriage by the innocent party." Let's examine this statement only in the light of Holy Scripture - the Bible. It will be seen, that such a statement will not bear the light of Divine authority. The Lord's meaning, when He spoke about divorce and re-marriage, was quite clear to His immediate followers - this is evident. This: "all things whatsoever I have commanded you," which they taught to succeeding generations of Christians, was the doctrine of the absolute indissolubility of marriage. Accordingly, for the first years of the Christian era, divorce was unheard of among Christians.

Is it possible that the early Christian teachers

Notes

had mistaken (or purposely misused) the Lord's meaning, and that men of today have rediscovered it? Was it not a sign of the worldliness (the flesh) of the 4th century, that divorce began to creep into the Christian walk at that time? Is it not a symptom of the worldliness (the flesh) of this day that it again rears its ugly head, even to its appearance among professing assemblies of God's people, let alone the Christian body at large?

If one teaches, permits, and/or recognizes "divorce" and "remarriage" of divorced persons, one is placing a stumbling block before the body of Christ, and this is not in line with God's Word - it also gives a mixed message before the world. It will show the unbelievers, that it (the body) has departed from the fundamental Christian doctrine of the absolute sacred state of marriage - allowing the flesh to dictate truth. **Ephesians 5:23-33** likens the marriage of man and woman to the marriage of our Heavenly Bridegroom to His bride - the body of Christ. If either marriage is breakable, wouldn't the truth of the **Ephesians 5** verses be compromised? Didn't God solidify the unbreakable condition of both marriage situations in these verses - making it scripturally impossible for man to cause the oneness of a married couple to be put asunder? The unbreakable marriage between Jesus Christ and his bride, and the marriage between a man and his wife are both "covered" here. If not, would our perfect God use this illustration if either marriage tie could be broken in His sight?

A Note on "Fornication"

1.- Fornication never means adultery. They are different words with different meanings: "adultery" means infidelity, disloyalty, betrayal, faithlessness - it applies to married partners who break the condition of the oneness of their marriage agreement by forbidden sexual contact with another party. "Fornication" refers to the sexual misbehavior between unmarried people - even when only one is unmarried. Yet people today take away the chosen word of the Holy Spirit, "fornication," in **Matt. 5:32, 19:9** and put the word "adultery" in its place. Unless they do this, they can offer no "ground" for divorce. Yet they have no authority to do so, and fall into the act of adding or detracting from God's Word - which carries a heavy penalty.

2.- In **Matthew 5:32, Matthew 15:19, Matthew 19:9, 1 Corinthians 6:9** and **Galatians 5:19** the Holy Spirit-inspired scriptures use both words in the same writings. This establishes the fact, that the two words are distinguished one from another - they have different meanings. The term "fornication" does not cover all forms of sexual evil - as stated in: **Galatians 5:19** Now the works of the flesh are manifest, which are these; *Adultery, fornication*, uncleanness, lasciviousness, Man has interchanged the meanings of these words in order to skirt around the Truth to satisfy the leadings of the flesh - we know the harsh self-inventory, that God's Word can inflict on us. (Check out **Hebrews 4:12.**)

3. **1 Corinthians 5:1** It is reported commonly that there is fornication among you, and such fornication as is not so much as named among the Gentiles, that one should have *his father's wife.* Only the man is dealt with here, and is treated as a single man as regards his behavior. God's Word refers to the woman as still being "his father's wife" - not his. So God did not recognize as marriage, that he had "his father's wife." Such a connection would have been unlawful. Accordingly, the proper word, which describes his sin is "fornication" - this the Holy Spirit uses.

Now, as fornication does not mean adultery, the current idea that adultery is scriptural grounds for divorce is a fallacy. No one has the right to change (add or detract) from God's Word. Substituting "adultery" for God's chosen Word "fornication" as given in **Matthew 5:32** and **Matthew 19:9** is doing just that - for which a price will be paid.

SUMMARY:

Matthew 19:6 Wherefore they are no more twain, but one flesh. What therefore God hath joined together, let not man put asunder.

1 Corinthians 7:11 But and if she depart, let her remain unmarried or be reconciled to her husband: and let not the husband put away his wife.

Notes

Comment: Everything else is "hardness of heart", and against the clear meanings of God's Word (s)!!

God's Word tells believers in Christ Jesus, that we are to be of one mind, judgment and spirit. We are to speak the same words - the oracles of God. We are to rightly divide the Word of Truth. The only way this can all be accomplished is that we interpret, use and teach through the sharing of God's Word with the leading of our true Teacher, the Holy Spirit. We must stop misusing **Matthew 5:32** and **Matthew 19:9** - accepting and standing fast on what they actually say. These words were for the ears of those, who belonged to the dispensation of the law, and applied to men under it, who wanted to put away their wives for whatever reason. They reveal, that the believer's use of these two verses as an authority to divorce on the grounds of adultery, is a mistaken and unwarranted misuse of Scriptures.

CHRIST'S SECOND COMING

We have been ask several about our "opinion" concerning the second coming of our Lord and Savior Jesus Christ. Our answer is always the same, "We have no opinion-God covers this subject completely in His Word".

Matthew 24:36 But of that day and hour knoweth no man, no, not the angels of heaven, but my Father only.

Matthew 24:44 Therefore be ye also ready: for in such an hour as ye think not the Son of man cometh.

Luke 12:40 Be ye therefore ready also: for the Son of man cometh at an hour when ye think not.

Matthew 25:13 Watch therefore, for ye know neither the day nor the hour wherein the Son of man cometh.

2 Peter 3:10 But the day of the Lord will come as a thief in the night;

Acts 1:7 And he said unto them, It is not for you to know the times or the seasons, which the Father hath put in his own power.

1 Thessalonians 5:2 For yourselves know perfectly that the day of the Lord so cometh as a thief in the night.

Revelation 3:3 I will come on thee as a thief, and thou shalt not know what hour I will come upon thee.

Mark 13:32 But of that day and that hour knoweth no man, no, not the angels which are in heaven, neither the Son, but the Father.

Deuteronomy 29:29 The secret things belong unto the LORD our God

Man can ponder and figure this question all he wants, but the secret things *do* belong unto the Lord, and He is in control. The above scriptures clearly state that God is the only one, who knows when Jesus will return. Too many of us wonder and worry about when our Lord Jesus Christ will return to assume his throne here on earth. Many of us want it to be soon so that we can be delivered from the things of this world. It speaks to us that we should

Notes

not be concerned about the time, only that we should ***be ready*** as the five virgins, who had oil for their lamps were. God tells us how Christ will return in **Rev 1:7, Acts 1:9-11,** and **Luke 21:27.**

Anyone, who claims to possess special knowledge about when Christ will return in a manner not consistent with God's Word, is suspect.

GOD'S WORD IS FINAL

Many believers are disturbed about the arguments and/or disagreements over God's Words that occur in Christians gatherings. They also bemoan the fact that, with so many different versions of the Bible in use, the possibility of different interpretations often causes problems and confusion. They seek advice about an answer to their dilemma in handling this problem. After placing them in an "attitude of gratitude" by sharing the thank-you scriptures, we share the following:

In the Old Testament:

Psalm 89:34 My covenant will I not break, nor alter the thing that is gone out of my lips.

Psalm 119:89 For ever, O LORD, thy word is settled in heaven.

Isaiah 40:8 The grass withereth, the flower fadeth: but the word of our God shall stand for ever.

Proverbs 30:5 Every word of God is pure: he is a shield unto them that put their trust in him.

Proverbs 30:6 Add thou not unto his words, lest he reprove thee, and thou be found a liar.

Psalm 12:6 The words of the LORD are pure words:

Psalm 19:7 The law of the LORD is perfect, converting the soul: the testimony of the LORD is sure, making wise the simple.

Psalm 19:8 The statutes of the LORD are right, rejoicing the heart: the commandment of the LORD is pure, enlightening the eyes.

Deuteronomy 4:2 Ye shall not add unto the word which I command you, neither shall ye diminish ought from it,

Psalm 18:30 As for God, his way is perfect: the word of the LORD is tried:

Psalm 119:140 Thy word is very pure:

Deuteronomy 12:32 What thing soever I command you, observe to do it: thou shalt not add thereto, nor diminish from it.

Joshua 1:8 This book of the law shall not depart out of thy mouth; but thou shalt meditate therein day and night, that thou mayest observe to do according to all that is written therein:

Notes

In the New Testament:

Matthew 24:35, Mark 13:31, Luke 21:33 - Heaven and earth shall pass away: but my words shall not pass away.

1 Peter 1:23 Being born again, not of corruptible seed, but of incorruptible, by the word of God, which liveth and abideth for ever.

Hebrews 13:8 Jesus Christ the same yesterday, and to day, and for ever.

Titus 3:9 But avoid foolish questions, and genealogies, and contentions, and strivings about the law; for they are unprofitable and vain.

John 17:17 Sanctify them through thy truth: thy word is truth.

Acts 19:20 So mightily grew the word of God and prevailed.

James 3:17 But the wisdom that is from above is first pure, then peaceable, gentle, and easy to be entreated,

1 Corinthians 2:7 But we speak the wisdom of God in a mystery, even the hidden wisdom, which God ordained before the world unto our glory:

1 Peter 4:11 If any man speak, let him speak as the oracles of God;

Philippians 2:16 Holding forth the word of life; that I may rejoice in the day of Christ,

Romans 1:16 For I am not ashamed of the gospel of Christ: for it is the power of God unto salvation to every one that believeth;

Hebrews 1:3 and upholding all things by the word of his power,

Revelation 22:18 For I testify unto every man that heareth the words of the prophecy of this book, *If any man shall add* unto these things, God shall add unto him the plagues that are written in this book:

Revelation 22:19 And *if any man shall take away* from the words of the book of this prophecy, God shall take away his part out of the book of life, and out of the holy city, and from the things which are written in this book.

We have no idea how these scriptures speak to you-that is up to you and the Holy Spirit. We can, however, share how these verses speak to us. God's

Word is Final. No matter what man tries to do with His Word, it endureth forever in purity and truth. Man has pounded on the anvil, God's Word for centuries-The hammers have all worn out, but the Word of God remains. All the hammers have worn out, and will always wear out. So we counsel believers, who have questions and concerns in this area, to refer also to: **Philippians 4:11, John 14:1, John 14:27, Philippians 4:6, 1 Thessalonians 5:16**, and other like scriptures. Then we suggest that they accept **1 Corinthians 16:13**, which says: .."stand fast in the faith", **and Ephesians 6:13**, which says: "...and having done all, to stand".

Notes

Notes

FORGIVENESS

By this time you are either experiencing new spiritual awareness, or you are harboring some negative and judgmental feelings toward me-it's OK, get in line. If you don't have the inclination to review the section called, "People Bug Me", allow me to share a short section on forgiveness-short, but sweet. (Then refer back to "People Bug Me", if you are so led by the Spirit).

Colossians 3:13 Forbearing one another, and forgiving one another, if any man have a quarrel against any: even as Christ forgave you, so also do ye.

Matthew 6:14 For if ye forgive men their trespasses, your heavenly Father will also forgive you:

Matthew 6:15 But if ye forgive not men their trespasses, neither will your Father forgive your trespasses.

Mark 11:25 And when ye stand praying, forgive, if ye have ought against any: that your Father also which is in heaven may forgive you your trespasses.

Mark 11:26 But if ye do not forgive, neither will your Father which is in heaven forgive your trespasses.

Ephesians 4:32 And be ye kind one to another, tenderhearted, forgiving one another, even as God for Christ's sake hath forgiven you.

Matthew 18:35 So likewise shall my heavenly Father do also unto you, if ye from your hearts forgive not every one his brother their trespasses.

Mat thew18:21 Then came Peter to him, and said, Lord, how oft shall my brother sin against me, and I forgive him? till seven times?

Matthew 18:22 Jesus saith unto him, I say not unto thee, Until seven times: but, Until seventy times seven.

Luke 6:37 forgive, and ye shall be forgiven:

Question: Is this saying that, if you do not forgive, you will not be forgiven?

Luke 23:34 Then said Jesus, Father, forgive them; for they know not what they do.

Matthew 6:15 But if ye forgive not men their trespasses, neither will your Father forgive your trespasses.

Comment: I guess this answers the question asked directly above, doesn't it?

Luke 17:3 Take heed to yourselves: If thy brother trespass against thee, rebuke him; and if he repent, forgive him.

Luke 17:4 And if he trespass against thee seven times in a day, and seven times in a day turn again to thee, saying, I repent; thou shalt forgive him.

2 Corinthians 2:7 So that contrariwise ye ought rather to forgive him, and comfort him, lest perhaps such a one should be swallowed up with overmuch sorrow.

2 Corinthians 12:13 For what is it wherein ye were inferior to other churches, except it be that I myself was not burdensome to you? forgive me this wrong.

NOTE: The above verses are not just "pretty" words-they mean what they say.

Notes

Notes

BLESSINGS

Many Christians ask us to pray God to provide certain blessings. The blessings involve an number of subjects. Some are pointed, others are more general. We share the following:

Psalm 5:12 For thou, LORD, wilt bless the righteous; with favour wilt thou compass him as with a shield.

Psalm 119:1 Blessed are the undefiled in the way, who walk in the law of the LORD.

Psalm 119:2 Blessed are they that keep his testimonies, and that seek him with the whole heart.

Psalm 106:3 Blessed are they that keep judgment, and he that doeth righteousness at all times.

Luke 11:28 But he said, Yea rather, blessed are they that hear the word of God, and keep it.

Ephesians 1:3 Blessed be the God and Father of our Lord Jesus Christ, who *hath* blessed us with all spiritual blessings in heavenly places in Christ: (*WOW!!*)

Psalm 72:17 and men shall be blessed in him:

Hebrews 6:14 Saying, Surely blessing I will bless thee,

1 Peter 3:9 Not rendering evil for evil, or railing for railing: but contrariwise blessing; knowing that ye are thereunto called, that ye should inherit a blessing.

Acts 3:26 Unto you first God, having raised up his Son Jesus, sent him to bless you,

John 20:29 blessed are they that have not seen, and yet have believed.

There are many other scriptures that have to do with blessing (s). **Matt 5:3-11** tells about certain specific people, who will be blessed.

Matthew 5:3-11
3 Blessed are the poor in spirit: for theirs is the kingdom of heaven.
4 Blessed are they that mourn: for they shall be comforted.
5 Blessed are the meek: for they shall inherit the earth.

⁶ Blessed are they which do hunger and thirst after righteousness: for they shall be filled.

⁷ Blessed are the merciful: for they shall obtain mercy.

⁸ Blessed are the pure in heart: for they shall see God.

⁹ Blessed are the peacemakers: for they shall be called the children of God.

¹⁰ Blessed are they which are persecuted for righteousness' sake: for theirs is the kingdom of heaven.

¹¹ Blessed are ye, when men shall revile you, and persecute you, and shall say all manner of evil against you falsely, for my sake.

We find no instance of anyone praying for blessings in the Bible. The verses we read only tell us who will qualify for blessings. When they qualify, they are blessed as promised. **Ephesians 1:3** clearly tells us that God *hath* blessed us with all spiritual blessings in heavenly places in Christ Jesus. Since he has already blessed us with all spiritual blessings, we find it not necessary to ask or pray for more. We accept God's Word-he wrote it, we accept and believe it, and that's all there is to it.

All spiritual blessings are ours, if we satisfy God's qualifications.

Notes

GOD'S WILL

Many Christians have shared with us that they are waiting for God to express His will for their lives. They wonder what God's Will for their lives will be-what great and special thing (s) they will be called upon to do. They ask if there is anything they can do to speed up the process. We share with them that there is no necessity to speed up a process that is already a fact. After agreeing on the thank-you scriptures, we share the following:

Romans 13:8 - Love one another.
Matthew 5:44 - Love your enemies.
Romans 13:9 - Love thy neighbor as thyself.
Mark 11:25 - Forgive.
Luke 6:38 - give.
Ephesians 6:10 - Be strong in the Lord.
Galatians 5:1 - Stand fast.
Ephesians 4:32 - Be ye kind.
Philippians 4:11 - Be content.
Mark 16:15 - Preach the gospel.
Ephesians 4:25 - Speak truth.
Ephesians 4:27 - Neither give place to the devil.
Matthews 5:16 - Let your light so shine.
Matthews 5:25 - Agree with thine adversary.
Matthews 5:34 - Swear not at all.
Matthews 5:37 - Let your communication be, Yea, yea; Nay, nay.
Matthews 6:20 - Lay up for yourselves treasures in heaven.
Matthews 6:33 - Seek ye first the kingdom of God.
Matthews 6:34 - Take therefore no thought for the morrow.
Matthews 7:1 - Judge not.
Matthews 24:44 - Be ye also ready.
Matthews 28:19 - and teach all nations.

The above scriptures barely scratch the surface of things God has already willed us to do. There are many more things he has commanded us to do in his Word in order to fulfill his will. What we are trying to say here is, that we do not have to wait for God to express his will for our lives-he has already done so in his Word. >From our vantage point the problem here stems mainly from Christians believing that God has more to do. If one accepts that God has done it all, that it is finished-the burden of waiting for God to do more is eliminated. The challenge is for believers to accept, and act upon God's Word, as not only suggestions - but commands, which cry for obedience.

In a later section, we devote an entire section to this question-it is entitled "**It is Finished**". We will share scriptures that cause us to believe that God has done all-that his will is complete. All we have to do is obey the leading of his Holy Spirit.

We realize that it is not easy for most believers to accept this position-we have been led to participate in a result-oriented walk. We have been encouraged to bombard God with our requests, and then stand by for deliverance; treating God as we should a short-order cook. To all of a sudden stop this activity, and stand on the promises of God's Word is not an easy gear-shift change to make. For some it amounts to moving a car forward at 60 MPH, and then suddenly shifting into reverse. We encourage you to spend quality time in the "It is Finished" chapter. We will be content-however it speaks to you.

Isn't it strange that many of us want to do great things for God and the world, yet we won't help our neighbor?

Notes

INHERITED HABITS

B elievers sometimes confess that some bad habits they had in their old lives continue to manifest themselves in their born-again lives. They seek relief from these old habits. After sharing the thank-you scriptures, we share the following:

2 Corinthians 5:17 Therefore if any man be in Christ, he is a new creature: old things are passed away; behold, all things are become new.

James 1:14 But every man is tempted, when he is drawn away of his own lust, and enticed.

Comment: The temptation can be put away by God's Word (**Psalm. 119:11**).

Philippians 3:13 Brethren, I count not myself to have apprehended: but this one thing I do, *forgetting those things which are behind*, and reaching forth unto those things which are before,

Philippians 3:14 I press toward the mark for the prize of the high calling of God in Christ Jesus.

Luke 9:62 And Jesus said unto him, No man, having put his hand to the plow, *and looking back*, is fit for the kingdom of God.

Romans 13:14 But put ye on the Lord Jesus Christ, and make not provision for the flesh, to fulfill the lusts thereof.

Romans 14:5 Let every man be fully persuaded in his own mind.

Hebrews 12:1 let us lay aside every weight, and the sin which doth so easily beset us,

1 Peter 1:18 Forasmuch as ye know that ye were not redeemed with corruptible things, as silver and gold, from your vain conversation received by tradition from your fathers;

These scriptures, if claimed and accepted, will deliver a believer from any old habits. In other words, any "old habits", if they stay after one becomes saved, have been asked to remain. Some believers blame their earthly lineage for bad habits, that continue to manifest themselves in their Christian walks. They say, "I inherited this or that from my father". **Matthews 23:9** says, "And call no man your father upon the earth: for one is your Father, which is in heaven" Maybe we should be "taking after" our heavenly Father once we are saved.

1 John 1:9 If we confess our sins, he is faithful and just to forgive us our sins, and to cleanse us from all unrighteousness.

God's Word says that all unrighteousness is sin, and that whatsoever in not of faith is sin. It says also that to him that knows to do good, and does it not, to him it is sin. Look at the "inherited" habits, and accept that they are yours alone-not passed on to you. Then accept **Psalm 119:11**, and hide God's Word in your heart. If the habits qualify as sin according to God's definition, be not concerned or of a doubtful heart.

If you decide to do-it-yourself, without the help of God's Word, you are flying in the face of **Psalm 55:22**. The undesired habits will remain, and you may find yourself falling under the following scriptures:

Galatians 6:7 Be not deceived; God is not mocked: for whatsoever a man soweth, that shall he also reap.

2 Corinthians 13:5 Examine yourselves, whether ye be in the faith; prove your own selves.

(And many others)!

How about the following scriptures as they pertain to those, who insist on hanging on to inherited habits?

2 Peter 2:22 But it is happened unto them according to the true proverb, The dog is turned to his own vomit again; and the sow that was washed to her wallowing in the mire.

Proverbs 26:11 As a dog returneth to his vomit, so a fool returneth to his folly.

Note: Seeing that we are not fools-we do not return to our own vomit of folly, and we do not entertain the so-called "inherited" habits. We stand fast in the liberty wherewith Christ has made us free.

PERSECUTIONS AND TRIBULATIONS

Believers suffering persecution and/of tribulation contact us asking for prayer in order to relieve them from their burden. Christians are going through this or that, and want God to deliver them- even though he already has. After agreeing on the thank-you scriptures, we share the following:

2 Timothy 3:12 Yea, and all that will live godly in Christ Jesus shall suffer persecution.

Comment: "Suffer" means to experience, and endure.

Romans 5:3 And not only so, but we glory in tribulations also: knowing that tribulation worketh patience;

Comment: If you know of any scriptures that instructs us to moan, groan, and seek prayer concerning deliverance from tribulations, please advise us-we have found none. However, The Word does tell us to glory in, be thankful for, and to rejoice in all things.

Acts 14:22 and that we *must* through much tribulation enter into the kingdom of God.

Comment: Not may, not might possibly, not could, not can, or whatever. God says we **must**- Could this be the answer to, "Why me, Oh Lord"?

Psalm 34:19 Many are the afflictions of the righteous: but the LORD delivereth him out of them all.

Comment: Claim and stand fast on this one, and know the deliverance will come according to God's Will-not our prayers or whatever.

Romans 8:18 For I reckon that the sufferings of this present time are not worthy to be compared with the glory which shall be revealed in us.

Question: Are we being told here that we should look past the sufferings, and think on the glory that will be revealed? We believe so. What do you think?

Acts 9:16 For I will show him how great things he must suffer for my name's sake.

2 Corinthians 7:4 I am filled with comfort, I am exceeding joyful in all our tribulation.

Comment: "Joyful in all our tribulation?" No moaning or groaning here-no direction to pray about it.

2 Thessalonians 1:4 So that we ourselves glory in you in the churches of God for your patience and faith in all your persecutions and tribulations that ye endure:

Comment: We are being told here to endure-to endure means to persist, to bear up under adversity, to bear with patience. Nothing is said in the definition about praying for deliverance (s).

2 Corinthians 4:9 Persecuted, but not forsaken; cast down, but not destroyed;

Comment: The persecution can't defeat us-we can only defeat ourselves. God said in **Hebrews 13:5-..."I will never leave thee, nor forsake thee".**

1 Corinthians 4:12 being persecuted, we suffer it:

John 16:33 These things I have spoken unto you, that in me ye might have peace. In the world ye shall have tribulation: but be of good cheer; I have overcome the world.

Hebrews 5:8 Though he were a Son, yet learned he obedience by the things which he suffered;

2 Corinthians 1:7 that as ye are partakers of the sufferings, so shall ye be also of the consolation.

Confirmation: **Romans 8:17** And if children, then heirs; heirs of God, and joint-heirs with Christ; if so be that we suffer with him, that we may be also glorified together.

Philippians 1:29 For unto you it is given in the behalf of Christ, not only to believe on him, but also to suffer for his sake;

Mark 10:30 But he shall receive an hundredfold now in this time, houses, and brethren, and sisters, and mothers, and children, and lands, with persecutions; and in the world to come eternal life.

2 Corinthians 12:10 Therefore I take pleasure in infirmities, in reproaches, in necessities, in persecutions, in distresses for Christ's sake: for when I am weak, then am I strong.

Question: What? Take pleasure in all those things? That is what God said through Paul-sorry.

Notes

Notes

It speaks to us that all these scriptures attest to the fact that persecutions and tribulations are part and parcel of the Christian walk-they are promised and should be expected. In our counseling ministry, when these verses are cited in response to a plea for help, the usual comment is, "That's easy for you to say-you don't have my problems". Our answer is always the same-we didn't say these Words; God did. We also ask if the seeker's problem is so unique, that God didn't make provision for it in his Word. Did our Lord Jesus Christ shed his blood on the cross for everyone's problems, but yours?

We are told to be thankful in and for all things. The attitude of gratitude is seldom easy to assume, when faced with adversity-even though we are told to do it. However, the born-again spirit can soar by claiming and accepting God's Word as his promise to us. God's Words are as sweet as honey, and they have set us free.

Heb 12:5-11 And ye have forgotten the exhortation which speaketh unto you as unto children, My son, despise not thou the chastening of the Lord, nor faint when thou art rebuked of him: For whom the Lord loveth he chasteneth, and scourgeth every son whom he receiveth. If ye endure chastening, God dealeth with you as with sons; for what son is he whom the father chasteneth not? But if ye be without chastisement, whereof all are partakers, then are ye bastards, and not sons Furthermore we have had fathers of our flesh which corrected us, and we gave them reverence: shall we not much rather be in subjection unto the Father of spirits, and live? For they verily for a few days chastened us after their own pleasure; but he for our profit, that we might be partakers of his holiness. Now no chastening for the present seemeth to be joyous, but grievous: nevertheless afterward it yieldeth the peaceable fruit of righteousness unto them which are exercised thereby.

Hebrews 6:15 And so, *after* he had patiently endured, he obtained the promise.
Note: He obtained the promise *after* he patiently endured-not after he prayed.

God's Word(s) stands on its own merit, because it is Truth. It doesn't need a wrap-up exercise. However, the following may sum up this section:

2 Corinthians 12:8-9 For this thing I besought the Lord thrice, that it might depart from me. And he (Jesus) said unto me, My grace is sufficient for thee: for my strength is made perfect in weakness. Most gladly therefore will I rather glory in my infirmities, that the power of Christ may rest upon me. Therefore I take pleasure in infirmities, in reproaches, in necessities, in persecutions, in distresses for Christ's sake: for when I am weak, then am I strong.

(Does this say, that we should glory in, and take pleasure in our various challenges-or that should we pray for deliverance from them?)

2 Thessalonians 4:9 Persecuted, but not forsaken; cast down, but not destroyed;

Comment: These things will not defeat us; we are covered.)

1 Corinthians 4:2 being persecuted, we suffer it:

Comment: To suffer is to bear; to endure; to put up with - not to pray about it.

John 16:33 In the world ye shall have tribulation: but be of good cheer; I have overcome the world.

Question: Tribulations are promised? That's what it says.

2 Corinthians 1:7 that as ye are partakers of the sufferings, so shall ye be also of the consolation.

Question - The consolation is ours only if we partake of the sufferings? Hmmm.

Philippians 1:29 For unto you it is given in the behalf of Christ, not only to believe on him, but also to suffer for his sake;

Question: Sort of goes along with the scripture verse, that tells us, that we should rejoice when we suffer for Christ's sake, doesn't it?

Notes

QUENCHED SPIRIT

We have been approached by Christians complaining about their reaching a place of spiritual "dryness". Their fire (zeal) for the Lord is not burning as brightly as it once did. They are looking for a way to rekindle their spiritual zeal. After agreeing on the thank-you scriptures, we exhort any believer to stop making negative confessions, and start claiming and standing fast on God's Word. **Proverbs 6:2** says, "Thou art snared with the words of thy mouth, thou art taken with the words of thy mouth." Negative confessions breed negative non-action, and will keep us in the place we are professing-we suggest the believer should utter God's Words, which will release the power that will promise delivery. After all, God did say that his Word will not return to him void, didn't he? Let's look at some of these wonderful Words:

John 5:39 Search the scriptures;

Comment: This is not a suggestion-it is a command from God. It will help reduce the number of the 80% of believers, who do not know what is in their Bible.

Isaiah 34:16 Seek ye out of the book of the LORD, *and read*:

Acts 17:11 in that they received the word with all readiness of mind, and searched the scriptures *daily*, whether those things were so.

Question: DAILY? Yes, *daily!!* When we obey these three verses, we will begin to enjoy God's promises in our lives. Our spirits will soar.

1 Thessalonians 5:19 Quench not the Spirit.

Romans 12:2 And be not conformed to this world: but be ye transformed by the renewing of your mind, that ye may prove what is that good, and acceptable, and perfect, will of God.

Comment: The only true way to renew our minds (and lift our spirits) is by reading and claiming as fact the Word of God. Doing this will prove his will for us, which also is found in his Word.

While we are fueling up on the above cited scriptures, we might want to claim these verses:

Philippians 4:11 Not that I speak in respect of want: for I have learned, in whatsoever state I am, therewith to be content.

1 Timothy 6:6 But godliness with contentment is great gain.

Philippians 4:8 Finally, brethren, whatsoever things are *true,* whatsoever things are *honest,* whatsoever things are *just,* whatsoever things are *pure,* whatsoever things are *lovely,* whatsoever things are of *good report*; if there be any virtue, and if there be any praise, think on these things.

Question: Would you not agree, that all those "things" are actually God's Words?

Hebrews 4:12 For the word of God is quick, and powerful, and sharper than any twoedged sword, piercing even to the dividing asunder of soul and spirit, and of the joints and marrow, and is a discerner of the thoughts and intents of the heart.

Saints, if the above doesn't get you back on track, we are at a loss as to what else we can recommend. We do know that God's Word will work, if we work it. The only way you can fail to enjoy God's promises is not to walk according to his Will. The only way to stay on his pathway is to read, and heed, his signposts-his Word.

Those of us, who refuse to obey God's Word, may be considered as rebellious. God says in **Isaiah 63:10**, But they rebelled, and vexed his holy Spirit: therefore he was turned to be their enemy, and he fought against them.

2 Corinthians 4:16 For which cause we faint not; but though our outward man perish, yet the inward man is renewed day by day.

Maybe another reading of the "Rejoice" section will help spark up the quenched spirit, and thereby buoy up the inward man. Try it - you have nothing to lose, and everything to gain.

Notes

Notes

IDLE TALK

We have had brethren, who come to us and reveal that they are victims of idle talk. It is bothering them, and they are seeking prayer for relief. After sharing aloud the thank-you scriptures, we share the following:

Galatians 6:17 From henceforth let no man trouble me: for I bear in my body the marks of the Lord Jesus.

Romans 8:28 And we know that all things work together for good to them that love God, to them who are the called according to his purpose.

John 14:1 Let not your heart be troubled:

John 14:27 Peace I leave with you, my peace I give unto you: not as the world giveth, give I unto you. Let not your heart be troubled, neither let it be afraid.

Matthew5:44 But I say unto you, Love your enemies, bless them that curse you, do good to them that hate you, and pray for them which despitefully use you, and persecute you;

Romans 12:14 Bless them which persecute you: bless, and curse not.

Luke 6:27 But I say unto you which hear, Love your enemies, do good to them which hate you,

Luke 6:28 Bless them that curse you, and pray for them which despitefully use you.

Philippians 4:11 for I have learned, in whatsoever state I am, therewith to be content.

1 Peter 5:7 Casting all your care upon him; for he careth for you.

Psalm 112:7 He shall not be afraid of evil tidings: his heart is fixed, trusting in the LORD.

Psalm 112:8 His heart is established,

The foregoing scriptures offer deliverance to the believer, who is being victimized by idle talk. How about the Christian, who is engaging in idle talk? How do we exhort him? We share the following:

Ephesians 5:3 But fornication, and all uncleanness, or covetousness, let it not be once named among you, as becometh saints;

Ephesians 5:4 Neither filthiness, nor foolish

talking, nor jesting, which are not convenient: but rather giving of thanks.

Titus 2:1 But speak thou the things which become sound doctrine:

Comment: The only things that are sound doctrine are God's Words.

1 Peter 4:11 If any man speak, let him speak as the oracles of God;

Comment: God's oracles are his Words.

1 Timothy 6:3 If any man teach otherwise, and consent not to wholesome words, even the words of our Lord Jesus Christ, and to the doctrine which is according to godliness;

1 Timothy 6:4 He is proud, knowing nothing,

1 Corinthians 1:10 Now I beseech you, brethren, by the name of our Lord Jesus Christ, that ye all speak the same thing, and that there be no divisions among you; but that ye be perfectly joined together in the same mind and in the same judgment.

Comment: It would be impossible for anyone, who subscribes to this verse to indulge in idle talk.

Mathew 12:34 for out of the abundance of the heart the mouth speaketh.

Comment: If the mouth speaks idle talk, idle talk is in the heart.

James 4:11 Speak not evil one of another, brethren. He that speaketh evil of his brother, and judgeth his brother, speaketh evil of the law, and judgeth the law:

Matthew 12:36 But I say unto you, That every idle word that men shall speak, they shall give account thereof in the day of judgment.

Matthew 12:37 For by thy words thou shalt be justified, and by thy words thou shalt be condemned.

Comment: If this doesn't stifle idle talk-nothing will.

Titus 3:2 To speak evil of no man,

Discussing someone else's sin amounts to idle talk-gossip, if you will. When we are asked about our position or opinion concerning believers, who are found in sin, we suggest that our opinion is found in **1 Corinthians 12:18** But now hath God set

Notes

the members every one of them in the body, as it hath pleased him. If that doesn't stem the tide of idle talk, we ask what Jesus Christ would say if the sinner were brought into his presence and accused. He would probably say something like: **John 8:7** He that is without sin among you, let him first cast a stone... This should do it. However, if it doesn't-you may want to cite**: Luke 13:2** And Jesus answering said unto them, Suppose ye that these Galilaeans were sinners above all the Galilaeans, because they suffered such things?

Luke 13:3 I tell you, Nay: but, except ye repent, ye shall all likewise perish.

Luke 13:4 Or those eighteen, upon whom the tower in Siloam fell, and slew them, think ye that they were sinners above all men that dwelt in Jerusalem?

Luke 13:5 I tell you, Nay: but, except ye repent, ye shall all likewise perish.

COMMENT: God's Word brought the responsibility back where it belongs-at our front door.

Ephesians 4:29 Let no corrupt communication proceed out of your mouth, but that which is good to the use of edifying, that it may minister grace unto the hearers.

God said it, I believe it, and that's all there is to it. **AMEN!!**

TEACHING:

Colossians 4:17 says, "Take heed to the ministry which thou hast received in the Lord, that thou fulfill it." All of us are expected to be teachers of one sort or another in our Christian walks. Witnessing Jesus Christ to non-believers is teaching of a kind-a very rewarding kind. However, there are some, who are led to teaching as an overall ministry. This is a significant and important calling. The teacher must be aware of the responsibility placed on him. The teacher, who teaches men's doctrines and falsities will be rewarded according to his works. Teaching God's doctrines will also bring the teacher rewards according to his works.

We said earlier that all Christian ministries amount to rightly dividing the Word of Truth, God's Word. Of course, this includes teaching. Please allow the sharing of scriptures that may address the area of teaching. They will reveal to you who does the teaching, and what should be taught.

In the Old Testament we have:

Psalm 32:8 I will instruct thee and teach thee in the way which thou shalt go: I will guide thee with mine eye.

Psalm 19:7 The law of the LORD is perfect, converting the soul: the testimony of the LORD is sure, making wise the simple.

Psalm 19:8 The statutes of the LORD are right, rejoicing the heart: the commandment of the LORD is pure, enlightening the eyes.

Psalm 19:9 The fear of the LORD is clean, enduring for ever: the judgments of the LORD are true and righteous altogether.

Psalm 119:12, 33, 64, 68, 124, 135, 171 - Teach me *thy* statutes.

Psalm 119:24 Thy testimonies also are my delight and my counselors.

Psalm 119:34 Give me understanding, and I shall keep thy law;

Psalm 119:66 Teach me good judgment and knowledge: for I have believed thy commandments.

Notes

Psalm 119:102 I have not departed from thy judgments: for thou hast taught me.

Psalm 119:108 Accept, I beseech thee, the freewill offerings of my mouth, O LORD, and teach me thy judgments.

Psalm 119:130 The entrance of thy words giveth light; it giveth understanding unto the simple.

Comment: These *Psalm 119* verses show God as our Teacher. Jesus sent the Holy Spirit to us to be our Teacher. Is there a link here? Hmmm!

Isaiah 34:16 Seek ye out of the book of the LORD, and read:

Isaiah 48:17 Thus saith the LORD, thy Redeemer, the Holy One of Israel; I am the LORD thy God which teacheth thee to profit, which leadeth thee by the way that thou shouldest go.

Isaiah 58:11 And the LORD shall guide thee continually,

Proverbs 3:5 Trust in the LORD with all thine heart; and lean not unto thine own understanding.

Proverbs 3:6 In all thy ways acknowledge him, and he shall direct thy paths.

Jeremiah 42:3 That the LORD thy God may show us the way wherein we may walk, and the thing that we may do.

In the New Testament we have the following:

Matthew 28:18 And Jesus came and spake unto them, saying, All power is given unto me in heaven and in earth.

Matthew 28:19 Go ye therefore, and teach all nations, baptizing them in the name of the Father, and of the Son, and of the Holy Ghost:

Matthew 28:20 Teaching them to observe all things *whatsoever I have commanded you*: and, lo, I am with you alway, even unto the end of the world. Amen.

Luke 12:12 For the Holy Ghost shall teach you in the same hour what ye ought to say.

John 14:26 But the Comforter, which is the Holy Ghost, whom the Father will send in my name, he shall teach you all things, and bring all things to your remembrance, *whatsoever I have said unto you.*

John 6:45 It is written in the prophets, And they

shall be all taught of God.

1 Corinthians 2:13 Which things also we speak, not in the words which man's wisdom teacheth, but which the Holy Ghost teacheth; comparing spiritual things with spiritual.

Galatians 6:6 Let him that is taught in the word communicate unto him that teacheth in all good things.

Hebrews 5:12 For when for the time ye ought to be teachers, ye have need that one teach you again which be the first principles of the oracles of God;

Hebrews 8:10 saith the Lord; I will put my laws into their mind, and write them in their hearts:

Hebrews 10:16 saith the Lord, I will put my laws into their hearts, and in their minds will I write them;

1 John 2:27 But the anointing which ye have received of him abideth in you, and *ye need not that any man teach you*: but as the same anointing teacheth you of all things, and is truth, and is no lie, and even as it hath taught you, ye shall abide in him.

2 Timothy 3:16 All scripture is given by inspiration of God, and is profitable for doctrine, for reproof, for correction, for instruction in righteousness:

2 Peter 1:20 Knowing this first, that no prophecy of the scripture is of any private interpretation.

You probably can find other scriptures that speak to this area of teaching. The verses we have shared are enough to tell us that God does the teaching through the Holy Spirit, and it is his Word that should be taught. You may ask, "Well, if this true, why does God talk about teachers in the Word?" We must look for the agreement, as there are no conflicts in the Word. We believe that, since we accept that God does the teaching, and it is his Word that should be taught, it must be that God wants those, who have received a teaching ministry from him, to rightly dividing the truth-the Word of God. As discussed earlier, rightly divide means to share or disseminate-it doesn't mean to interpret or pass opinion on. Therefore, we feel that a Christian teacher should allow the Holy Spirit to speak to the understanding. Some have pointed out that God

Notes

allows interpreting as stated in:

1 Corinthians 14:27 and let one interpret. In this case, God was referring to the area of speaking in tongues-not general interpretation of His Word.

It does say in **2 Peter 1:20** - Knowing this first, that no prophecy of the scripture is of any private interpretation.

Comment: We believe this means that everyone must be personally responsible for searching the scriptures, and allowing the Holy Spirit to provide an understanding. Don't

accept another's interpretation unless it lines up with God's Word-in the end you will be held responsible-right or wrong. Don't accept ours either-seek ye out of the book of the Lord. Seek and ye shall find!

SIN

Sin is defined in the Bible. We find in **Romans 14:23**, "for whatsoever is not of faith is sin." We also find in **1 John 5:17**-"All unrighteousness is sin:" A third sin definition has been shouting loudly to my spirit of late: **James 4:17** Therefore to **him** that knoweth to do good, and doeth **it** not, to **him it** is **sin**.

To define sin is one thing, but to finally understand the consequences of sin in our lives is something else. Many have taken stands on sin, and have preached, taught, exhorted, rebuked, and whatever. It took the counseling of others in this area before the subject of sin began to sort itself out scripturally in my spirit.

1 John 1:8 If we say that we have no sin, we deceive ourselves, and the truth is not in us.

James 3:2 For in many things we offend all.

Galatians 3:22 But the scripture hath concluded *all* under sin,

Romans 3:23 For all have sinned, and come short of the glory of God;

1 John 2:1 My little children, these things write I unto you, that ye sin not. And if any man sin, we have an advocate with the Father, Jesus Christ the righteous:

1 John 2:2 And he is the propitiation for our sins: and not for ours only, but also for the sins of the whole world.

Hebrews 10:26 For if we sin willfully after that we have received the knowledge of the truth, there remaineth no more sacrifice for sins,

Romans 7:14-25

14 For we know that the law is spiritual: but I am carnal, sold under sin.

15 For that which I do I allow not: for what I would, that do I not; but what I hate, that do I.

16 If then I do that which I would not, I consent unto the law that it is good.

17 Now then it is no more I that do it, but sin that dwelleth in me.

Notes

¹⁸ For I know that in me (that is, in my flesh,) dwelleth no good thing: for to will is present with me; but how to perform that which is good I find not.

¹⁹ For the good that I would I do not: but the evil which I would not, that I do.

²⁰ Now if I do that I would not, it is no more I that do it, but sin that dwelleth in me.

²¹ I find then a law, that, when I would do good, evil is present with me.

²² For I delight in the law of God after the inward man:

²³ But I see another law in my members, warring against the law of my mind, and bringing me into captivity to the law of sin which is in my members.

²⁴ O wretched man that I am! who shall deliver me from the body of this death?

²⁵ I thank God through Jesus Christ our Lord. So then with the mind I myself serve the law of God; but with the flesh the law of sin.

Comment: God's Words, by way of Paul, indicate here that we have two natures-the spirit and the flesh. With one we serve God, and with the other the law of sin. It would appear that sin *is* in us. We are of the flesh, and of the spirit. We are told in **1 John 1:9** - "If we confess our sins, he is faithful and just to forgive us our sins, and to cleanse us from all unrighteousness." The act of confessing our sins admits there are sins to confess. All of the preceding scriptures indicate the existence of the propensity to sin in all of us.

Let us look at another position taken by many, that we are not to sin at all. In **1 John 3:4-9** it speaks too some that if we sin, we are not of God.

1 John 3:4-9

⁴ Whosoever committeth sin transgresseth also the law: for sin is the transgression of the law.

⁵ And ye know that he was manifested to take away our sins; and in him is no sin.

⁶ Whosoever abideth in him sinneth not: whosoever sinneth hath not seen him, neither known him.

⁷ Little children, let no man deceive you: he that doeth righteousness is righteous, even as he is

righteous.

[8] He that committeth sin is of the devil; for the devil sinneth from the beginning. For this purpose the Son of God was manifested, that he might destroy the works of the devil.

[9] Whosoever is born of God doth not commit sin; for his seed remaineth in him: and he cannot sin, because he is born of God.

We further find the following in **Romans 6:**

Romans 6:1 What shall we say then? Shall we continue in sin, that grace may abound?

Romans 6:2 God forbid. How shall we, that are dead to sin, live any longer therein?

Romans 6:7 For he that is dead is freed from sin.

Romans 6:12 Let not sin therefore reign in your mortal body, that ye should obey it in the lusts thereof.

Romans 6:13 Neither yield ye your members as instruments of unrighteousness unto sin:

Rom ans6:14 For sin shall not have dominion over you:

Romans 6:18 Being then made free from sin, ye became the servants of righteousness.

Romans 6:20 For when ye were the servants of sin, ye were free from righteousness.

Romans 6:22 But now being made free from sin,

Romans 6:23 For the wages of sin is death;

Comment: If you have been with us throughout this book, you know of our belief that there is no conflict in God's Word. Our perfect God would not saddle us with an imperfect book-the Bible is perfect. If you accept this, you can honestly ask, "Where is the agreement here"? What understanding should we accept? This is between you and the Holy Spirit. All we can do is share how this area speaks to us with the understanding we have been given. We are not asking you to accept our point of view-we are content to allow God's Holy spirit to finish his work in you. If you are led to accept another view than ours, we will say, "Praise the

Notes

Lord". There is no problem in differences as long as we do not participate in foolish questions, and genealogies, and contentions, and strivings. Disagreements between believers are not salvation issues. We will not argue. One, who is content with where he stands, does not argue. He makes a decision, states his case, and then stands. It speaks to us that God spoke about decision-making, when he said in **Matthew 5:37**, "But let your communication be, Yea, yea; Nay, nay: for whatsoever is more than these cometh of evil." God wants us to say yes or no: he makes no reference to being right or wrong. Decision causes action. If the action is right, something good will be accomplished. If the action is wrong, the decision maker will be able to discern it, and change course. The man who wavers, the double-minded man, does not have this ability. He is being driven with the wind and tossed , which does not lead to fruitful action.

Please allow us to share our understanding of the scriptures that speak to sin. First of all, we accept and believe all the scriptures referred to in this segment. They are God's Words, and they are perfect. The challenge is to find the agreement with scriptures that seem to be in conflict. We believe as God indicated through Paul that a sin nature is present in us. God says in **1 Corinthians 15:44**, "There is a natural body, and there is a spiritual body." We agree with God's Word in **Romans 7:14-25**, as spoken through Paul. We also relate to Paul's agonizing in verse 24: "O wretched man that I am!" We also go along with Paul in verse 25, "thank god through Jesus Christ our Lord." We again claim the thank-you scriptures-**Ephesians 5:20, Colossians 3:17**, and **1 Thessalonians 5:18.** We would now like to share how we were led into seeing the agreement in the scriptures.

Comment: To "commit" is to absolutely transfer power or final authority. It speaks to us here that if one "commits" sin, one makes sin a way of life-this is different that being guilty of an occasional sin. We have been given an understanding, that there is a difference in God's eyes between a sinner, who makes sin a way of life, and the sinner, who occasionally sins.

Romans 6:1 Shall we continue in sin,

Comment: This is not saying we won't sin. It is saying that we shouldn't make sin a continuing way of life.

Romans 6:2 How shall we, that are dead to sin, live any longer therein?

Comment: To "live in" is to abide in-to take residence in. We are not to abide in sin. This does not say we will not sin.

Romans 6:6 that henceforth we should not serve sin.

Comment: This tells us not to be servants of sin-not that we will not sin.

Romans 6:12 Let not sin therefore reign in your mortal body,

Comment: In other words, let not sin establish dominion over you.

Romans 6:13 Neither yield ye your members as instruments of unrighteousness unto sin:

Comment: To yield is to give, or render, sin as fitting. Although sin occurs, we do not render it as fitting-it is only a reaction of the flesh.

Romans 6:14 For sin shall not have dominion over you:

Comment: This doesn't say we will not sin-it tells us not to let sin take us over, and run our lives.

Romans 6:23 For the wages of sin is death;

Comment: A wage is a pledge of security, that one will do something, or will abide by the result of something. It speaks to us that, if one abides in sin and its results, his wage is death. An occasional sin, when forgiven and forgotten by God, does not qualify as a death sentence. Our advocate, the propitiation for our sins (Christ Jesus), is alive and on the job.

We are now content, that all the scriptures are in agreement in our spirits. There is a distinct difference between the sinner, who makes sin a way of life, and the sinner, who falls off the wagon once and a while and sins. The one has left the protection of God's Word, and will be rewarded according to his work. The other, although having given in to the

Notes

flesh for the moment, can confess the sin and receive God's forgiveness. (which he has already done; He has forgiven and forgotten all our sins.)

We referred earlier in this section to **Matthew 5:37** as one scripture that deals with decision-making. We can also cite: **Revelation 3:15-16** I know thy works, that thou art neither cold nor hot: I would thou wert cold or hot. So then because thou art lukewarm, and neither cold nor hot, I will spue thee out of my mouth. (I never want to hear the sound of God clearing his throat in preparation for "spewing" me out of his mouth). I can't think of a more horrible sound to hear and endure.

BLAME WHO?

When a Christian is suffering persecution or tribulation, is it all right to lay the blame off on someone or something else? If you accept the previous treatment of these things in the "Persecution and Tribulation" section, your answer would have to be, "No"! Is it right to blame Satan? (Not if you obey God's command not to give place to him.). In general, it speaks to us, that getting involved in the process of laying blame elsewhere is negative and counter-productive.

As far as blaming the devil is concerned, it amounts almost to blaming ourselves-after all, we have dominion over him. If we accept the scriptural fact that he is defeated, how can we blame him? Please refer to ahead to the section entitled, "Satan's Power"?. and read **Ephesians 4:27**, **Luke 10:19**, **Genesis 1:28**, and **1 John 5:18**. You may also want to read **2 Timothy 3:12**, **Romans 5:3**, **Acts 14:22**, and **Psalm 34:19**. (Searching the scriptures is always a blessing to one's spirit.)

We have heard many believers rebuking and binding the devil in order to get him off their backs, and out of their lives. Since he is not on their backs (he was defeated at the cross of Christ), this exercise is a negative thing-it only serves to give him place. We prefer leaving the rebuke and binding to the Word of God.

Jude 1:9 Yet Michael the archangel,...said, The Lord rebuke thee.
Zechariah 3:2 And the LORD said unto Satan, The LORD rebuke thee,
Romans 16:20 And the God of peace shall bruise Satan under your feet shortly.
Revelation 12:10 for the accuser of our brethren is cast down,
Revelation 12:11 And they overcame him by the blood of the Lamb, and by the word of their testimony;

When our Lord Jesus was tempted of the devil

Notes

in the wilderness, he chose the perfect way to rebuke that deceiver and liar—he rebuked him with his Word (s).

> **Matthew 4:4** But he answered and *said,*
> **Matthew 4:7** Jesus said unto him, *It is written* again,
> **Matthew 4:10** Then *saith* Jesus unto him, Get thee hence, Satan: for it is written,
> **Luke 4:4** And Jesus answered him, *saying*, It is written,
> **Luke 4:8** And Jesus answered *and said* unto him,...for it is written,
> **Luke 4:12** And Jesus answering said unto him, It is said,
> **Addition:** Please add this to your spirit: **Matthew 8:16** ..and he (Jesus) cast out the spirits with his *word,*

Jesus overcame with his Word. It speaks to us that we should be doing the same thing. We should overcome Satan by the blood of the Lamb, and by the Word of God. After all, are we not joint-heirs with Christ Jesus?

Many Christians have been convinced that we are in a warfare with the enemy, and that we should get involved in an active war-like campaign against him. We have no argument with those, who choose this posture. We, however, prefer to stand fast on what is written in **2 Corinthians 10:3-4**: For though we walk in the flesh, we do not war after the flesh:

(For the weapons of our warfare are not carnal, but mighty through God to the pulling down of strong holds;)

Question: If our weapons are not carnal, what are they? They must be spiritual-they must be those that are sharper than any two-edged sword. They must be God's Words.

According to the Word of God, we are not to battle the devil on his terms, that is, with weapons of the flesh. (Why battle someone, who is already defeated-anyway)?

Matthew 5:39 But I say unto you, That ye resist not evil:

2 Timothy 2:5 And if a man also strive for masteries, yet is he not crowned, except he strive lawfully.

Comment: Our striving is done lawfully in line with the Bible-we use spiritual weapons, God's Words.

2 Timothy 2:24 And the servant of the Lord must not strive; but be gentle unto all men, apt to teach, patient,

1 Peter 3:9 Not rendering evil for evil,

1 Thessalonians 5:15 See that none render evil for evil...

Romans 12:17 Recompense to no man evil for evil.

Deuteronomy 32:35 To me belongeth vengeance, and recompense;

Proverbs 20:22 Say not thou, I will recompense evil; but wait on the LORD, and he shall save thee.

We are not to resist of strive against evil, according to God's Word-it is our position that the devil can not tempt us. He doesn't have that power in the life of a Christian-after all, the Word says that we are drawn away of our own lust and enticed. You may ask how he was able to tempt our Lord-he was able, because he was not yet sentenced by the death of our Lord and Savior. Once Jesus gave up his life on the cross, the devil's power was neutralized in the life of the born-again person.

2 Corinthians 7:4 I am filled with comfort,

Philippians 4:11 for I have learned, in whatsoever state I am, therewith to be content.

2 Corinthians 12:10 Therefore I take pleasure in infirmities, in reproaches, in necessities, in persecutions, in distresses for Christ's sake:

Romans 8:28 And we know that all things work together for good to them that love God,

All of **Psalm 37** carries a positive and powerful message about the fact that the days of the wicked are numbered-he will perish. We recommend you read all of Psalm 37-we hope to whet your appetite

Notes

Notes

with these few verses:

Psalm 37:3 Trust in the LORD, and do good;

Psalm 37:4 Delight thyself also in the LORD;

Psalm 37:7 Rest in the LORD, and wait patiently for him:

Psalm 37:10 For yet a little while, and the wicked shall not be:

Psalm 37:13 The Lord shall laugh at him: for he seeth that his day is coming.

Psalm 37:34 Wait on the LORD, and keep his way,

Psalm 37:38 the end of the wicked shall be cut off.

Psalm 37:40 And the LORD shall help them, and deliver them: he shall deliver them from the wicked, and save them, because they trust in him.

If you will review the section on Rejoicing, and accept, believe, and claim the scriptures entered therein, you will find it easier to put the devil in his place of nothingness-where he belongs. You will become content to let him do his worst in the world (of which we are no longer a part). We know that our position is not a popular one with most believers, who have been ingrained with the doctrine of "spiritual warfare"-so be it. Many have not been exposed to our persuasion here (many are probably whispering, "Thank God") That's fine, but don't judge us too harshly-remember that in the beginning of this offering, we did cite:

Acts 5:38-39 And now I say unto you, Refrain from these men, and let them alone: for if this counsel or this work be of men, it will come to nought: But if it be of God, ye cannot overthrow it; lest haply ye be found even to fight against God.

There is a place in God's Word where he tells us to resist the devil. It is found in **1 Peter 5:9,** which says, Whom resist stedfast *in the faith*,

Comment: God tells us to resist, and he tells us how to do it-"stedfast *in the faith*". We know that faith cometh by hearing, and hearing by the Word of God. It speaks to us, therefore, that faith is trusting in God's Word-we should resist the devil with God's

Word. Blaming him or anyone else for whatever happens is a negative and wasted exercise.

Again, it says in **Matthew 8:16**: and he cast out the spirits with his word, He did it, and since we are joint-heirs with him, we also can-it doesn't take striving to do it. All we need is God's Word.

Blame who? **2 Corinthians 13:5** says: Examine yourselves, whether ye be in the faith; prove your own selves. Know ye not your own selves, how that Jesus Christ is in you, except ye be reprobates? **1 Corinthians 11:28** says: But let a man examine himself, **Galatians 6:4** says: But let every man prove his own work,. If we stay busy obeying God's Words in this area, we won't have time to point fingers of blame at the devil-or anyone else. This is why I counsel believers as follows: "Our problems can be found in our individual mirrors, and the all the answers can be found in our Bibles.

Notes

EVIL

It is often asked of us Why God allows evil to exist. They wonder how a loving God could allow so much evil in the world. They ask if evil is part of God's plan-his Will. After sharing the thank-you scriptures, we follow with:

Revelation 4:11 for thou hast created *all* things,

2 Corinthians 5:18 And *all* things are of God,

Isaiah 45:7 I form the light, and create darkness: I make peace, *and create evil*: I the LORD do *all* these things.

Proverbs 16:4 The LORD hath made *all* things for himself: yea, even the wicked for the day of evil.

Romans 11:36 For of him, and through him, and to him, are *all* things: to whom be glory for ever. Amen.

1 Corinthians 8:6 But to us there is but one God, the Father, of whom are *all* things,

Colossians 1:16 For by him were *all* things created, that are in heaven, and that are in earth, visible and invisible, whether they be thrones, or dominions, or principalities, or powers: *all* things were created by him, and for him:

John 1:3 *All* things were made by him; and without him was not any thing made that was made.

Daniel 9:14 Therefore hath the LORD watched upon the evil, and brought it upon us: for the LORD our God is righteous in *all* his works which he doeth:

Jeremiah 18:11 Behold, I frame evil against you, and devise a device against you:

Amos 3:6 shall there be evil in a city, and the LORD hath not done it?

Nehemiah 9:33 Howbeit thou art just in *all* that is brought upon us; for thou hast done right, but we have done wickedly:

Revelation 16:7 Even so, Lord God Almighty, true and righteous are thy judgments.

Revelation 19:2 For true and righteous are his judgments:

Psalm119:137 Righteous art thou, O LORD, and upright are thy judgments.

Romans 9:22 What if God, willing to show his

wrath, and to make his power known, endured with much longsuffering the vessels of wrath fitted to destruction:

These scriptures clearly tell us the God created ***all*** things; evil was on of those things. When **Isaiah 45:7** was cited in support of God creating evil, the leader of a fellowship we attended became offended. He loudly disputed this position, and maintained that our loving God could not have done this. He ended with the accusation that we were blaming God unjustly-it moved in our spirit to say nothing at that moment. After the meeting the leader offered a genuine apology for his angry outburst. As is often the case, it was a few days later that I thought of an example I could have shared with the fellowship. This example is expressed whenever the "blaming God" accusation is made. Almost every-one has heard of Joe DiMaggio, who was a baseball legend with the New York Yankees. Do we blame Joe for being a star player? Do we blame him for being elected to baseball's Hall of Fame? Of course, we don't — it'a just the way it is. By the same token, we do not blame God for creating all things-it's just the way it is.

The Joe DiMaggio example may be considered by some as reaching into the world for an explana-tion. We believe, however, that since all things are of God, the example is valid. In any case, we can also offer support for not "blaming" God for evil out of His Word.

Romans 9
[17] For the scripture saith unto Pharaoh, Even for this same purpose have I raised thee up, that I might shew my power in thee, and that my name might be declared throughout all the earth.

[18] Therefore hath he mercy on whom he will have mercy, and whom he will he hardeneth.

[19] Thou wilt say then unto me, Why doth he yet find fault? For who hath resisted his will?

[20] Nay but, O man, who art thou that repliest against God? Shall the thing formed say to him that formed it, Why hast thou made me thus?

[21] Hath not the potter power over the clay, of the

Notes

same lump to make one vessel unto honour, and another unto dishonour?

[22] What if God, willing to shew his wrath, and to make his power known, endured with much long-suffering the vessels of wrath fitted to destruction:

[23] And that he might make known the riches of his glory on the vessels of mercy, which he had afore prepared unto glory,

Yes, evil is in the world. Yes, God created it. Yes, it is part of God's perfect plan. Let us thank God for **Psalm 23:4** Yea, though I walk through the valley of the shadow of death, I will fear no evil: for thou art with me; thy rod and thy staff they comfort me.

Romans 16:19 but yet I would have you wise unto that which is good, and simple concerning evil.

Traditional teachings have claimed that our good, gracious, merciful, and loving God could not have created evil. He couldn't be responsible for all that is bad in the world. They claim, that evil comes only from man's sinful nature (who created man?), or from the devil. If you are led to believe with this- Praise the Lord. As it written: **Romans 14:5** Let every man be fully persuaded in his own mind. We prefer to believe, accept, and stand fast on God's Word as the final authority and answer as indicated earlier in this section.

We agree that God is a wonderful, caring, forgiving, gracious, and good Father. The Word of God says he is also:

1. **A *jealous* God** - **Exodus 34:14, Exodus 20.5, Joshua 24:10**

2. **A *vengeful* God** - **Deuteronomy 4:14, Deuteronomy 34:35, Psalm 94:1, Romans 12:19, Hebrews 10:30, Isaiah 34:8, Jeremiah 51:6, 2 Thessalonians 1:8**

3. **A *consuming fire*** - **Hebrews 12:29, Deuteronomy 4:24, Deuteronomy 9:3, Psalm 97:3, Isaiah 66:15, 2 Thessalonians 1:8**

4. **An *angry* God** - **Exodus 33:22, Psalm 30:5, Psalm 78:38, Isaiah 48:9, Isaiah 5:25, Joshua 7:26**

5. **God as an *enemy*** - **Isaiah 63:10**

SATAN'S POWER ?

Please allow us to make a little confession. We have been chomping at the bit to get into this area. As far as I am personally concerned, the liberty that God's Word revealed to me concerning this subject has been thoroughly blessed, and is heaven-sent. The "religion", in which we were raised, taught fear of satan. In spite of the hundreds of admonitions given in the Bible about not being afraid, we were told to fear the devil. Even after being born-again, the fear of satan was still being taught and preached. In spite of God's Word, which told us not to give place to the devil, too much place was given to that deceiving, rat-fink liar. Believers were confessing the devil's interference in their lives, and how he was coming against them. Others were binding satan at every turn. It was almost as if they enjoyed the confrontation. unnecessary, though it is.

The following scriptures delivered us from all this-thank God in the name of Jesus Christ. If you will permit us to do so, we will probably comment on almost every verse. We think it is important to explain how the many scriptures to us.

Hebrews 2:14 Forasmuch then as the children are partakers of flesh and blood, he also himself likewise took part of the same; that through death he might destroy him that had the power of death, that is, the devil;

Comment: Christ's death on the cross destroyed the power of the devil.

1 John 3:8 For this purpose the Son of God was manifested, that he might destroy the works of the devil.

John 12:31 now shall the prince of this world be cast out.

Colossians 1:13 Who hath delivered us from the power of darkness,

Comment: We have been delivered-it is a fact, so enjoy the freedom.

Genesis 1:28 And God blessed them, and God said unto them, Be fruitful, and multiply, and replenish the earth, and subdue it: and have dominion over

Notes

the fish of the sea, and over the fowl of the air, and over every living thing that moveth upon the earth.

Comment: We admit that the devil is a living thing on earth. This admission gives us dominion over him-according to the Word of God.

Ephesians 4:27 Neither give place to the devil.

Comment: With pleasure-we won't. (Will you - or do you??

James 4:7 Submit yourselves therefore to God. Resist the devil, and he will flee from you.

Comment: How do you submit yourselves to God? You do it through his Word. When God's Words become your words, the devil has no choice-he must flee from you. We are blessed to report that the only part of him we see is his back as he flees from us. Thank you, Father, in the name of Jesus! No need for ":spiritual warfare" - the battle was fought and won by Christ Jesus - The victory is ours!!

1 John 5:18 but he that is begotten of God keepeth himself, and *that wicked one toucheth him not.*

Acts 26:18 To open their eyes, and to turn them from darkness to light, and from the power of Satan unto God,

Psalm 112:10 the desire of the wicked shall perish.

Comment: For believers, that desire perished by Jesus' death on the cross.

Romans 12:21 Be not overcome of evil, but overcome evil with good.

Comment: We are commanded not to be overcome of evil-and how to do it.

1 John 4:4 Ye are of God, little children, and have overcome them: because greater is he that is in you, than he that is in the world.

Comment: Thank you Father for being greater in us than he that is in the world.

Isaiah 54:17 *No* weapon that is formed against thee shall prosper;

Comment: *No weapon*-including the devil's fiery darts.

2 Corinthians 2:14 Now thanks be unto God, which always causeth us to *triumph in Christ*, and maketh manifest the savour of his knowledge by us in every place.

1 John 5:4 For whatsoever is born of God

Notes

overcometh the world: and this is the victory that overcometh the world, even our faith.

Comment: We can't speak for you-for us, we claim the victory.

John 16:33 but be of good cheer; I have overcome the world.

Ephesians 6:10 Finally, my brethren, be strong in the Lord, and in the power of his might.

Ephesians 6:11 Put on the whole armour of God, that ye may be able to stand against the wiles of the devil.

Comment: We are commanded to put on the armor. God's armor is his Word-sharper that any twoedged sword. Put it on, and stand fast.

Ephesians 6:16 Above all, taking the shield of faith, wherewith ye shall be able to quench all the fiery darts of the wicked.

Comment: Again, we accept that the shield of faith is God's Word.

John 14:30 for the prince of this world cometh, and hath *nothing* in me.

Comment: As joint-heirs with Christ Jesus, satan has nothing in us either.

Luke 10:19 Behold, I give unto you *power to tread* on serpents and scorpions, and *over all the power* of the enemy: and *nothing* shall by any means hurt you.

Question: Why do we not accept this power in faith?: Can you accept this power? We have-we are content!

Luke 1:74 that we being delivered out of the hand of our enemies might serve him without fear,

Comment: We are delivered-it is finished.

Proverbs 16:7 When a man's ways please the LORD, he maketh even his enemies to be at peace with him.

Galatians 1:4 Who gave himself for our sins, that he might deliver us from this present evil world,

Comment: He gave himself-we are delivered.

2 Thessalonians 3:3 But the Lord is faithful, who shall stablish you, *and keep you from evil.*

John 17:15 but that thou shouldest keep them from the evil.

1 Samuel 2:10 The adversaries of the LORD *shall be broken to pieces*; out of heaven shall he

Notes

thunder upon them: the LORD shall judge the ends of the earth; and he shall give strength unto his king, and exalt the horn of his anointed.

We don't know how all of the above scriptures and comments speak to you-all we can do is share how they speak to us. satan is a toothless lion, and arrowless bow, a bulletless gun, a nothing in the life of a believer-if the believer claims and stands fast on God's Word. We have claimed, and we stand fast on God's Promise.

We are often asked why it says in **1 Peter 5:8-9** Be sober, be vigilant; because your adversary the devil, as a roaring lion, walketh about, seeking whom he may devour: Whom resist *stedfast in the faith,* On the surface these verses seem to be in contradiction with the other scriptures, and how they speak to us. These verses are often employed to keep believers in fear of the devil. Finding agreement between **1 Peter 5:8-9** and all of the other scriptures cited in this work is up to the spirit of each individual. As for us, he can roar all he wants-we are not afraid. He can seek all he wants-he just won't find us. Resisting in the faith is simply resisting with God's Word (s).

Yes, the devil is an adversary, and Mohammed Ali would have been, if I would have crawled into the ring with him. I would not have done so under most circumstances. However, if Ali had been first securely bound hand and foot, I would have had no problem in getting into that ring. Daniel had no problem in the lion's den, when the king cried unto Daniel. Daniel replied, "My God hath sent his angel, and hath shut the lion's mouths, that they have not hurt me". My answer to those, who warn me about what the devil can do to me if I speak so severely against him is quite similar. I reply that God, through his Son Jesus Christ, has given me dominion and power over the devil. I accept this condition, and stand on it in faith. After all, we are commanded by God in **Philippians 1:2**8 that we should be terrified by our adversaries *by nothing.* **Isaiah 41:10** says: Fear thou not; for I am with thee: be not dismayed; for I am thy God:

The devil was bound by the death or our Lord Jesus Christ-the devil is defeated. If satan has no power over believers, how come it says in **1 Thessalonians 2:18** Wherefore we would have come unto you, even I Paul, once and again; but *satan hindered us*? again we must look for agreement. The word, "hinder" means to checkor obstruct. It does not mean to stop or defeat. satan is the prince of the world-we are the children of God. He can manipulate the things of the world in order to slow us down, but he cannot stop or defeat us.

It boils down to this-we believe that God has given us dominion over the wicked one (**Genesis 1:28**). We believe that God has destroyed the works of the devil (**Hebrews 2:14**). We believe that we should not give place to the devil (**Ephesians 4:27**). We believe that the prince of this world has nothing in us (**John 14:30**). God has given us all power against the devil to take authority and dominion over him. Now the choice is ours (and yours)-after being given dominion, it is up to us whether or not we take it. We prefer to take it. How about you? It is your choice.

How about the unbeliever? Where does stand in all this? **2 Corinthians 4:4** says: In whom the god of this world hath blinded the minds of them which believe not,...The devil has power only in the minds and lives of unbelievers.

SPIRITUAL WARFARE?

Many have expounded the necessity for our taking part in "spiritual warfare." Many also have asked me of my position on the subject. I always reply, that I accept the leading of the Holy Spirit as he reveals answers to me in the pure light of God's Word. This answer may not please the many, who have said we should actively join in a "fight" for the Lord. God's Word (s) has spoken to me differently in this area, and I am content.

Following are many scripture verses, that were given me as regards this subject:

Notes

1 Corinthians 9:25 And every man that striveth for the mastery is temperate in all things. Now they do it to obtain a corruptible crown; but we an incorruptible.

Matthew 5:39 But I say unto you, That ye resist not evil

The following Ephesians verses have always been cited by the brethren, who "hawk" the spiritual warfare agenda:

Ephesians 6-10-17
[10] Finally, my brethren, be strong in the Lord, and in the power of his might.
[11] Put on the whole armour of God, that ye may be able to stand against the wiles of the devil.
[12] For we wrestle not against flesh and blood, but against principalities, against powers, against the rulers of the darkness of this world, against spiritual wickedness in high places.
[13] Wherefore take unto you the whole armour of God, that ye may be able to withstand in the evil day, and having done all, to stand.
[14] Stand therefore, having your loins girt about with truth, and having on the breastplate of righteousness;
[15] And your feet shod with the preparation of the gospel of peace;
[16] Above all, taking the shield of faith, wherewith ye shall be able to quench all the fiery darts of the wicked.
[17] And take the helmet of salvation, and the sword of the Spirit, which is the word of God

Comment: One can "use" these verses to justify the need for a warfare, however, they speak differently to my spirit. All the emphasized points: *be strong*; *armour of God*; *truth*; *breastplate of righteousness*; *gospel of peace; shield of faith; helmet of salvation; sword of the spirit;* all these are, in my judgment, the Word (s) of God. God's Word does the fighting and protecting. After all, why should we fight a battle, that has already been won by Christ's suffering and death. Jesus gave us freedom, liberty and peace. He paid the ultimate price. Why do we insist on continuing to send him a bill

Notes

2 Timothy 2:4 No man that warreth entangleth himself with the affairs of this life; that he may please him who hath chosen him to be a soldier.

Question: Isn't carrying on a spiritual warfare an *affair of this life*?) If evil, sin, the devil, etc. are affairs of this life is this verse telling to avoid these affairs of this life?

2 Timothy 2:5 And if a man also strive for masteries, yet is he not crowned, except he strive lawfully. (Question: How does one strive lawfully? We strive lawfully, when we stay in line with the spirit of God's commands.)

2 Corinthians 10:4 (For the weapons of our warfare are *not carnal*, but mighty through God to the pulling down of strong holds;

Question: If our weapons are not carnal (of the flesh) just what are they? They must be God's Words - the truth and two-edged sword.

Philippians 4:5 Let your moderation be known unto all men. The Lord is at hand (Note: Moderation means the act of keeping in bounds, and our "bounds" are God's commands.

Philippians 4:8 Finally, brethren, whatsoever things are true, whatsoever things are honest, whatsoever things are just, whatsoever things are pure, whatsoever things are lovely, whatsoever things are of good report; if there be any virtue, and if there be any praise, think on these things.

Note: All of these things negate the reasons given for taking part in spiritual warfare. These things are all descriptive of God's Word (s). Thinking on these things leaves no room for participating in a so-called spiritual warfare.

1 Timothy 1:18 This charge I commit unto thee, son Timothy, according to the prophecies which went before on thee, that thou by them mightest war a *good* warfare;

Question: Would you not agree, that a good warfare is one which is "fought" according to (and in line with) God's Word?

2 Timothy 2:24 And the servant of the Lord *must not strive*; but be gentle unto all men, apt to teach, patient

Question: How can this particular "servant"

Notes

serve God in truth by engaging in any kind of warfare?)

1 Timothy 6:12 Fight the good fight of faith.

Note: Synonyms for "faith": assurance, sureness, reliance, trust. We exercise all these in line with God's Words, as faith comes by hearing, and hearing by the Word of God. We "fight" within the bounds of scripture.)

2 Timothy 2:4 I have fought a good fight, I have finished my course, I have kept the faith

Question: Doesn't this verse tie in beautifully with the verse directly above? We think so!)

Revelation 2:16 Repent; or else I will come unto thee quickly, and will fight against them with the sword of my mouth (Comment: Jesus fights with the sword of his mouth, which is his Word. Question: As joint-heirs with Christ, shouldn't we brandish the same "sword"? We think so!)

Now the basic question: Where does all this leave "spiritual warfare" as a viable action for a believer? Your call, again. I am content.

PROPHECY

PROPHECY - The work, function, or vocation of a prophet. Inspired utterance, interpretation or declaration or the will or purpose of God.

PROPHESY - To speak for, or as, God. To utter with divine inspiration.

PROPHET - Proclaimer of a revelation; interpreter of an oracle. An inspired spokesman. One whose office is to deliver a message. One inspired or instructed by God to speak in his name.

<u>Revelation 19:10</u> worship God: *for the testimony of Jesus is the spirit of prophecy*.

Question: What is the testimony of Jesus? We believe it is his Word (God's Word), that is the true spirit of prophecy. That's prophecy enough for me.

<u>Hebrews 1:1</u> God, who at sundry times and in divers manners spake in time past unto the fathers by the prophets,

<u>Hebrews 1:2</u> Hath in these last days *spoken unto us by his Son*, whom he hath appointed heir of all things, by whom also he made the worlds;

<u>Romans 12:6</u> whether prophecy, let us prophesy according to the proportion of faith;

Comment: If we believe that faith cometh by hearing, and hearing by the Word of God-it follows that prophesying is simply rightly dividing the Word of God.

<u>1 Peter 4:11</u> If any man speak, let him speak *as the oracles of God;*

Question: Does this verse also apply to prophets? Wouldn't this make anyone who speaks the oracles of God a prophet? (We believe so).

<u>1 Corinthians 2:13</u> Which things also we speak, not in the words which man's wisdom teacheth, but which the Holy Ghost teacheth;

Comment: This applies also to prophecy-don't you agree?

<u>Romans 1:2</u> (Which he had promised afore by his prophets *in the holy scriptures*,)

<u>Revelation 22:7</u> blessed is he that keepeth the sayings of the *prophecy of this book.*

Note: Of course, the book here is the Word of God.

Notes

Revelation 22:19 And if any man shall take away from the ***words of the book of this prophecy,***

Revelation 1:3 Blessed is he that readeth, and they that hear the words of this prophecy,

1 Corinthians 14:3 But he that prophesieth speaketh unto men to edification, and exhortation, and comfort.

Comment: Only the Word of God can successfully do this-the Word must be prophecy.

2 Peter 1:20 Knowing this first, that no ***prophecy of the scripture*** is of any private interpretation.

2 Peter 1:21 For the prophecy came not in old time by the will of man: but holy men of God spake as they were moved by the Holy Ghost

In the book of Jeremiah we find warnings concerning prophecy that is not inspired of God.

Jeremiah 14:13-16
[13] Then said I, Ah, Lord GOD! behold, the prophets say unto them, Ye shall not see the sword, neither shall ye have famine; but I will give you assured peace in this place.

[14] Then the LORD said unto me, The prophets prophesy lies in my name: I sent them not, neither have I commanded them, neither spake unto them: they prophesy unto you a false vision and divination, and a thing of nought, and the deceit of their heart.

[15] Therefore thus saith the LORD concerning the prophets that prophesy in my name, and I sent them not, yet they say, Sword and famine shall not be in this land; By sword and famine shall those prophets be consumed.

[16] And the people to whom they prophesy shall be cast out in the streets of Jerusalem because of the famine and the sword; and they shall have none to bury them, them, their wives, nor their sons, nor their daughters: for I will pour their wickedness upon them.

Jeremiah 23:11-40
[11] For both ***prophet*** and priest are profane; yea, in my house have I found their wickedness, saith the LORD.

12 Wherefore their way shall be unto them as slippery ways in the darkness: they shall be driven on, and fall therein: for I will bring evil upon them, even the year of their visitation, saith the LORD.

13 And I have seen *folly in the prophets* of Samaria; they prophesied in Baal, and caused my people Israel to err.

14 I have seen also in the *prophets of Jerusalem* an horrible thing: they commit adultery, and walk in lies: they strengthen also the hands of evildoers, that none doth return from his wickedness; they are all of them unto me as Sodom, and the inhabitants thereof as Gomorrah.

15 Therefore thus saith the LORD of hosts concerning the prophets; Behold, I will feed them with wormwood, and make them drink the water of gall: for from the prophets of Jerusalem is profaneness gone forth into all the land.

16 Thus saith the LORD of hosts, Hearken not unto the words of the prophets that prophesy unto you: they make you vain: they speak a vision of their own heart, and not out of the mouth of the LORD.

17 They say still unto them that despise me, The LORD hath said, Ye shall have peace; and they say unto every one that walketh after the imagination of his own heart, No evil shall come upon you.

18 For who hath stood in the counsel of the LORD, and hath perceived and heard his word? who hath marked his word, and heard it?

19 Behold, a whirlwind of the LORD is gone forth in fury, even a grievous whirlwind: it shall fall grievously upon the head of the wicked.

20 The anger of the LORD shall not return, until he have executed, and till he have performed the thoughts of his heart: in the latter days ye shall consider it perfectly.

21 *I have not sent these prophets*, yet they ran: I have not spoken to them, yet they prophesied.

22 But if they had stood in my counsel, and had caused my people to hear my words, then they should have turned them from their evil way, and from the evil of their doings.

23 Am I a God at hand, saith the LORD, and not a God afar off?

Notes

24 Can any hide himself in secret places that I shall not see him? saith the LORD. Do not I fill heaven and earth? saith the LORD.

25 I have heard what the prophets said, *that prophesy lies in my name,* saying, I have dreamed, I have dreamed.

26 How long shall this be in the heart of the *prophets that prophesy lies*? yea, they are prophets of the deceit of their own heart;

27 Which think to cause my people to forget my name by their dreams which they tell every man to his neighbour, as their fathers have forgotten my name for Baal.

28 The prophet that hath a dream, let him tell a dream; *and he that hath my word, let him speak my word faithfully.* What is the chaff to the wheat? saith the LORD.

29 Is not my word like as a fire? saith the LORD; and like a hammer that breaketh the rock in pieces?

30 Therefore, behold, I am against the prophets, saith the LORD, that steal my words every one from his neighbour.

31 *Behold, I am against the prophets, saith the LORD, that use their tongues, and say, He saith.*

32 Behold, I am against them that prophesy false dreams, saith the LORD, and do tell them, and cause my people to err by their lies, and by their lightness; yet I sent them not, nor commanded them: therefore they shall not profit this people at all, saith the LORD.

33 And when this people, or the prophet, or a priest, shall ask thee, saying, What is the burden of the LORD? thou shalt then say unto them, What burden? I will even forsake you, saith the LORD.

34 And as for the prophet, and the priest, and the people, that shall say, The burden of the LORD, I will even punish that man and his house.

35 Thus shall ye say every one to his neighbour, and every one to his brother, What hath the LORD answered? and, What hath the LORD spoken?

36 And the burden of the LORD shall ye mention no more: for every man's word shall be his burden; *for ye have perverted the words of the living God,* of the LORD of hosts our God.

37 Thus shalt thou say to the prophet, What hath

Notes

the LORD answered thee? and, What hath the LORD spoken?

³⁸ But since ye say, The burden of the LORD; therefore thus saith the LORD; Because ye say this word, The burden of the LORD, and I have sent unto you, saying, Ye shall not say, The burden of the LORD;

³⁹ Therefore, behold, I, even I, will utterly forget you, and I will forsake you, and the city that I gave you and your fathers, and cast you out of my presence:

⁴⁰ And I will bring an everlasting reproach upon you, and a perpetual shame, which shall not be forgotten.

Jeremiah 29:8 For thus saith the LORD of hosts, the God of Israel; *Let not your prophets and your diviners, that be in the midst of you, deceive you*, neither hearken to your dreams which ye cause to be dreamed.

Jeremiah 29:9 *For they prophesy falsely unto you in my name: I have not sent them, saith the LORD.*

COMMENTS: Saints, we can't speak for you, but after reading these Jeremiah verses, we have to believe that those, who prophesy against the Will of God-and those, who receive their prophesies-are in a lot of trouble. We have to caution any believer, who prophesies from his own heart, saying, "Thus saith the Lord"-when the Lord said no such thing. There are many believers that feel since we are living under a new covenant, the Words of the Old Testament do not apply. Let us share: **2 Timothy 3:16** All scripture is given by inspiration of God, and: **Matthew 5:17** Think not that I am come to destroy the law, or the prophets: I am not come to destroy, but to fulfill.

Allow us to share some New Testament scriptures concerning prophets.

Matthew 7:15-16 Beware of false prophets, which come to you in sheep's clothing, but inwardly they are ravening wolves. Ye shall know them by their fruits.

Romans 16:17 Now I beseech you, brethren,

Notes

mark them which cause divisions and offences contrary to the doctrine which ye have learned; and avoid them.

Matthew 24:4 And Jesus answered and said unto them, Take heed that no man deceive you. (Including prophets.)

Ephesians 5:6-7 Let no man deceive you with vain words: for because of these things cometh the wrath of God upon the children of disobedience. Be not ye therefore partakers with them.

Comment: The word "prophet" does not appear, but we believe he is included under, "Let no man". It speaks to us here that God has placed the responsibility on us. We are commanded not to be deceived, and to not be partakers with them. If we disobey-shame on us. We have only ourselves to blame.

Colossians 2:8 Beware lest any man spoil you through philosophy and vain deceit, after the tradition of men, after the rudiments of the world, and not after Christ.

2 Peter 2:1 But there were false prophets also among the people, even as there shall be false teachers among you, who privily shall bring in damnable heresies, even denying the Lord that bought them, and bring upon themselves swift destruction.

1 John 4:1 Beloved, believe not every spirit, but try the spirits whether they are of God: because many false prophets are gone out into the world.

Matthew 12:36 But I say unto you, That every idle word that men shall speak, they shall give account thereof in the day of judgment.

Galatians 1:7 Which is not another; but there be some that trouble you, and would pervert the gospel of Christ.

Galatians 1:8 But though we, or an angel from heaven, preach any other gospel unto you than that which we have preached unto you, let him be accursed.

Galatians 1:9 As we said before, so say I now again, If any man preach any other gospel unto you than that ye have received, let him be accursed.

Matthew 24:24 For there shall arise false Christs, *and false prophets*, and shall show great signs and wonders; insomuch that, if it were possible, they shall deceive the very elect.

Revelation 20:10 And the devil that deceived them was cast into the lake of fire and brimstone, where the beast and the *false prophet* are, and shall be tormented day and night for ever and ever.

Matthew 24:11 And many false prophets shall rise, and shall deceive many.

Comment: Let the one, who falsely prophesies, and the one, who accepts the false prophecy be fairly warned. You are treading on very thin ice. As the Bible says, we are not to be deceived by any man, or by any means.

Notes

Notes

PRAYER

At the beginning of this work we talked about launching this boat into deeper waters. Well, stand by-we are about to sail into the deepest waters yet. We are now over the deepest part of the deepest ocean. We readily admit that we considered for a brief moment to exclude this section on prayer in our effort to provide a meaningful work concerning counseling. We thought, that most Christians, who have been satisfied with the milk, would not be able to suddenly switch to the pure meat of the Word. We then consulted God's Word, and he told us to be careful for nothing (**Philippians 4:6**). We also figured that, if you reached this point in our (His) Manual without caving in, you would be able to handle this segment on prayer. you may not agree with it, but you would handle it. The deeper water gave us pause, but it spoke to our spirit that walking on water is just as much a wonder whether the depth of the water is 2000 feet-or 20 feet.

Before we get into this subject, please allow us to emphasize that we believe in prayer with all our heart, soul, spirit, and mind. We are told by God to pray without ceasing(**1 Thessalonians 5:17**), that men ought always to pray (**Luke 18:1**), that we should continue in prayer (**Romans 12:12**), that we should pray always with all prayer and supplication (**Ephesians6:18**), that we should continue in prayer (**Colossians 4:2**). These are but a few of the scriptures that exhort us to pray, and to be in prayer-we agree. We are now going to steer this boat into deeper waters. Many of the prayer warriors may try to sink her, and that's OK. We will remain content, forgiving, patient, loving, longsuffering, etc.- not because we are special, but because God wills it. Again, disagreements between believers are not salvation issues. Here we go!

When people come to me and request prayer for the relief of what is bothering them, I immediately ask questions. Are you saved? (some aren't). If they are, I ask if they believe God wrote all the Words in the Bible-that they are his Words. I then ask if they believe that their answer is in the Bible. If yes, I first ask them to agree on the thank-you scriptures. Then I share whatever scriptures that come into my remembrance concerning their problem. Then I ask them to settle on the verses that speak to their hearts and spirits-then stand on them in faith, knowing that God will keep his promise. When I are through, the believer doesn't realize that I haven't "prayed"- although I did pray. I prayed the Words that will not return to God void-we prayed His Word.

Romans 8:26-28 Likewise the Spirit also helpeth our infirmities: for we know not what we should pray for as we ought: but the Spirit itself maketh intercession for us with groanings which cannot be uttered. And he that searcheth the hearts knoweth what is the mind of the Spirit, because he maketh intercession for the saints according to the will of God. And we know that all things work together for good to them that love God, to them who are the called according to his purpose.

Question: What are these verses saying to your spirit? They tell me that I really do *not* know how to pray effectively. So God has assigned the Holy Spirit to intercede for me in prayer with words I couldn't possibly begin to understand. God understands, because the Spirit is acting according to God's Will. Now if we accept verse 28, and know that all things work together for good, why would we want to ask God to change his Will as regards our situation? Aren't we doing just that when we pray for deliverance? In a way, aren't we actually "charging God foolishly" (**Job 1:22**)? Aren't we saying to God, "Your will isn't convenient or comfortable-please change it"? There are other scriptures that encourage us to look to the Holy Spirit as our prayer intercessor.

1 Corinthians 14:15 What is it then? I will pray with the spirit, and I will pray with the understanding also:

Ephesians 6:18 Praying always with all prayer and supplication *in the Spirit,*

Comment: When we pray God's Words, we are praying in and with the Sprit, because God's Words will not return to him void., but they shall accomplish

Notes

that which he pleases, and they shall prosper in the thing whereto he sent them. Is this said about men's words anywhere in the bible?

James 5:16 The effectual fervent prayer of a *righteous* man availeth much. The word "effectual" means having adequate power or force to produce an intended effect. The only prayers that are effectual in focusing God's power on a problem are his Words. A righteous man, one who is in right standing with God, knows that only God's Words will avail much. Therefore, a righteous man will pray only God's Words - of course, this is what Jesus did. He spoke God' Words.

Proverbs 15:29 The LORD is far from the wicked: but he heareth the prayer of the righteous.

Question: Is God saying here that he doesn't hear the prayers of the unrighteousness?

Let's look at some of the common areas for which believers seek prayer. Please get a sheet of paper, and draw a "T" on the page. On the left side of the "T" (on the line) write, "Things to pray for"- on the right line write, "Things not to pray for". Let us first decide under which category "Wants" should be listed.

WANTS
Psalm 23:1 The LORD is my shepherd; I shall not want.

Philippians 4:11 Not that I speak in respect of want:

Psalm 34:9 O fear the LORD, ye his saints: for there is no want to them that fear him.

Psalm 34:10 but they that seek the LORD shall not want any good thing.

James 1:4 But let patience have her perfect work, that ye may be perfect and entire, wanting nothing.

Hebrews 13:5 and be content with such things as ye have:

Comment: If you believe that these verses are asking us to pray about wants, please enter "Wants" on the left side of the "T". If you believe the verses are telling us not to want enter "Want" on the right side. (We favored the right side).

NEEDS

Philippians 4:19 But my God shall supply all your need according to his riches in glory by Christ Jesus.

Matthew 6:8 for your Father knoweth what things ye have need of, before ye ask him.

Matthew 6:32 for your heavenly Father knoweth that ye have need of all these things.

Luke 12:30 and your Father knoweth that ye have need of these things.

Hebrews 4:16 Let us therefore come boldly unto the throne of grace, that we may obtain mercy, and find grace to help in time of need.

Hebrews 13:5 and be content with such things as ye have: Psalm 23:5 my cup runneth over.

Question: If your cup runneth over-what else is there to need?

Comment: Do the same here that you did in the Wants part of this exercise. If you believe as we do, that "Needs" belongs in the right column-please place it there.

Hebrews 4:16 above says that we may obtain mercy and find grace in time of need at the throne of grace. Does it ask us to pray about our time of need? No, it simply asks us come boldly into the throne of grace and obtain.

Many other subjects (many of which are found in this Manual) could be covered here in like manner, but I think you probably get the idea. When you look at all the problems for which believers seek counsel and prayer (many of which are in this Manual) you should be able to scripturally place them on the "T" page. We have no idea what your page looks like-mine has all the subjects listed on the right side. The left side is blank. Just a minute-hold the phone. It has already been said that we believe in prayer, and we have accepted that God has told us to pray. I admit that prayer is an important and necessary part of the Christian walk. Well, then, what goes in our left column? We have written: *GOD'S WORD*. I pray the Words of God. **2 Corinthians 12:9-10** tells me, that I should glory in and take pleasure in any challenge or problem, that comes my way.

Notes

Notes

There is another reason why I pray God's Words instead of my own, when claiming anything. It is found in **Romans 8:32**: He that spared not his own Son, but delivered him up for us all, how shall he not with him also *freely give us all things*? "Freely" is defined as follows:

1. not determined by anything beyond its own nature or being;

2. not necessitated by an external cause or agency;

3. not unduly influenced;

4. spontaneous of independent.

When God said he shall with Jesus *freely* give us all things, he does it independently of us.

He does it because of his nature-not because of our prayers, but because of his Word and Promise.

We are often told that we are directed in God's Word to *ask*. One of the definitions of the word "ask" is to *claim, demand, or expect*. Since this definition lines up more readily with God's Word, this is the one upon which I stand. It follows therefore that my method of asking is different than most. I claim God's promise through his Word in the Name of Jesus Christ; then I stand fast in faith for delivery - adding, "Father, not my will, but thine be done." **Ephesians 3:20** Now unto him that is able to do exceeding abundantly above all that we ask or think, according to the power that worketh in us, This verse tells me that we need not "ask" for anything, if we believe that God freely gives us all things, and is able to do more than we ask or think. **1 John 5:14** And this is the confidence that we have in him, that, if we ask any thing *according to his will*, he heareth us:**1 John 5:15** And if we know that he hear us, whatsoever we ask, we know that we have the petitions that we desired of him. Notice that the verse says, "if we ask anything *according to his will..*". What is his Will, but his Word? We must ask according to His Will, and the Holy Spirit does just that.

I pray the scriptures, because they are quick and powerful, and they will not return void to God. When we have prayed with someone by offering scripture (s) as answers, they often do not accept this as prayer. They do not realize that we have

Notes

prayed for them in the most pure and powerful fashion. They expect the traditional men's prayers-asking for things that God has already done. Men will pray, "May God bless you in this"-he has already blessed us with all spiritual blessings (**Ephesians 1:3**). Often men will pray, "May God curse this evil", when He has already cursed and delivered us from evil. Some pray for God to bind this or that, when He has already bound it. It speaks to me that these kinds of traditional prayers may actually border on being sinful, because they are not of faith-but of fear. When I exhort in this area without being heard or received, I simply shake and/or wipe the dust off my feet as I am commanded to do in **Matthew 10:14** and **Luke 10:11**, while reminding dissenters, that we must be fully persuaded in our own mind. I also find joy in standing on **1 Corinthians 14:37-38** and **Titus 3:9**.

Holy scripture is prayer. Whenever a believer rightly divides the Word of Truth, when ministering in any situation, he has prayed. The problem here arises, because the saints have become so used to hearing men's watered-down prayers from men's doctrines, they do not understand, or accept, a real prayer when they hear it. Instead of asking God to do things he has already done, wouldn't it be better to know, and stand, on what he has already promised us? I think so, and this is what this section is all about

In my ministry I meet believers, who say they are having trouble with their prayer life. They often express that they can't seem to find the words that others seem to have no trouble in expressing. After agreeing on the thank-you scriptures, I share:

Matthew 6:5-13 And when thou prayest, thou shalt not be as the hypocrites are: for they love to pray standing in the synagogues and in the corners of the streets, that they may be seen of men. Verily I say unto you, They have their reward.

But thou, when thou prayest, enter into thy closet, and when thou hast shut thy door, pray to thy Father which is in secret; and thy Father which seeth in secret shall reward thee openly.

Notes

But when ye pray, use not vain repetitions, as the heathen do: for they think that they shall be heard for their much speaking.

Be not ye therefore like unto them: for your Father knoweth what things ye have need of, before ye ask him.

After this manner therefore pray ye: Our Father which art in heaven, Hallowed be thy name.

Thy kingdom come. Thy will be done in earth, as it is in heaven.

Give us this day our daily bread.

And forgive us our debts, as we forgive our debtors.

And lead us not into temptation, but deliver us from evil: For thine is the kingdom, and the power, and the glory, for ever. Amen.

After reading the above verses, how can anyone confess a problem with their prayer life? Here God has taken all the question out of it. God tells us how not to pray, where to pray, to whom we should pray, not to use vain repetitions (men's words), and what to say in our prayer. Read these verses until they really begin to speak to you. They are full of wonderful deliverances and protection. God liked his prayer so much he repeated it in:

Luke 11:2-4

2 And he said unto them, When ye pray, say, Our Father which art in heaven, Hallowed be thy name. Thy kingdom come. Thy will be done, as in heaven, so in earth.

3 Give us day by day our daily bread.

4 And forgive us our sins; for we also forgive every one that is indebted to us. And lead us not into temptation; but deliver us from evil.

Thank you Father in the Name of Jesus Christ for your precious Word. There are many scriptures that tell us that God knows all things. He knows our needs; he knows our hearts and spirits; he knows our wants; we are manifest in his sight; all things are naked and open unto him. He knows our words before we even speak them **Isaiah 65:24** says:

And it shall come to pass, that before they call, I

will answer; and while they are yet speaking, I will hear. When we truly accept that God knows all , doesn't it seem just a bit redundant to pray our own words, while asking for various things he has already delivered? What has happened here is, that man has caused the believer's prayer life to go way beyond what God has designed for us.

Yes, the Word of God commands us to pray-I do. It speaks to me that, in order to be in line with God's Word, all I have to do is pray his Words. **James 5:15** refers to the prayer of faith; **Romans 10:17** says: So then faith cometh by hearing, and hearing by the word of God. I accept from this that the prayer of faith is God's Word-this is why I pray his Words, and not my own.

1 Corinthians 3:21 Therefore let no man glory in men. For all things are yours;

Question: If all things are ours-why do we pray about these things?

2 Peter 1:3 According as his divine power hath ***given unto us all things*** that pertain unto life and godliness,

Question: If has already give us all things-why don't we stop asking him for more favors and various other "things"? I don't anymore-I'm too busy thanking him for his precious grace and blessings.

Think of all the things for which you normally would petition God; things for which you usually pray. Aren't they all covered by: **Matthew 6:33** But seek ye first the kingdom of God, and his righteousness; and all these things shall be added unto you.? How about: **Luke 12:31** But rather seek ye the kingdom of God; and all these things shall be added unto you.?

Question: Is this saying that all we have to do is "seek the kingdom of God"? God said, that all things shall be added unto me - so why should I pray specifically for these things?

After sharing this section with a fellowship we attended, I received the usual expected resistance and rebuke. None of what was said was scripturally based-they were the usual opinions fostered by

Notes

Notes

years of "traditional" teachings in this area. However, what followed is what usually comes about after these sessions-I was driven back into the Bible for more understanding. The Holy Spirit presented the following to me:

Psalm 119:67 Before I was afflicted I went astray: but now have I kept thy word.

Psalm 119:71 It is good for me that I have been afflicted; that I might learn thy statutes.

Question: Are these verses saying that the afflictions are meant to lead us into

God's Word? (You decide).

Hebrews 12:11 Now no chastening for the present seemeth to be joyous, but grievous: nevertheless afterward it yieldeth the peaceable fruit of righteousness unto them which are exercised thereby.

Question: If we pray for and receive deliverance, are we not saying we are willing

to forego the "peaceable fruit of righteousness"? (Again, you decide)!

Jeremiah 30:15 Why criest thou for thine affliction?

Question: Is this a way of saying, "What are you moaning about"?

Ecclesiastes 7:14 In the day of prosperity be joyful, but in the day of adversity consider: God also hath set the one over against the other, to the end that man should find nothing after him.

Note: Yes, "All things are of God." God has set joy against adversity-one over against the other. If we pray for deliverance from adversity, isn't it only fair to be delivered from joy also? (Gives one pause to consider, doesn't it)?

2 Thessalonians 1:4-5 So that we ourselves glory in you in the churches of God for your patience and faith in all your persecutions and tribulations *that ye endure*: Which is a manifest token of the righteous judgment of God, that ye may be counted worthy of the kingdom of God, for which ye also suffer:

Question: Is praying for deliverance saying that we do not want to be counted

worthy of the kingdom of God? What is your answer? (Aren't we supposed to endure)?

Acts 20:23-24 Save that the Holy Ghost witnesseth in every city, saying that bonds and a afflictions abide me. But none of these things move me,

Question: Do none of these things move us-or do we pray for deliverance?

2 Corinthians 4:17 For our light affliction, which is but for a moment, worketh for us a far more exceeding and eternal weight of glory;

2 Timothy 4:5 But watch thou in all things, endure afflictions,

Hebrews 11:25 Choosing rather to suffer affliction with the people of God, than to enjoy the pleasures of sin for a season;

James 5:11 Behold, we count them happy which endure.

Hebrews 11:35 Women received their dead raised to life again: and others were tortured, not accepting deliverance; that they might obtain a better resurrection:

1 Thessalonians 3:3-4 That no man should be moved by these afflictions: for yourselves know that we are appointed thereunto. For verily, when we were with you, we told you before that we should suffer tribulation; even as it came to pass, and ye know.

Psalm 34:19 Many are the afflictions of the righteous: but the LORD delivereth him out of them all.

Question: If we are to endure, why waste time praying about the afflictions and tribulations?

1 Pet 4:19 Wherefore let them that suffer according to the will of God commit the keeping of their souls to him in well doing, as unto a faithful Creator.

The following scriptures may also add to the truth that persecutions and tribulations are part and parcel of the Christian walk-to be suffered and endured.

Mark 10:30; John 16:23; Acts 9:16; Acts 14:22; Romans 5:3; Romans 8:18; 1 Corinthians 4:12; 2 Corinthians 7:4; 2 Corinthians 12:10; 2 Corinthians 1:7;

2 Corinthians 4:8-9; Phil 1:29; 2 Thessalonians 1:4; 2 Tim 3:12; Hebrews 5:8

(These verses are printed out on later pages.)

Notes

It is accepted that I am a joint-heir with Christ (**Romans 8:17**). Accepting this has shown me that I should pray as Christ prayed (**John 18:11, Matthew 26:42, Mark 14:36,** and **Luke 22:42).**

2 Corinthians 4:17-18 For our light affliction, which is but for a moment, worketh for us a far more exceeding and eternal weight of glory; While we look not at the things which are seen, but at the things which are not seen: for the things which are seen are temporal; but the things which are not seen are eternal.

Question: Don't our prayers asking for deliverance reflect on things which are seen-such as our afflictions, persecutions and tribulations? We are directed by God to look at the things unseen, which are eternal. Is praying about things that are seen going against God's Word? I think it is. What do you think-how readest thou? We are told in:**2 Corinthians 5:7** For we walk by faith, not by sight:

Just in case some of you saints are not moved to search the scriptures for the five verses cited above, here they are:

Matthew 26:42 He went away again the second time, and prayed, saying, O my Father, if this cup may not pass away from me, except I drink it, ***thy will be done.***

Matthew 26:39 And he went a little farther, and fell on his face, and prayed, saying, O my Father, if it be possible, let this cup pass from me: ***nevertheless not as I will, but as thou wilt.***

Mark 14:36 And he said, Abba, Father, all things are possible unto thee; take away this cup from me: nevertheless not what I will, ***but what thou wilt.***

John 18:11 the cup which my Father hath given me, shall I not drink it?

Luke 22:42 Saying, Father, if thou be willing, remove this cup from me: nevertheless ***not my will, but thine, be done.***

We all know the terrible load that Jesus Christ carried to the cross. Yet, he did not pray for deliverance-he left the outcome in God's hands. It is true that every man must be fully persuaded in his own mind, and here is my persuasion. As a joint-heir with Christ Jesus, I prefer to pray as he did. Since accepting the leading that persecutions, afflictions, tribulations, and all other challenges, that God has willed for my life, are part and parcel of my Christian walk, I pray not for deliverance. pray as Christ did in the above verses. These are God's Words, and they give me the spiritual strength to endure, to be patient, and to be long-suffering as they exhort me to have faith in God's Will for my life. (It may be beneficial to review the "Persecutions and Tribulations" chapter of this Manual.)

When we have asked many brethren to share with us any scriptures that direct us to pray for deliverance from our challenges, a few have shared:**2 Corinthians 12:8** For this thing I besought the Lord thrice, that it might depart from me. The few claim that Paul was asking the Lord for deliverance, and he was for the moment, but it was the flesh speaking to his problem. The following two verses put Paul back in line with the Holy Spirit and God's Will. He then began to take pleasure in his infirmities, reproaches, necessities, persecutions, and distresses for Christ's sake. Let's look deeper into **2 Corinthians 12:9-10** "And he said unto me, My grace is sufficient for thee: for my strength is made perfect in weakness. Most gladly therefore will I rather glory in my infirmities, that the power of Christ may rest upon me. Therefore I take pleasure in infirmities, in reproaches, in necessities, in persecutions, in distresses for Christ's sake: for when I am weak, then am I strong. Let us look at the definitions of the five conditions stated in verse 10:

Infirmities: ill-health; illness; medical condition; sickness; frailty. (Ant: health)

Reproaches: criticism; blame; scolding; censure; reprimand; accusation; rebuke; reproof:

Necessity: need; requirement; inevitability; obligation; stipulation.

Persecutions: harassment; maltreatment; bullying; singling out; hounding; bullying; harrying; discrimination.

Distress: suffering; pain; sorrow; anguish;

Notes

agony; grief; misery.
(Ant. Peace.)

Question: Can you think of any problems or challenges, that are not included in these five conditions? I cannot! If you agree, then you must accept, that we must take pleasure and glory in all these things as God has commanded us to do.

God' Word says: **Romans 10:17** So then faith cometh by hearing, and hearing by the word of God. It also says in: **James 5:15** And the prayer of faith shall save the sick, Again it speaks loudly to my spirit that the Word of God is the only effectual prayer language. Maybe God said it all through the publican in **Luke 18:13**, when he said: "God be merciful to me a sinner. (while smoting his breast)."

It is felt that a wrap-up of this section is demanded here. It is known, and accepted, that much of what has been shared here goes against what the prayer warriors are practicing. This chapter can be considered a controversial view of what has been accepted as a good prayer life. This is understandable, so please suffer me to share some definitions with you.

Webster's International Dictionary:
Prayer: 1. act of beseeching, petition, supplication.
2. act of adoration, confession, thanksgiving
The Winston Dictionary:
Pray: 1. to ask earnestly; to ask with humility and reverence; *to speak to God in request, confession, or praise*
Prayer: 1. the act of entreating earnestly; *thanks and praise words to God*

It is once again time to be fully persuaded in your own minds. You may elect to honor the first definitions found in the above reference sources. If you do-Praise the Lord. This decision would make your staying in the traditional posture much easier to maintain. However, if you decide (as I have) to honor the second definitions, which are fact also-Praise the Lord again. Just remember that all things are of God-no matter which direction you choose.

Please allow me to refresh your memory as to the definitions of the word, "ask": to ask is to claim, demand, expect. Choosing only the first definitions will certainly justify the traditional prayer practice of asking God for the granting of various petitions. It would support the idea that God has not yet done it all-that he has more to do. It is my belief that God has "finished" his work. After all, God is the Alpha and the Omega-the beginning and the end. This belief encourages me to pray God's Words, which are the only Words that the Bible says will not return to him void. These Words, his Words, wonderfully express my adoration for him, my confession to him, and my grateful thanks for all he has done. "It is finished".

Thank you Father in the Name of Jesus.

Maybe you will allow me to relate this entire scenario to Peter's plight, when he stepped out of the ship onto the water to meet Jesus. Whether or not you accept what follows is again a matter of being fully persuaded in your own minds. In other words, "What thinkest thou"?

Peter's faith in Jesus allowed him to step out of the boat, and walk on the water. Then he saw the wind boisterous, became afraid, and took his eyes off Jesus. Can't you just picture the winds disturbing the calm of the sea, and causing waves to cascade around Peter's feet? He lost his faith in the Savior, and focused his attention on the sea. He began to sink, and prayed to Jesus- , "Lord save me". Jesus said in **Mattthew 14:31**: "O thou of little faith, wherefore didst thou doubt"? Let us look at our own situation concerning faith. We accepted Jesus Christ as Savior and Redeemer, and received the Holy Spirit and a measure of faith. We accepted that Jesus is the Word of God-we stepped out in faith. We soon discovered that the boisterous winds of promised persecutions and tribulations began to disturb the seas of our lives. Instead of keeping our eyes on Jesus, and enduring and suffering as commanded by the Word-we sought deliverance by pleading, "Lord save me". It speaks to me that our

Notes

Lord's answer is as always, "O thou of little faith, wherefore didst thou doubt"?

Note: Verse 32 says that, "they were come into the ship". It doesn't say that Jesus dragged Peter through the water back to the ship. Apparently Peter regained his faith, put his eyes back on Jesus, and walked on the water back to the boat.

Can it be that all we have to do is regain as much faith as a grain of mustard seed, and stand fast on God's Word and Promises-that we don't have to pray for what he has already done?

Are your prayers of faith, or of fear?

Have you honestly inventoried your prayers to ascertain whether they are truly based on faith? Or are they based on fear-the flesh?

My present stance as regards my prayer life was triggered by: **Romans 8:26-27** Likewise the Spirit helpeth our infirmities: for we know not what we should pray of as we ought: but the Spirit itself maketh intercession for us with groanings which cannot be uttered. And he that searcheth the hearts knoweth what is the mind of the Spirit, because he maketh intercession for the saints according to the will of God". When I really began to understand and accept these verses for what they said, it spoke to my spirit that:

1. I do not how to pray effectively.

2. The Spirit automatically helps me without communications from me.

3. The Spirit acts strictly according to the Will of God-the flesh does not enter into the mix.

When I fully accepted this posture, I stopped praying in the traditional manner-I started only to claim God's promises as stated in his Word with a thankful attitude.

A search was made to locate any scripture verses that stated, that we should pray for deliverance in any situation, and none were found. In my search it became clear to me that God's Word held all the answers, and not my own attempt to "pray" my own words. As you can imagine, much rebuke and criticisms were forthcoming from the traditional prayer warriors. Most of them took me to task by leading me to **James 5:13-15**, which says: Is any among you afflicted? let him pray. Is any merry? let him sing psalms. Is any sick among you? let him call for the elders of the church: and let them pray over him, anointing him with oil in the name of the Lord: And the *prayer of faith* shall save the sick, and the Lord shall raise him up..."

It is my persuasion that God's Word is perfect, and there is total agreement in the scriptures. How then does my position, and the verses in the book of James, line up in agreement? The key words are *"prayer of faith"*. Faith is defined in **Hebrews 11:1** - Now faith is the substance of things hoped for, and the evidence of things not seen". Please consider how this speaks to my spirit. The things hoped for must be God's promises-the evidence of things not seen must be the results manifested by those promises. This is why I have chosen to pray God's Words, and thereby to release the power of the Holy Spirit in my life.

There was a period in my walk, where I insisted to see in order to believe. By praying God's Words, my spirit began to believe first-then followed a patient waiting to see the results. God tells us that they, who see not and yet believe, will be blessed.

Thank you Father in the Name of Christ Jesus for your promises.

SUFFER IT - OR BE DELIVERED

The following verses tell me, that we are to suffer all things. ("How readest thou"-**Luke 10:26**)

Matthew 3:15 And Jesus answering said unto him, *Suffer* it to be so now: for thus it becometh us to fulfil all righteousness. Then he suffered him.

Mark 8:31 And he began to teach them, that the Son of man *must suffer* many things, and be rejected of the elders, and of the chief priests, and scribes, and be killed, and after three days rise again.

Luke 9:22 Saying, The Son of man *must suffer* many things, and be rejected of the elders and chief priests and scribes, and be slain, and be raised the third day.

Notes

Luke 17:25 But first *must he suffer* many things, and be rejected of this generation.

Luke 22:51 And Jesus answered and said, *Suffer ye* thus far.

Acts 5:41 And they departed from the presence of the council, rejoicing that they were counted worthy *to suffer* shame for his name.

Acts 9:16 For I will show him how great things he *must suffer* for my name's sake.

Romans 8:17 And if children, then heirs; heirs of God, and joint-heirs with Christ; if so be that we *suffer* with him, that we may be also glorified together.

1 Corinthians 4:12 And labour, working with our own hands: being reviled, we bless; being persecuted, we *suffer* it:

1 Corinthians 6:7 Now therefore there is utterly a fault among you, because ye go to law one with another. Why do ye not rather take wrong? why do ye not rather *suffer* yourselves to be defrauded?

1 Corinthians 9:12 If others be partakers of this power over you, are not we rather? Nevertheless we have not used this power; but *suffer all things*, lest we should hinder the gospel of Christ.

1 Corinthians 10:13 There hath no temptation taken you but such as is common to man: but God is faithful, who will not suffer you to be tempted above that ye are able; but will with the temptation also make a way to escape, that ye may be able to bear it.

1 Corinthians 12:26 And whether one member *suffer,* all the members **suffer** with it; or one member be honoured, all the members rejoice with it

2 Corinthians 1:6 And whether we be afflicted, it is for your consolation and salvation, which is effectual in the enduring of the same *sufferings* which we also *suffer:* or whether we be comforted, it is for your consolation and salvation.

Philippians 1:29 For unto you it is given in the behalf of Christ, not only to believe on him, but also to *suffer* for his sake;

Philippians 4:12 I know both how to be abased, and I know how to abound: every where and in all things I am instructed both to be full and to be hungry, both to abound and *to suffer* need.

1 Thessalonians 3:4 For verily, when we were with you, we told you before that we *should suffer tribulation;* even as it came to pass, and ye know.

2 Thessalonians 1:5 Which is a manifest token of the righteous judgment of God, that ye may be counted worthy of the kingdom of God, for which ye also *suffer:*

1 Timothy 4:10 For therefore we both labour and *suffer reproach*, because we trust in the living God, who is the Saviour of all men, specially of those that believe.

2 Timothy 1:12 For the which cause I also *suffer* these things:

2 Timothy 3:12 Yea, and all that will live godly in Christ Jesus *shall suffer persecution*.

Hebrews 11:25 Choosing rather to *suffer affliction* with the people of God, than to enjoy the pleasures of sin for a season;

Hebrews 13:3 Remember them that are in bonds, as bound with them; and them which *suffer adversity*, as being yourselves also in the body.

1 Peter 2:20 For what glory is it, if, when ye be buffeted for your faults, ye shall take it patiently? but if, when ye do well, and *suffer* for it, ye take it patiently, this is acceptable with God.

1 Peter 3:14 But and if ye *suffer* for righteousness' sake, happy are ye:

1 Peter 3:17 For it is better, if the will of God be so, that ye *suffer for well doing,*

1 Peter 4:16 Yet if any man *suffer as a Christian*, let him not be ashamed; but let him glorify God on this behalf.

1 Peter 4:19 Wherefore let them that *suffer* according to the will of God

Revelation 2:10 Fear none of those things which thou shalt *suffer:*

Comment: Looks as if there is, and will be, much suffering going on in our walk with the Lord and "praying" about it will not change a thing.

DELIVER - DELIVERED - DELIVERANCE

Luke 4:18 The Spirit of the Lord is upon me, because he hath anointed me to *preach the gospel* to the poor; he hath sent me to heal the brokenhearted,

Notes

Notes

to *preach deliverance* to the captives, and recovering of sight to the blind, to set at liberty them that are bruised,

2 Corinthians 1:10 Who delivered us from so great a death, and doth deliver: in whom we trust that he will yet deliver us;

Colossians 1:13 Who *hath delivered* us from the power of darkness, and hath translated us into the kingdom of his dear Son:

1 Thessalonians 1:10 And to wait for his Son from heaven, whom he raised from the dead, even Jesus, which delivered us from the wrath to come.

2 Timothy 3:11 Persecutions, afflictions, which came unto me at Antioch, at Iconium, at Lystra; what persecutions *I endured:*

2 Timothy 4:18 And the Lord shall deliver me from every evil work,

Hebrews 11:35 Women received their dead raised to life again: and others were tortured, *not accepting deliverance*; that they might obtain a better resurrection:

2 Peter 2:9 The Lord knoweth how to deliver the godly out of temptations,

This entire exercise was a tremendous blessing for me. I hope it has stirred up some questions in your spirit.

The question to be addressed now is: do you believe that you should stand in faith on God's promises-or do you feel it is necessary to pray for deliverances from whatever?

"Let every man be fully persuaded in his own mind".

WE ARE TO ENDURE

Matthew 10:22 And ye shall be hated of all men for my name's sake: but *he that endureth* to the end shall be saved.

Matthew 24:13 But he that *shall endure* unto the end, the same shall be saved.

Mark 13:13 And ye shall be hated of all men for my name's sake: but he that *shall endure* unto the end, the same shall be saved.

1 Corinthians 13:7 Beareth all things, believeth

all things, hopeth all things, *endureth all things.*

2 Thessalonians 1:4 So that we ourselves glory in you in the churches of God for your patience and faith in all your persecutions and tribulations *that ye endure*:

2 Timothy 2:3 Thou therefore *endure hardness*, as a good soldier of Jesus Christ

2 Timothy 2:10 Therefore I *endure all things* for the elect's sakes, that they may also obtain the salvation which is in Christ Jesus with eternal glory.

2 Timothy 3:11 Persecutions, afflictions, which came unto me at Antioch, at Iconium, at Lystra; what persecutions *I endured*: but out of them all the Lord delivered me.

2 Timothy 4:5 But watch thou in all things, *endure afflictions*, do the work of an evangelist, make full proof of thy ministry.

Hebrews 6:15 And so, after he had *patiently endured*, he obtained the promise.

Hebrews 10:32 But call to remembrance the former days, in which, after ye were illuminated, *ye endured* a great fight of afflictions;

Hebrews 12:2 Looking unto Jesus the author and finisher of our faith; who for the joy that was set before him **endured the cross**, despising the shame, and is set down at the right hand of the throne of God.

Hebrews 12:7 If ye *endure chastening*, God dealeth with you as with sons; for what son is he whom the father chasteneth not?

James 1:12 Blessed is the man that *endureth temptation*: for when he is tried, he shall receive the crown of life, which the Lord hath promised to them that love him.

James 5:11 Behold, we count them happy which *endure*

1 Peter 2:19-21 [19] For this is thankworthy, if a man for conscience toward God *endure grief,* suffering wrongfully.

[20] For what glory is it, if, when ye be buffeted for your faults, ye shall take it patiently? but if, when ye do well, and suffer for it, ye take it patiently, this is acceptable with God.

[21] For even hereunto were ye called: because Christ also suffered for us, leaving us an example,

Notes

that ye should follow his steps:

While doing my memory scripture recitations this morning, this verse was on one of my memory cards. While I recited it, the Holy Spirit provided me with one of his "Wow" experiences. Thanks to his leading, my position, as regards the praying for deliverances was further solidified. Praying for deliverances, in my humble belief, is not part of God's plan for my prayer life. God's promises are all stated in His Word, the Holy Bible, and they are enough to satisfy all that could possibly happen to me. I do not have to bring them up before Him in any fashion; He knows them all beforehand, as He created them all. I am content and at peace- I patiently endure, and am thankful in and for all things as I am commanded to do. His promises are mine.

PRAYER ADDENDUM

Matthew 5:44 But I say unto you, Love your enemies, bless them that curse you, do good to them that hate you, and pray for them which despitefully use you, and persecute you; Combine this with: **Luke 23:34** Then said Jesus, Father, forgive them; for they know not what they do. And they parted his raiment, and cast lots. (Comment: These prayers answer any persecution, that could ever come against me. How readest thou?)

Matthew 6:6-13 - traditionally called "The Lord's Prayer", although it was a prayer taught to his followers to be prayed by them. What speaks to me as the true "Lord's Prayer" is found in **John 1:1-17**. In these Matthew verses, God tells us how to pray - what our prayer should actually be.

Matthew 9:38 Pray ye therefore the Lord of the harvest, that he will send forth labourers into his harvest. (**Comment**: Here's one that needs more action in our own prayer lives. We need more laborers, and fewer entertained believers.)

Matthew 26:39 And he went a little farther, and fell on his face, and prayed, saying, O my Father, if it be possible, let this cup pass from me: nevertheless not as I will, but as thou wilt. (**Commen**t: Jesus left it up to God's Will - he didn't pray for deliverance.)

Matthew 26:41 Watch and pray, that ye enter not into temptation: the spirit indeed is willing, but the flesh is weak. (**Comment**: This prayer is telling us to enter not into temptation - not to pray for deliverance.)

Mathew 26:42 He went away again the second time, and prayed, saying, O my Father, if this cup may not pass away from me, except I drink it, thy will be done. (**Comment**: Again, Jesus gave it over to God's Will.)

Matthew 26:44 And he left them, and went away again, and prayed the third time, saying the same words. (**Comment**: As we have often asked, "How many times must we be told?"

Mark 12:40 Which devour widows' houses, and for a pretence make long prayers: these shall receive greater damnation. (**Question**: Could our long prayers for deliverance be considered "pretence?" Your call.

Mark 13:18 And pray ye that your flight be not in the winter. (**Comment** This is not asking - it is claiming.)

Mark 14:35 And he went forward a little, and fell on the ground, and prayed that, if it were possible, the hour might pass from him. (**Comment**: Not praying for deliverance - only that the hour might pass from him.)

Luke 6:28 Bless them that curse you, and pray for them which despitefully use you. (**Comment**: Please refer back to **Matthew 5:44** above.)

Luke 11:2-4 2 And he said unto them, When ye pray, say, Our Father which art in heaven, Hallowed be thy name. Thy kingdom come. Thy will be done, as in heaven, so in earth.

3 Give us day by day our daily bread.

4 And forgive us our sins; for we also forgive every one that is indebted to us. And lead us not into temptation; but deliver us from evil. (**Wondering**: This prayer (along with **Matthew 6:9-13**) covers it all for me. How about you?)

Luke 17:5 Increase our faith. (**Comment**: Here's a prayer we should be repeating over and over again.)

Luke 31:36 Watch ye therefore, and pray always, that ye may be accounted worthy to escape

Notes

Notes

all these things that shall come to pass, and to stand before the Son of man. (**Question**: Is this prayer worthy of daily repetition - or what?)

Luke 22:32 But I have prayed for thee, that thy faith fail not (**Comment**: I pray this often for myself, and for my dear brethren in the Lord.)

Acts 8:15 Who, when they were come down, prayed for them, that they might receive the Holy Ghost: (**Comment**: This is a potent prayer.)

Acts 8:22 Repent therefore of this thy wickedness, and pray God, if perhaps the thought of thine heart may be forgiven thee (**Comment**: Another worthy of much repetition.)

Romans 8:26 Likewise the Spirit also helpeth our infirmities: for we know not what we should pray for as we ought: but the Spirit itself maketh intercession for us with groanings which cannot be uttered. (**Comment**: This spoke to my spirit long ago, and caused me to pray only God's Words, and allow the Holy Spirit to stand in the breach as my prayer warrior and intercessor.)

Romans 10:1 Brethren, my heart's desire and prayer to God for Israel is, that they might be saved

2 Corinthians 5:20 Now then we are ambassadors for Christ, as though God did beseech you by us: we pray you in Christ's stead, be ye reconciled to God. (**Comment**: Praying God's Words is my most direct route to my reconciliation with Him.)

Note: I am separating the following gems, because they were most influential in my ceasing from praying for any deliverances of any kind. Enjoy!!

2 Corinthians 12:9-10 [9] And he said unto me, My grace is sufficient for thee: for my strength is made perfect in weakness. Most gladly therefore will I rather glory in my infirmities, that the power of Christ may rest upon me.

[10] Therefore I take pleasure in infirmities, in reproaches, in necessities, in persecutions, in distresses for Christ's sake: for when I am weak, then am I strong. (**Comment**: I will refrain from further commenting on these Words, and allow the Holy Spirit to lead you in understanding.)

Notes

2 Corinthians 13:7 Now I pray to God that ye do no evil; not that we should appear approved, but that ye should do that which is honest, though we be as reprobates.

Philippians 1:9 And this I pray, that your love may abound yet more and more in knowledge and in all judgment; (**Comment:** This one also bears much voicing by us.)

Philippians 1:29 - For unto you it is given in the behalf of Christ, not only to believe on him, but also to suffer for his sake; (**Comment:** There is joy in suffering for Christ's sake - not in praying for deliverances. No joy in praying for deliverances.)

Colossians 1:9 For this cause we also, since the day we heard it, do not cease to pray for you, and to desire that ye might be filled with the knowledge of his will in all wisdom and spiritual understanding; (**Comment**: Praying this for one another should deliver the desire.)

Colossians 4:3 Withal praying also for us, that God would open unto us a door of utterance, to speak the mystery of Christ, for which I am also in bonds: along with: **Ephesians 6:19** And for me, that utterance may be given unto me, that I may open my mouth boldly, to make known the mystery of the gospel, (**Comment:** Worthy prayers.)

Colossians 4:12 Epaphras, who is one of you, a servant of Christ, saluteth you, always labouring fervently for you in prayers, that ye may stand perfect and complete in all the will of God. (**Comment:** Another prayer worthy of much repetition.)

1 Thessalonians 3:10 Night and day praying exceedingly that we might see your face, and might perfect that which is lacking in your faith?

I Thessalonians 5:23 And the very God of peace sanctify you wholly; and I pray God your whole spirit and soul and body be preserved blameless unto the coming of our Lord Jesus Christ. (**Comment:** It would be a blessing to have someone praying this one over me.)

2 Thessalonians 1:11 Wherefore also we pray always for you, that our God would count you worthy of this calling, and fulfil all the good pleasure of his goodness, and the work of faith with power: (**Question:** Who needs deliverance prayers,

Notes

when this prayer is answered?)

My prayers are all the utterance of God's Words, and standing fast on His promises. It spoke to my spirit long ago, that praying for deliverances from any problems promised by God, that I would be faced with, was, in effect, telling God I have no faith in His promises - His Word.

Many cite the following adage: "Prayer changes things," Based on the sharing of this entire Prayer section, I must disagree. Prayer does not change anything but the spirit of the one doing the praying; only if the one praying is uttering God's Word.

IT IS FINISHED
(God's Will)

We presented a section entitled, "God's Will" earlier, which treated believers, who were waiting for God to express his will in their lives (He already has). This segment looks at the Will of God as a completed whole. There are many, who believe that God is continually expressing his will-some even say that God talks directly to them audibly, revealing revelations as regards his will for them. **Hebrews 1:1** God, who at sundry times and in divers manners spake in time past unto the fathers by the prophets, **Hebrews 1:2** Hath in these last days spoken unto us by his Son, whom he hath appointed heir of all things, by whom also he made the worlds; (**Comment**: One wonders just whose voice they are hearing). **Colossians 2:9** For in him dwelleth all the fullness of the Godhead bodily (**Comment**: That is, in Christ). **John 5:37** And the Father himself, which hath sent me, hath borne witness of me. Ye have neither heard his voice at any time, nor seen his shape. (**Comment**: These verses tell us that, with the coming of Jesus Christ on earth, God has (and does) speak to us through His Son. In **John 1:1** we are told that Jesus is the Word. Since God doesn't speak directly to us, his Will can only be expressed through his Word-his Word must be his Will.

John 6:29 Jesus answered and said unto them, This is the work of God, that ye believe on him whom he hath sent.

John 6:40 And this is the will of him that sent me, that every one which seeth the Son, and believeth on him, may have everlasting

John 1:14 And the Word was made flesh, and dwelt among us,

Comment: Now then, since we are taught to believe on Jesus Christ, and it is spoken that Jesus was the Word made flesh-it follows that we are to believe on the Word, which God has left us. The Word is God's Will and his work. How readest thou?

The following scripture verses speak to the point

Notes

that God's Will must be an established fact, and that it does exist as completed.

Acts 21:14 The will of the Lord *be* done.
Comment: The word, *"be"*, means exists, lives, has a place in fact.
Luke 22:42 nevertheless not my will, but thine, be done.
Matthew 6:10 Thy kingdom come. Thy will *be* done in earth, as it *is* in heaven.
Comment: *"Is"* also means exists, lives, has a place in fact. His will for the earth *is* the same as it *is* for heaven.
Ephesians 5:17 Wherefore be ye not unwise, but understanding what the will of the Lord is.
1 Thessalonians 4:3 For this is the will of God,
Romans 12:2 that ye may prove what is that good, and acceptable, and perfect, will of God.
John 6:39 And this is the Father's will which hath sent me,
Luke 11:2 Thy will be done, as in heaven, so in earth.
Comment: We are fully persuaded by these verses that the Will of God is; it exists, it has a place in fact. His Will is not something that is going to be in the future-it is now, and it is forever.

What are we to *do* as regards God's Will?

John 6:38 For I came down from heaven, not to do mine own will, but the will of him that sent me.
John 4:34 Jesus saith unto them, My meat is to do the will of him that sent me,
Matthew 7:21 Not every one that saith unto me, Lord, Lord, shall enter into the kingdom of heaven; but he that doeth the will of my Father which is in heaven.
Hebrews 13:21 Make you perfect in every good work to do his will,
Ephesians1:11 being predestined according to the purpose of him who worketh all things after the counsel of his own will:
Revelation 17:17 For God hath put in their hearts to fulfil his will,
Acts 13:22 a man after mine own heart, which

shall fulfil all my will.

Hebrews 10:9 Then said he, Lo, I come to do thy will, O God.

Ephesians 6:6 but as the servants of Christ, doing the will of God from the heart;

Hebrews 10:36 For ye have need of patience, that, after ye have done the will of God,

1 John 2:17 but he that doeth the will of God abideth for ever.

Mark 3:35 For whosoever shall do the will of God, the same is my brother, and my sister, and mother.

Psalm 143:10 Teach me to do thy will; for thou art my God:

Matthew 12:50 For whosoever shall do the will of my Father which is in heaven,

QUESTION: Are you getting the message? Is it reasonable to believe that, with all the mentioning of doing his Will, that there must be a Will to be done? Right-it is more that reasonable. In the face of all the scriptural evidence, we believe that God's Will is his Word-we are to obey, and carry out, his Word. We are to do it.

Luke 11:28 But he said, Yea rather, blessed are they that hear the word of God, *and keep it. (Or do it).*

In other references to God's Will, we find:

John 5:30 because I seek not mine own will, but the will of the Father which hath sent me.

1 John 5:14 And this is the confidence that we have in him, that, if we ask any thing according to his will, he heareth us:

Hebrews 2:4 and gifts of the Holy Ghost, according to his own will?

Romans 8:27 because he maketh intercession for the saints according to the will of God.

2 Corinthians 8:5 but first gave their own selves to the Lord, and unto us by the will of God.

Colossians 4:12 that ye may stand perfect and complete in all the will of God.

1 Peter 4:19 Wherefore let them that suffer according to the will of God

Notes

Colossians 1:9 and to desire that ye might be filled with the knowledge of his will in all wisdom and spiritual understanding;

Comment: With all these references to the Will of God, isn't it reasonable that it *must exist* somewhere? God would not have referred to his Will as he has, unless it was a tangible thing able to be touched by man. If his Will is not his Word, then where and what is it?

There are those, who believe that God's Will is not finished-that he still has more to do. They pray to God as if he will change his Will, and grant them a special dispensation of some sort.

Let's consider the following:

John 19:30 he said, *It is finished*:

John 17:4 I have glorified thee on the earth: I have finished the work which thou gavest me to do.

Romans 10:4 For Christ is the end of the law for righteousness to every one that believeth.

John 4:34 Jesus saith unto them, My meat is to do the will of him that sent me, and to finish his work.

John 5:36 But I have greater witness than that of John: for the works which the Father hath given me *to finish*,

Romans 9:28 For he will finish the work, and cut it short in righteousness: because a short work will the Lord make upon the earth.

Hebrews 12:2 Looking unto Jesus the author and *finisher* of our faith;

Revelation 1:8 I am Alpha and Omega, the beginning *and the ending*,

Revelation 1:11 Saying, I am Alpha and Omega, the first *and the last*:

Revelation 21:6 And he said unto me, It is done. I am Alpha and Omega, the beginning *and the end.*

Revelation 22:13 I am Alpha and Omega, the beginning and the end, the first and the last.

Revelation 16:17 *It is done.*

Hebrews 4:3 although the works were finished from the foundation of the world.

Comment: This verse tells us that it was all

Notes

done at the beginning.

Matthew 6:10 Thy will be done

Luke 11:2 Thy will *be* done, (*is* done.)

Acts 4:28 For to do whatsoever thy hand and thy counsel *determined before to be* done.

Revelation 4:11 for thou hast created *all* things,

Luke 22:22 And truly the Son of man goeth, as it *was* determined:

Ephesians 3:11 According to the eternal purpose which he purposed in Christ Jesus our Lord:

Matthew 25:34 Come, ye blessed of my Father, inherit the kingdom prepared for you *from the foundation of the world:*

1 Peter 1:2 Elect according to the *foreknowledge* of God the Father,

Philippians 2:13 For it is God which worketh in you both to will and to do of his good pleasure.

Romans 8:29 For whom he did foreknow, he also did *predestinate*

Ephesians 1:11 In whom also we have obtained an inheritance, *being predestinated*

Ephesians 1:3 Blessed be the God and Father of our Lord Jesus Christ, who *hath* blessed us with all spiritual blessings in heavenly places in Christ:

Ephesians 1:4 According as he hath chosen us in him *before the foundation of the world,* that we should be holy and without blame before him in love:

Ephesians 1:5 Having *predestinated* us unto the adoption of children by Jesus Christ to himself, according to the good pleasure of his will,

Acts 15:18 *Known unto God are all his works from the beginning of the world.*

Ephesians 1:9 Having made known unto us the mystery of his will, according to his good pleasure which he hath purposed in himself:

Comment: The scriptures cited above tell us that God's Will, his work, *is* finished. His word *is* done; it *is* ended. He *is* the Alpha and the Omega-the beginning and the end. He began his work with the creation, and it seems plausible to accept, that he finished it right to the end-according to scripture. God's Word says that we were chosen before the foundation of the world. Is it that hard to also accept, that the last one to be chosen is already chosen? Some have asked, "If God's work is done, finished to

Notes

the end, how is it that he placed us here with a free will? This is more than a fair question. The only answer we can offer is that, by the many scriptures cited above, God's Will *is* complete. We stand by faith on his Word-men's words will not change our belief. Only God's Word, by the leading of the Holy Spirit, will change our posture here. As believers we must accept many mysteries by faith. It speaks to us that, putting us here with a free choice in a will already completed is one of these mysteries. "With God all things are possible".

Hebrews 13:8 Jesus Christ the same yesterday, and to day, and for ever.

Note: We are persuaded by God's Word that his Will *is* finished, completed, done. When this persuasion was first given us, we resisted it as many of you are doing. A dear Christian brother shared with us his position concerning the results-oriented walk of most of the brethren. It was his spiritual insight, that led us around results-orientation to our present place of belief. Accepting God's Will as finished has cleared the way for the wonderful freedom we now enjoy. The "clutter" has been cleared away, and we can now concentrate on thanking God for his Will, and standing on his promise. We no longer ask God for this or, that we no longer ask God to readjust his Will to suit our lives. We no longer gamble on charging God foolishly. Now we have more time to spend in the thank-you scriptures; we now can stand fast in faith on his promise, his Word. God's Word has all the answers necessary for a fruitful Christian walk. Thank you Father in the Name of Jesus Christ.

The following is another thought that spoke to my spirit well after this section was put together; so, here it is:

Mark 13:19 For in those days shall be affliction, such as was not from the beginning of the creation *which God created unto this time,* neither shall be.

WOMAN

Well saints, here is another "hot potato". This subject is seldom a topic for an in-depth sermon. In fact, almost every time it is brought up in a Christian fellowship, the discussion is reduced to argument. We know, because we used to get involved in the arguing. We did until it spoke to us that we are to be content, patient, comforted, etc.. We found that we must make our decision as led, and stand.

We made this one of the later subjects in this effort for a good reason; no, it is not because we fear the subject.. On the contrary, we fear nothing (for God has not given us a spirit of fear.) We figured that if you had the spiritual leading to get this far in this work, you would be able to "handle" this topic.

Unfortunately, this subject also has been tainted by the world's influence. All the talk about equal rights, male chauvinism, etc. has filtered into the Christian view of this matter. We hope to cut through all the frills, and see what God says about it. Now, as we have stated before, please take up any objections you may have with the Author-God wrote the book, not us.

Proverbs 31:10 Who can find a virtuous woman? for her price is far above rubies.
Proverbs 31:11 The heart of her husband doth safely trust in her, so that he shall have no need of spoil.
Proverbs 31:12 She will do him good and not evil all the days of her life.
Proverbs 31:30 but a woman that feareth the LORD, she shall be praised.
Proverbs 11:16 A gracious woman retaineth honour: and strong men retain riches.
Proverbs 14:1 Every wise woman buildeth her house: but the foolish plucketh it down with her hands.
Proverbs 12:4 A virtuous woman is a crown to her husband:
Titus 2:5 To be discreet, chaste, keepers at

Notes

home, good, obedient to their own husbands, that the word of God be not blasphemed.

1 Corinthians 11:7 For a man indeed ought not to cover his head, forasmuch as he is the image and glory of God: but the woman is the glory of the man.

1 Corinthians 11:8 For the man is not of the woman; but the woman of the man.

Jeremiah 31:22 A woman shall compass a man.

Proverbs 21:19 It is better to dwell in the wilderness, than with a contentious and an angry woman.

Colossians 3:18 Wives, submit yourselves unto your own husbands, as it is fit in the Lord.

Ephesians 5:33 and the wife see that she reverence her husband.

1 Tim 3:11 Even so must their wives be grave, not slanderers, sober, faithful in all things.

1 Corinthians 11:3 But I would have you know, that the head of every man is Christ; and the head of the woman is the man;

Ephesians 5:22 Wives, submit yourselves unto your own husbands, as unto the Lord.

Ephesians 5:23 For the husband is the head of the wife, even as Christ is the head of the church: and he is the saviour of the body.

Ephesians 5:24 Therefore as the church is subject unto Christ, so let the wives be to their own husbands in every thing.

1 Peter 3:5 For after this manner in the old time the holy women also, who trusted in God, adorned themselves, being in subjection unto their own husbands:

Ecclesiastes 7:26 And I find more bitter than death the woman, whose heart is snares and nets, and her hands as bands: whoso pleaseth God shall escape from her; but the sinner shall be taken by her.

Ecclesiastes 7:27 Behold, this have I found, saith the preacher, counting one by one, to find out the account:

Ecclesiastes 7:28 Which yet my soul seeketh, but I find not: one man among a thousand have I found; but a woman among all those have I not found.

Ecclesiastes 7:29 Lo, this only have I found, that God hath made man upright; but they have sought out many inventions.

1 Corinthians 14:34 Let your women keep silence in the churches: for it is not permitted unto them to speak; but they are commanded to be under obedience, as also saith the law.

1 Corinthians 14:35 And if they will learn any thing, let them ask their husbands at home: for it is a shame for women to speak in the church.

Comment: Whenever we stand fast on **1 Corinthians 14:34-35**, we are often told two things. First, we are against women. Nothing could be further from the truth; we are simply for God's Word. The second thing, that is pointed out to us, is scriptural. We are made aware of **Acts 21:9**, which says, And the same man had four daughters, virgins, which did prophesy. We are also reminded of **Acts 2:17-18**, which says, And it shall come to pass in the last days, saith God, I will pour out of my Spirit upon all flesh: and your sons and your daughters shall prophesy, and your young men shall see visions, and your old men shall dream dreams: And on my servants and on my handmaidens I will pour out in those days of my Spirit; and they shall prophesy:

We must again affirm our belief that God's Word is pure, perfect, and is Truth. We believe that there are no disagreements or conflicts in the Bible, the Word of God. Accepting this as fact caused us to seek understanding concerning the apparent conflict of these verses. We sought out of the book of the Lord-we searched the scriptures. We received an understanding. One scripture says that women are to be silent in the churches-that it is a shame for women to speak in the church. The other scriptures say that women will prophesy. It appears that women *will* prophesy-but *not* in the churches. Their prophesying must apparently be done elsewhere; in the home, in their prayer closets, in the gathering of women, or whatever, but not in the churches.

Please allow us again to repeat that we did not write the scriptures-God did. All we are trying to do is bring agreement into our spirits.

1 Timothy 2:11 Let the woman learn in silence with all subjection.

Notes

Notes

1 Timothy 2:12 But I suffer not a woman to teach, nor to usurp authority over the man, but to be in silence.

When faced with these scriptures, many believers point out what they believe to be "equality" verses which are as follows:

Matthew 19:6 Wherefore they are no more twain, but one flesh.

Galatians 3:28 There is neither Jew nor Greek, there is neither bond nor free, there is neither male nor female: for ye are all one in Christ Jesus.

Romans 10:12 For there is no difference between the Jew and the Greek: for the same Lord over all is rich unto all that call upon him.

Acts 15:9 And put no difference between us and them, purifying their hearts by faith.

Romans 2:11 For there is no respect of persons with God.

Deuteronomy 10:17 For the LORD your God is God of gods, and Lord of lords, a great God, a mighty, and a terrible, which regardeth not persons, nor taketh reward:

Ephesians 6:9 neither is there respect of persons with him.

1 Peter 1:17 And if ye call on the Father, who without respect of persons judgeth according to every man's work,

Colossians 3:25 and there is no respect of persons.

Acts 10:34 Then Peter opened his mouth, and said, Of a truth I perceive that God is no respecter of persons:

Proverbs 24:23 These things also belong to the wise. It is not good to have respect of persons in judgment.

Now it appears that a decision must be made. You can "use" these scriptures to negate what is said in the first group of verses; if you are led to continue doing this, Praise the Lord! However, you may be acting in opposition to **Titus 3:9** But avoid foolish questions, and genealogies, and contentions, and strivings about the law; for they are unprofitable and vain. You may also be counter to **2 Timothy 2:23-24**

But foolish and unlearned questions avoid, knowing that they do gender strifes. And the servant of the Lord must not strive; but be gentle unto all men, apt to teach, patient, You may feel you are not running in the face of these scriptures-if not, Praise the Lord! Or maybe you are subscribing to the idea, that one verse can contradict and negate another.

We, on the other hand, prefer to believe and accept, that God's Word is perfect, pure, and true. We believe God is perfect, and would not have given us an imperfect book. In believing that we must take the position, that there is no conflict or disagreement in the Bible. We always look for the agreement in scriptures-and if we perservere, the Holy Spirit shows us the agreement in his timing.

God has given woman a beautiful and wondrous role to play in his perfect plan. A woman, who faithfully plays out that role, is a blessing to God, and to the world. Instead of trying to justify the equality theory, that women and men can serve the same functions in God's eyes, let us look further at what God says.

1 Corinthians 12:18 But now hath God set the members every one of them in the body, as it hath pleased him. **Comment**: God created everything-all things are of God-he even created his own three-fold nature. He is God the Father, the Son, and the Holy Spirit. There are a multitude of scriptures in which Jesus refers to his Father God-thereby making Jesus God's Son. **2 Corinthians 3:17** Now the Lord is that Spirit: **John 4:24** God is a Spirit: and they that worship him must worship him in spirit and in truth. **Matthew 28:19** Go ye therefore, and teach all nations, baptizing them in the name of the Father, and of the Son, and of the Holy Ghost: Evidently, the three are God-God is all three. Although he is all three, God laid out his perfect plan, and he assigned the proper tasks to be performed by Jesus and the Holy Spirit.

God also set us all in the body of believers as it has pleased him. He gave certain responsibilities to man, and others to woman. We are to carry out his

Notes

will as stated in his Word. We are structured in the body of faith much as various body parts are structured in the human body. Each part has its function; we do not ask the toes to do the job given to the fingers. We don't run on our arms and hands-we use our legs and feet. We don't see with our ears, or hear with our eyes. In the same fashion, man does what he is supposed to do, and women are to carry out their scripturally-ordered roles. This is all to be done according to God's Will.

Genesis 1:1 In the beginning God created the heaven and the earth. Do you believe that God created all this in disorder? Anyone, who looks upon the wonderful order of things He created, has to see God's hand in the perfect design of things. One has only to look at the universe, and how it functions, to realize the order of God's glorious plan. Is there not an order of the sun, moon, stars, and earth? The moon revolves around the earth, and both revolve around the sun. God says in **Jeremiah 31:22** that, A woman shall compass a man. The woman revolves around the man, and both revolve around the Son-we all revolve around our Father God. God said through Paul in:**1 Corinthians 11:3** But I would have you know, that the head of every man is Christ; and the head of the woman is the man; and the head of Christ is God. In the beginning the woman was made as a help meet for man. **1 Corinthians 11:8** For the man is not of the woman; but the woman of the man. 1 Corinthians 11:9 Neither was the man created for the woman; but the woman for the man.

This all has been made very clear to us. HOW READEST THOU?

NO MORE MIRACLES?

2 Tim 2:9 but the word of God is not bound.

Is there such a thing as the end of the "apostolic period"? We have often heard that miracles ended with the end of apostolic or biblical times. Our ministry has never been asked about this position. However, we did attend a debate concerning this issue. We were contented with our posture in this area, but we wanted to witness two Christians debating the Word of God. We have found nothing scriptural in favor of debating God's Word. On the contrary, we can cite a multitude of scriptures that clearly indicate that God's perfect Word is not to be debated. **Acts 17:2** was given as the basis for the rightness of debating God's Truth-it says, "**Acts 17:2** And Paul, as his manner was, went in unto them, and three sabbath days *reasoned* with them out of the scriptures,". The dictionary definition of the word, "reason", doesn't list debate.

We are fully persuaded and content in our own minds about the position to be supported in this matter. You will readily see how the Spirit speaks to us, after considering the scripture verses we will cite.

Are miracles possible today, or did they end with the end of the so-called apostolic age? Before citing verses, it may well be advisable to establish what a miracle is by definition. One source states, "Miracle is defined as a supernatural occurrence-an act or happening in the material or physical sphere that apparently departs from the laws of nature, or goes beyond what is known concerning these laws". Another dictionary defines miracle as an "event or effect in the physical world beyond or out of the ordinary course of things, deviating from the known laws of nature, or transcending our knowledge of these laws; an extraordinary event brought about by super-human agency as a manifestation of its power, or for the purpose of revealing or manifesting spiritual force." We will discuss our points of view concerning miracles, after we share the following scriptures.

Notes

Notes

Matthew 5:17 Think not that I am come to destroy the law, or the prophets: I am not come to destroy, but to fulfil. **Matthew 5:18** For verily I say unto you, Till heaven and earth pass, one jot or one tittle shall in no wise pass from the law, till all be fulfilled.

Matthew 17:20 And Jesus said unto them, Because of your unbelief: for verily I say unto you, If ye have faith as a grain of mustard seed, ye shall say unto this mountain, Remove hence to yonder place; and it shall remove; and nothing shall be impossible unto you.

Matthew 21:22 And all things, whatsoever ye shall ask in prayer, believing, ye shall receive.

Matthew 24:35 Heaven and earth shall pass away, but my words shall not pass away.

Mark 11:23 but shall believe that those things which he saith shall come to pass; he shall have whatsoever he saith.

Luke 17:6 And the Lord said, If ye had faith as a grain of mustard seed, ye might say unto this sycamine tree, Be thou plucked up by the root, and be thou planted in the sea; and it should obey you.

Luke 21:33 Heaven and earth shall pass away: but my words shall not pass away.

Matthew 18:18 Verily I say unto you, Whatsoever ye shall bind on earth shall be bound in heaven: and whatsoever ye shall loose on earth shall be loosed in heaven.

Mark 9:23 Jesus said unto him, If thou canst believe, all things are possible to him that believeth.

Mark 10:27 And Jesus looking upon them saith, With men it is impossible, but not with God: for with God all things are possible.

Mark 13:31 Heaven and earth shall pass away: but my words shall not pass away.

John 14:12 Verily, verily, I say unto you, He that believeth on me, the works that I do shall he do also; and greater works than these shall he do; because I go unto my Father.

John 14:13 And whatsoever ye shall ask in my name, that will I do, that the Father may be glorified in the Son. John 14:14 If ye shall ask any thing in my name, I will do it.

John 15:16 whatsoever ye shall ask of the

Father in my name, he may give it you.

1 Corinthians 12:10 To another the working of miracles;

Philippians 4:13 I can do all things through Christ which strengtheneth me.

1 Corinthians 15:19 tells says: If in this life only we have hope in Christ, we are of all men most miserable. In view of all the scriptures cited above, I would be of all men most miserable, if I accepted the premise that miracles ended with the apostolic age. It speaks to me, that if any of God's Words cease to apply, and have no effect, then all have can be suspect. I would be of all men most miserable if, upon reading **Revelation 22:21**, I could close my Bible-never to open it again. There are a multitude of scripture verses, that tell us of the power, perfection, purity, wisdom, sureness, rightness, cleanliness, sweetness, and righteousness attributed to the Word of God. Many of them tell us, that God's Word is eternal and forever. I accept this, and I accept all of God's promises. I know that his promises are as alive today as they were before, and will be forever more.

Now the opponents of this position usually ask, "If this is so, where are the miracles? Why don't we see Christians walking into hospitals, and emptying them out by healing the sick? Why aren't the dead brought back to life? Why are the demons of madness allowed to live on in the insane? Why isn't someone giving sight to the blind, and giving hearing ears to the deaf? It is my hope, that the answer given to me doesn't disturb my Christian brethren. If it does, they will find deliverance by standing on **Galatians 6:17** and **Philippians 4:11** and the like. The reason we have no miracles being manifested today is, that few of us are acting purely according to the will of God. Few of us are standing fast in the faith, and are doing what God has commanded us to do. Oh, we are quoting God's Words, and asking in the name of Jesus Christ all right. However, we must not be asking in faith-not according to God's Will. We must be asking amiss. If we were asking correctly, and

Notes

according to the Will of God-he would deliver. After all, God promised, and God does not lie; He is Truth

Let us take a small inventory. How many of us are satisfying completely what God has commanding us to in **1 Corinthians 15:58?** I am not. Are we totally in line with **Philippians 4:9**? I am not. How about **Luke 9:23-24**; are we faithfully doing this? I'm not. How many of us have done all the things we are ordered to do in **Mattthews chapters 5, 6, and 7?** I haven't. Have you completely taken **Matthew 19:29** to heart, and done it? I have not. When in need or want, how many of us stand fast on what Jesus said in **Matthew 26:42** O my Father, if this cup may not pass away from me, except I drink it, thy will be done. (Or have we been asking God to bend to *our* will)? Have you entirely satisfied **Mark 8:34**? I haven't. Have you ever taken inventory, and decided what ground on which you stand? **Luke 8** talks about the four conditions upon which the seed, God's Word, falls. In the beginning I did not enjoy facing where I qualified in these verses. How many of us have truly accepted that we cannot serve God and mammon? I have accepted it; the challenge lies in living it. I guess it comes under the heading of "am I walking the walk, or only talking the talk?" How many of us have truly received the Kingdom of God as a little child? I haven't. Enough inventory already-I'm sure that by now you are getting the point. Why take this inventory, anyway? Simple-if we don't know where we are, it becomes difficult to move ahead. What most of us have been doing is described in **Matthews 9:16-17**; we have been trying to put the new cloth onto the old garment, and making the rent worse. We have also been putting the new wine into the old bottle-such a waste of good wine! Take heart, and don't despair-Our Father God knows our hearts. What we have been doing is better than nothing in God's eyes, and his mercy and grace has us covered by **1 Corinthians 3:11-15**. Thank God we are still saved, yet so as by fire.

You may have decided that this exercise has been a negative one. If you have, you may be experiencing being convicted by God's Word, which is wonderfully described in **Hebrews 4:12** For the word of

God is quick, and powerful, and sharper than any twoedged sword, piercing even to the dividing asunder of soul and spirit, and of the joints and marrow, and is a discerner of the thoughts and intents of the heart. This has not been a negative exercise for me, because of **Psalm 119:11**. God's Word is being hidden in my heart more and more every day, because of this I know; that he will deliver on his promises. Admittedly, I have a long way to go; I just thank God for the distance I have come.

Romans 8:4 says: That the righteousness of the law might be fulfilled in us, who walk not after the flesh, but after the Spirit. The reason for taking a self-inventory should be obvious now. If we can't take care of our own houses, how can we expect God to entrust us with the effectual care of others? How can we expect God to freely bestow his gifts, that would result in the manifestation of miracles-when we are not acting in accordance with his will? God has not given me many of his gifts, which are listed in **1 Corinthians 12:8-10.** He has, however, given me a measure of a few of them. There is no concern on my part about what I have not received from God; I am too busy thanking God for what he has given me. It speaks to my spirit that we cannot charge God foolishly because of the miracles we are not seeing manifested today. The answer is in our mirrors, and not in the opinion that miracles are not for today. In the flesh, one could use syllogism to support the position that miracles ended with the close of the apostolic period. In syllogistic reasoning you have a major premise, a minor premise, and a conclusion. This form of reasoning purports that, if the major and minor premises are true, the conclusion is automatic and true. The supporters of the "no miracles today" posture cite the following:

Major premise: There were miracles in the time or the early apostles.

Minor premise: There are no miracles today.

Conclusion: Miracles ceased, when the apostolic period ended.

In the spirit we know, that we are debtors not to the flesh, to live after the flesh. We know, that if the conclusion reached through the syllogistic reasoning

Notes

is counter to God's Word, it is not true. It must be a lie, because God's Word is truth.

Please allow me to share a short look at miracles, and what they are. You will remember that we discussed the definitions of miracles at the beginning of this section. Those definitions came from two dictionaries you can buy at any store. In short, they say that a miracle is something that happens, which cannot be explained by normal laws of nature. In the spiritual realm a miracle would exist, if God interceded and did something miraculous without the request of his saints asking according to his will. If, however, a believer stands on the faith provided by God's Word, and claims a deliverance based entirely on God's promises-deliverance would not be considered a miracle. By all worldly definitions, miracles are unexplainable; in the Spirit God simply delivered on his promise, which rules out a miraculous event. God's reaction to a believer making a claim in accordance to his Will does not result in a miracle-it is explainable. The miracle to me is, that God knew he would do this before the foundation of the world; it was part of his completed will.

CONCLUSION: If you believe Jesus Christ is alive, you must believe that his Word (God's Word) is also alive-I do. Jesus Christ is the Word (**John 1:1**). He was in the beginning, is now, and ever will be. His Words lived then, are alive now, and will endure forever. Miracles are as much a part of God's now as they were then, and ever will be. There are a host of other scripture verses that speak to the truth of this-Search the scriptures-seek and ye shall find.

DEBATE

In the beginning of this chapter, we stated that we have found nothing scriptural in favor of the debating of God's Word. The Spirit has moved on us to expand discussion in this area. Debate is defined as follows: to engage in strife or combat; to contend, quarrel, to contend in words; to dispute; a controversial discussion.

Notes

After reading the following verses, the Holy Spirit should speak to your spirit concerning this issue. We will be content to allow the Spirit to help you decide the right or wrong of this issue of debating God's Word.

1 Corinthians 1:10 Now I beseech you, brethren, by the name of our Lord Jesus Christ, that ye all speak the same thing, and that there be no divisions among you; but that ye be perfectly joined together in the same mind and in the same judgment.

Matthew 5:39 But I say unto you, That ye resist not evil:

1 Corinthians 6:7 Why do ye not rather take wrong? why do ye not rather suffer yourselves to be defrauded?

1 Thessalonians 5:15 See that none render evil for evil unto any man; but ever follow that which is good, both among yourselves, and to all men.

1 **Peter 3:9** Not rendering evil for evil, or railing for railing: but contrariwise blessing;

1 Peter 4:11 If any man speak, let him speak as the oracles of God;

Matthew 12:19 He shall not strive,

Philippians 1:27 Only let your conversation be as it becometh the gospel of Christ:...that ye stand fast in one spirit, with one mind striving together for the faith of the gospel;

2 Timothy 2:5 And if a man also strive for masteries, yet is he not crowned, except he strive lawfully.

Matthew 12:37 For by thy words thou shalt be justified, and by thy words thou shalt be condemned.

Matthew 23:24 Ye blind guides, which strain at a gnat, and swallow a camel.

Romans 1:17 The just shall live by faith.

Rom 14:5 One man esteemeth one day above another: another esteemeth every day alike. Let every man be fully persuaded in his own mind.

Romans 15:5-7 Now the God of patience and consolation grant you to be likeminded one toward another according to Christ Jesus: That ye may with one mind and one mouth glorify God, even the Father of our Lord Jesus Christ. Wherefore receive

Notes

ye one another, as Christ also received us to the glory of God.

1 Corinthians 2:2 For I determined not to know any thing among you, save Jesus Christ, and him crucified.

1 Corinthians 2:5 That your faith should not stand in the wisdom of men, but in the power of God.

1 Corinthians 3:21 Therefore let no man glory in men. For all things are yours;

2 Corinthians 10:3 For though we walk in the flesh, we do not war after the flesh:

Galatians 3:25 But after that faith is come, we are no longer under a schoolmaster.

Ephesians 4:32 And be ye kind one to another, tenderhearted, forgiving one another, even as God for Christ's sake hath forgiven you.

Philippians 2:3 Let nothing be done through strife or vainglory; but in lowliness of mind let each esteem other better than themselves.

Philippians 2:14 Do all things without murmurings and disputings:

1 Thessalonians 4:11 And that ye study to be quiet, and to do your own business, and to work with your own hands, as we commanded you;

1 Timothy 2:5 For there is one God, and one mediator between God and men, the man Christ Jesus;

James 1:19 Wherefore, my beloved brethren, let every man be swift to hear, slow to speak, slow to wrath:

Let ever man be fully persuaded in his own mind (**Romans 14:5**). **Matthews 5:37** But let your communication be, Yea, yea; Nay, nay: for whatsoever is more than these cometh of evil. In other words, we should decide with no ifs, ands, of buts. What is your decision? Should Christians be debating one another about God's Word, which will remain forever no matter what? Yea or Nay?

STRIFE

One of the definitions attributed to debate is "strife". Let us look at some of the scriptures concerning strife:

Notes

James 3:14-16 But if ye have bitter envying and strife in your hearts, glory not, and lie not against the truth. This wisdom descendeth not from above, but is earthly, sensual, devilish. For where envying and strife is, there is confusion and every evil work.

Proverbs 20:3 It is an honour for a man to cease from strife:

Proverbs 16:28 A froward man soweth strife:

Proverbs 28:25 He that is of a proud heart stirreth up strife:

Romans 13:13 Let us walk honestly, as in the day; not in rioting and drunkenness, not in chambering and wantonness, *not in strife and envying.*

Galatians 5:19-20 Now the works of the flesh are manifest, Adultery, fornication, uncleanness, lasciviousness, Idolatry, witchcraft, hatred, variance, emulations, wrath, *strife,* seditions, heresies,

2 Corinthians 12:20 For I fear, lest, when I come, I shall not find you such as I would, and that I shall be found unto you such as ye would not: lest there be debates, envyings, wraths, *strifes*, backbitings, whisperings, swellings, tumults:

Note: I have to call attention to the various conditions with which debates and strifes are listed.

1 Timothy 6:4 He is proud, knowing nothing, but doting about questions and strifes of words, whereof cometh envy, strife, railings, evil surmisings,

---

Supporters of debating God's Word will often cite **Acts 9:29, 17:17**, and **19:8** in defense of the exercise. These verses all state that Paul "disputed." In all the cases he disputed with unbelievers-in one instance, he disputed with the Grecians (**Acts 9:29**). In the other two instances, he disputed with the Jews in their synagogues. We have found no scriptures that support the debating or disputing of God's Word with Christian brethren. **Philippians 2:14** says: Do all things without murmurings and disputings: Since we know that God's Word is perfect, and entertains no conflict and/or disagreement, we must conclude that disputing here means reasoning-not debating.

Now let's talk about the audience that is participating in the debate exercise. We are told by God's

Notes

Word, that we are to be careful what we listen to-
"Take heed how you hear" (**Luke 8:18, Mark 4:24**). We are also commanded not to be deceived(**1 Corinthians 6:9, Luke 21:8, Matthew 24:4, Ephesians 5:6, Colossians 2:18, 2 Thessalonians 2:3.**) Again, how many times must we be told? It speaks loudly to me, that, if I choose to sit in on a debate of God's Word, and allow myself to be deceived; shame on me. I can't blame the debaters; I have been warned. I would certainly not run afoul of **2 Timothy 4:3,** For the time will come when they will not endure sound doctrine; but after their own lusts shall they heap to themselves teachers, having itching ears;

Acts 5:38 And now I say unto you, Refrain from these men, and let them alone: for if this counsel or this work be of men, it will come to nought:

Acts 5:39 But if it be of God, ye cannot overthrow it; lest haply ye be found even to fight against God.

COUNSEL IS MINE ll

Matthew 15:7-8 Ye hypocrites, well did Esaias prophesy of you, saying, This people draweth nigh unto me with their mouth, and honoureth me with their lips; but their heart is far from me.

How do men's doctrines originate and take hold? Why do men devise their own commandments, and appear to substantiate them with God's Word (s)? It seems that it is easier to put the new cloth into the old garment, and to put the new wine into the old bottles. It appears more comfortable in the flesh to accept only the Words of God, that don't interfere too much with our own wills and with the old flesh. We skirt obedience to God's perfect and pure Word by establishing our own rules; then we "stretch" God's Word to justify our position.

Much of what passes for Christian principles today are merely men's doctrines and commandments. They are instilled in us early on, and are seemingly supported by scriptures. The scriptures are selectively chosen to mistakenly further the premise that the men's doctrines are inspired by God. The challenge lies with the ability one may have to lay aside the traditional spirit-washed condition he is in, and be open to what God is actually saying to us through His Word.

Proverbs 30:5 Every word of God is pure: he is a shield unto them that put their trust in him.
Proverbs 30:6 Add thou not unto his words, lest he reprove thee, and thou be found a liar.
Revelation 22:18 For I testify unto every man that heareth the words of the prophecy of this book, If any man shall add unto these things, God shall add unto him the plagues that are written in this book:
Revelation 22:19 And if any man shall take away from the words of the book of this prophecy, God shall take away his part out of the book of life, and out of the holy city, and from the things which are written in this book. **Comment**: These verses clearly warn us not to add or subtract from God's Word. When we stretch the import of God's Words

Notes

to justify a position of the flesh, we are, in effect, adding and/or subtracting from God's Words.

John 3:3 Except a man be born again, he cannot see the kingdom of God.

John 3:5 Except a man be born of water and of the Spirit, he cannot enter into the kingdom of God.

John 3:15 That whosoever believeth in him should not perish, but have eternal life.

John 3:16 For God so loved the world, that he gave his only begotten Son, that whosoever believeth in him should not perish, but have everlasting life.

John 14:6 ... no man cometh unto the Father, but by me.

John 10:9 I am the door: by me if any man enter in, he shall be saved, and shall go in and out, and find pasture.

Comment: There are many other scriptures that establish this clear message, but the above are enough to convince me that the only way to God is through his Son Jesus Christ. We have found no other words in the Bible that even hint about another route open to us, which leads to God.

There are some, who have claimed that God will eventually accept all into his kingdom-none will be lost (please refer to the **NONE LOST** segment of this Manual.) They cite scriptures that seem to support their stand. They say that all things are of God (which they are), that God is no respecter of persons (which he isn't), that we are all born with the same light (which we are), and that God is not willing that any shall perish, etc.. It is true that these are God's Words, however, they must in some way agree with the other verses that state the contrary.

These brethren also claim that God is like a refiner's fire-this fire will eventually try everyone, and bring them to God's salvation. The following verses are cited in support:

Malachi 3:2 But who may abide the day of his coming? and who shall stand when he appeareth? for he is like a refiner's fire, and like fullers' soap:

Malachi 3:3 And he shall sit as a refiner and purifier of silver: and he shall purify the sons of Levi, and purge them as gold and silver, that they may offer unto the LORD an offering in righteousness.

Zecheriah 13:9 And I will bring the third part through the fire, and will refine them as silver is refined, and will try them as gold is tried:

Isaiah 48:10 Behold, I have refined thee, but not with silver; I have chosen thee in the furnace of affliction.

Psalm 66:10 For thou, O God, hast proved us: thou hast tried us, as silver is tried.

Comment: Search the scriptures for **Ezekiel 22:14-22**. Let us look at the refiner's fire, and see what it actually does. Silver and gold are placed in the refiner's fire to free them from dross and alloys in order to reduce them to an unmixed or pure state. To achieve the pure state, you must first throw gold and silver into the fire. You cannot throw combustible materials like wood, hay, or stubble into the flames, and refine them into gold or silver. The refiner's fire does not take perishable items, and give them properties they did not possess-they end up as ashes. Silver and gold, however, will be made pure by the refiner's fire. (Now we know that with God nothing is impossible-but he won't go against his own Word).

The born-again believer, when tried by the refiner's fire, will be made more pure by the exercise. He entered in with the power of faith and belief, and was purified. He went in as dross-laden silver, and came out freed from the dross of sin in the flesh. As in the case of wood, hay, and stubble the unbeliever is consumed and destroyed when tried by the fire. To say that the unbelieving sinner will one day be tried by the refiner's fire, and come out as silver-a spirit acceptable to God-is stretching the point beyond credibility or belief. No, he will surely be consumed; his end is destruction. Again, we know that all things are of God, and that with God nothing is impossible. However, God is not a liar; he is Truth, and he won't go against his own Word. God's Word is perfect, and has no conflicts, contradictions, or disagreements.

It speaks to me that these scriptures say that there is destruction in God's perfect plan. They say that

Notes

ever worketh abomination, or maketh a lie: but they which are written in the Lamb's book of life.

<u>Romans 1:26</u> For this cause God gave them up unto vile affections: for even their women did change the natural use into that which is against nature:

Comment: We have never been approached by a homosexual-man or woman- seeking counsel in this area of abomination in God's eyes. However, if we were ever confronted with the opportunity to counsel in this area, we would first share the thank-you scriptures-then we would follow with the verses cited above. If the individual is honestly seeking deliverance, one or more of the above verses should speak to their spirit. After seeing how the scriptures affect the person involved, we would counsel as follows:

We would get agreement on <u>Romans 14:23</u> and <u>1 John 5:17</u> cited above. Then we would get agreement on whether homosexuality is, or is not, of faith; based on God's Word We would also have to agree that this condition is not of righteousness. All the scriptures we can find indicate that homosexuality is not of faith and/or righteousness. Therefore it must be sin. If this is not accepted, we are no doubt talking with one, who will not see. If it is accepted, and the troubled person is honestly seeking deliverance, we refer him to the **LUST** segment of this Manual. This section has at least two dozen applicable verses and many comments-many of which should speak heavily to the spirit, that is hungering for deliverance.

<u>Psalm 119:11</u> **Thy word have I hid in mine heart, that I might not sin against thee.**

THE ONLY FORCE WHICH HAS THE POWER TO DELIVER ONE FROM SIN IS THE WORD OF GOD; praying the prayers of man will not do it.

WINE OR WHINE

This segment our Manual deals with the often-sermonized subject of wine, hard drink, drunkenness, etc.. It would be nice if we could erase all you have heard and read from pastors, evangelists, writers, speakers, etc., who have expounded eloquently and with well-meaning fervor on this subject. Obviously we can't do this-God can, but we can't. What we can do is approach this topic in a refreshing different manner with the pure power and truth found in the Word of God. Before we start, we should find some agreement, and be in accord on some basic points. They are as follows:

1. The Word of God is just that-God's Words. He wrote the Bible's Words. His Word is forever.

2. God's Word is perfect. There are no disagreements or contradictions contained found.

3. Men's doctrines are not to be entertained here.

4. The Word, through the Holy Spirit, is accepted differently by each of us in direct

proportion to the reliance we place on the flesh. We will not argue any point, because of **Romans 14:5** Let every man be fully persuaded in his own mind. We also honor: **Titus 3:9** But avoid foolish questions, and genealogies, and contentions, and strivings about the about the law; for they are unprofitable and vain.

All right-let us steer this particular boat into deeper waters.

As in all our counseling activities we begin by claiming and standing fast on: **Acts 5:38** ...for if this counsel or this work be of men, it will come to nought: **Acts 5:39** But if it be of God, ye cannot overthrow it; lest haply ye be found even to fight against God. Whenever we voice understanding and/or interpretation of God's Word, we must be careful not to add or subtract from it. If we do, we fly in the face of **Proverbs 30:5-6** and **Revelation 22:18-19**. We could cite these scriptures, but it may be more beneficial for you to search the scriptures for them.

(When you find them, read them aloud). You might also look at:**1 Peter 4:11** If any man speak,

Notes

let him speak as the oracles of God; You might also check out **Philippians 1:27**.

In **Psalm 104**, God tells us many things that he has done-leading into verse 15 which says: And wine that maketh *glad* the heart of man, **Judges 9:13**, And the vine said unto them, Should I leave my wine, *which cheereth God and man*, **Matthew 11:19,** The Son of man came eating and drinking, and they say, Behold a man gluttonous, **and a winebibber**, It speaks to my spirit here, that they saw Jesus eating food and called him a glutton. They saw him drinking, and they say: Behold a man gluttonous, *and a winebibber* (a winebibber is one, who drinks wine to excess). Some maintain that he was mistakenly accused of drinking wine-that he actually drank water. If this is your position-praise the Lord. However, this view does not fit the situation.. When he was accused of being a glutton, what was he doing? He must have been over-eating food. Well, then, when he was accused of being a winebibber, isn't it obvious that he must have been drinking wine? He wasn't being called a "waterbibber", was he? You have to decide for yourself-as far I am concerned, he was drinking wine. **1 Timothy 5:23** Drink no longer water, but *use a little wine* for thy stomach's sake and thine often infirmities. **1 Timothy 3:8** Likewise must the deacons be grave, not double-tongued, *not given to much wine,* not greedy of filthy lucre; Does this mean that they can be given to a little wine? This is how I see it. **Romans14:14** I know, and am persuaded by the Lord Jesus, that there is nothing unclean of itself: but to him that esteemeth any thing to be unclean, to him it is unclean. Sort of leaves it to each individual decision-doesn't it?

The above scriptures speak to me that the taking of a little wine is acceptable to God. God said in **Ephesians 5:18:** And be not drunk with wine, wherein is excess; **1 Peter 4:3** says: when we walked in...excess of wine (In other words, we drank too much). In the Christian walk, as new creatures in Christ, we are commanded to "Let our moderation be known to all men". (Moderation is

Notes

limitation, control, keeping in bounds-it does not mean abstinence). God said in **1 Corinthians5:11** not to keep company with a drunkard. **Luke 21:34** warns as follows: And take heed to yourselves, lest at any time your hearts be overcharged with surfeiting, and drunkenness, (surfeiting means being excessive). We are told in **Romans13:13**: Let us walk honestly, as in the day; not in rioting and drunkenness,

Galatians 5:21 says that if we get involved with drunkenness, we will: "not inherit the kingdom of God". Everything here tells us that we are not to be drunkards-nowhere do we read that we must abstain. We are to have moderation in all things.

When we hear a sermon on the evils of drink, none of the above-cited scriptures are ever mentioned. Being of a spirit of fairness we, however, will cite the scriptures usually quoted in support of total abstinence. One of the most popular is: **Habakkuk 2:15** Woe unto him that giveth his neighbour drink, that puttest thy bottle to him, and makest him drunken also, One can stretch a point, and claim, that this says that we should not give a drink to a neighbor. Does it really say that? We read, that he should not be given the whole bottle-"wherein there is excess" (which will make him drunk). It does not say, that we cannot give him a drink wherein there is moderation. **Leviticus 10:9** Do not drink wine nor strong drink, However, those, who quote, conveniently fail to finish the verse, which says: when ye go into the tabernacle of the congregation, In **Luke 1:15**, we are given an instance when drink is nor acceptable-it says that John the Baptist "shall drink neither wine of strong drink". This states that John specifically is not to drink-it does not say that wine is forbidden in general for others.

It is my observation, based on God's Word, that the tirades against drinking have been the whining of men's doctrines. It may be that **Matthew 15:7-14** could come into the picture here. You will have to decide for yourself-read the verses aloud, and see how they speak to your spirit. You may look at this subject a little differently now, or at least with a

Notes

more open frame of mind and spirit. If you do, you may feel you have been deceived by false teachings in this area. If you do, you have only yourself to blame. We are told by God's Word not to be deceived by any man. If you blindly accept the understanding and interpretations of others without verifying, that they are not in line with scriptures, you are at fault (this includes our counsel as well). You have your Bible-all the protections against deceptions are included therein. All one has to do is search the scriptures, and allow the Holy Spirit to provide the understanding. We encourage you not to accept our understanding either-search the scriptures, and check us out also. **Proverbs 3:5-6** tells us not to lean on our own understanding-we are told not to be deceived (**Matthew 24:4**). The only answer is to get understanding from God's Word through the leading of the Holy Spirit.

All of God's admonitions are against the sot, the drunkard, and the winebibber.

against surfeiting, excessiveness, and the lack of moderation. God commands temperance and self-control in all things. We are not to be drunkards-we are not to drink wine to excess. In fact, we are not to do anything to excess-the sin is the excess, and is not in the drinking of wine. God has charged us in **Philippians 4:5**: Let your moderation be known unto all men. He said nothing about letting our abstinence be known.

There is one situation discussed in the old testament where it is commanded that no wine

or strong drink be taken. If one takes the vow of the Nazarite, no strong drink is to be taken (**Numbers 6:2-4**). We have yet to meet a Christian, who has taken that vow. Maybe it is because we are told in **Matthew 5:33-37** not to forswear ourselves-we are told not to swear at all. The taking of vows is treated in the old testament - but spoken against in the New Testament.

Hebrews 8:6-7: But now hath he obtained a more excellent ministry, by how much also he is the mediator of a better covenant, which was established upon better promises. For if that first covenant had been faultless, then should no place have been sought for the second. **Comment:** Even though Jesus came not to destroy the law, but to fulfill it-there was fault in the old law This understanding is further supported by **Hebrews chapters 7, 18, 19 and 22.** Please refer to them, and allow the Holy Spirit to give you the understanding. You can add all this to **Hebrews 8:13**, which says: In that he saith, A new covenant, he hath made the first old. Now that which decayeth and waxeth old is ready to vanish away. You almost have to accept the position that those of us, who came after the cross of Jesus Christ and are saved, are living under the New Testament. Citing old testament scriptures is support of dictating Christian life styles is an exercise in futility for the new creature described in **2 Corinthians 5:17** (old things are passed away) **Galatians 4:9** says: But now, after that ye have known God, or rather are known of God, how turn ye again to the weak and beggarly elements, whereunto ye desire again to be in bondage?

Well, it looks as if it is "yea, yea" or "nay, nay" time again. It is your decision to make. If you decide to continue accepting the traditional teachings and preachings concerning this subject, so be it; amen, and Praise the Lord in the name of Jesus Christ. We, however, prefer to claim, and stand fast in faith on **Galatians 5:1** Stand fast therefore in the liberty wherewith Christ hath made us free, and be not entangled again with the yoke of bondage. Many of us, who have accepted Jesus Christ as Redeemer and Savior, and became born-again, simply traded one bondage for another. We traded the bondage of unbelief for the bondage of men's teachings and commandments. It is more blessed to accept the freedom and rejoice in the fruits of the Spirit-in this case, the fruit of temperance cited in **Galatians 5:23**. Have you noticed, that abstinence is not listed as one of the fruits of the Spirit?

By the way (His Way). as I was reading in **Matthew** and **Luke** recently, the Spirit opened another tidbit you may want to throw into your decision-making process. **Matthew 9:17,** Neither do

Notes

10:14 For by one offering he hath perfected for ever them that are sanctified. **Hebrews 2:11** For both he that sanctifieth and they who are sanctified are all of one: for which cause he is not ashamed to call them brethren,

21. How long you will live in the flesh?

ANS. **Psalm 90:10** The days of our years are threescore years and ten; (at least).

22. Why ancient peoples set sail to prove the earth as flat-when they had?

ANS. **Isaiah 40:22** It is he that sitteth upon the <u>circle</u> of the earth,

23. What reasons God gives for people to get married?

ANS. **1 Corinthians 7:2** Nevertheless, to avoid fornication, let every man have his own wife, and let every woman have her own husband. **1 Corinthians 7:9** But if they cannot contain, let them marry: for it is better to marry than to burn.

24. What to say, when someone wants to engage in gossip?

ANS. **Ephesians 4:29** Let no corrupt communication proceed out of your mouth,

25. How God defines sin?

ANS. **James 4:17** Therefore to him that knoweth to do good, and doeth it not, to him it is sin. **1 John 5:17** All unrighteousness is sin: **Romans 14:23** for whatsoever is not of faith is sin. **1 John 3:4** for sin is the transgression of the law.

26. What the other fast is?

ANS. **Isaiah 58:6** Is not this the fast that I have chosen? to loose the bands of wickedness, to undo the heavy burdens, and to let the oppressed go free, and that ye break every yoke?

27. What you should be thinking about?

ANS. **Philippians 4:8** Finally, brethren, whatsoever things are true, whatsoever things are honest, whatsoever things are just, whatsoever things are pure, whatsoever things are lovely, whatsoever things are of good report; if there be any virtue, and if there be any praise, think on these things. **Philippians 4:9** Those things, which ye have both learned, and received, and heard, and seen in me, do: and the God of peace shall be with you.

28. Is the Word of God (the Bible) perfect?

ANS. **Hebrews 4:12** For the word of God is quick, and powerful, and sharper than any twoedged sword, piercing even to the dividing asunder of soul and spirit, and of the joints and marrow, and is a discerner of the thoughts and intents of the heart. **2 Peter 1:21** For the prophecy came not in old time by the will of man: but holy men of God spake as they were moved by the Holy Ghost. **Proverbs 30:5** Every word of God is pure: **Psalm 12:6** The words of the LORD are pure words: Psalm **119:140** Thy word is very pure: **2 Timothy 3:16** All scripture is given by inspiration of God, **Psalm 119:160** Thy word is true from the beginning: and every one of thy righteous judgments endureth for ever. **Psalm 19:7** The law of the LORD is perfect, converting the soul: the testimony of the LORD is sure, making wise the simple. **Psalm 19:8** The statutes of the LORD are right, rejoicing the heart: the commandment of the LORD is pure, enlightening the eyes. **John 17:17** Sanctify them through thy truth: thy word is truth.

29. When "women's lib" began?

ANS. **Genesis 3:6** And when the woman saw that the tree was good for food, and that it was pleasant to the eyes, and a tree to be desired to make one wise, she took of the fruit thereof, and did eat, and gave also unto her husband with her; and he did eat.

30. When you were actually saved?

ANS. **2 Thessalonians 2:13** because God hath from the beginning chosen you to salvation through sanctification of the Spirit and belief of the truth: **Ephesians 1:4** According as he hath chosen us in him before the foundation of the world, **1 Peter 1:2** Elect according to the foreknowledge of God the Father,

31. How you can spot a false prophet, and/or an anti-Christ?

ANS. **1 John 4:1** Beloved, believe not every spirit, but try the spirits whether they are of God: because many false prophets are gone out into the world. **1 John 4:2** Hereby know ye the Spirit of God: Every spirit that confesseth that Jesus Christ is come in the flesh is of God: **1 John 4:3** And every spirit that confesseth not that Jesus Christ is come in the flesh is not of God: and this is that spirit of

Notes

THE BUCK STOPS HERE
(With the Holy Spirit)

When you wish to turn on a light, do you go outdoors, face the power station, and yell for light? Certainly not! You go to the wall switch, and flick it on-then the light is lit. The power created the power-the power lines carried the charge into your home and to the switch. When you activated the switch, the power was loosed to the light bulb. You can make what you will of this analogy-it works for us. God is the power station for us; He created the power. The power lines are equated to Jesus Christ-he delivered God's power to earth, and brought it to the Holy Spirit through the Word. The Holy Spirit is our "light switch" with which we can release God's power in our lives. We receive deliverance and blessings not by praying, but by releasing the power of the Holy Spirit-we switch him on by the Word of God.

Let's say you have a two-ton, $50,000 car sitting in your garage. When wishing to start this vehicle, do you go outdoors, face Michigan (or wherever), and yell for the car company to start your car? Of course not! You take your 50-cent key, insert it into the ignition, turn it, and start the car. You have faith in the entire process, and know you will end up with a car that is running. When you want to start up your vacuum cleaner, do you go outdoors, face the Kirby plant, and holler for the cleaner to be turned on? No way! You plug the cord into a socket, and turn on the switch-it starts. Can you relate to these analogies? Can you accept the fact that your faith in the processes presented was sure and stedfast? Why can't we have the same faith in God's process? We often have more faith in flying in a plane, even though we do not know the planes mechanical condition or the true ability of the pilot (s), than we have in God's promises.

This section of the Manual deals with the role of the Holy Spirit in the life of the believer. You may not agree with what follows, and how the Holy Spirit speaks to us through scriptures about the relative roles of God the Father, his Son Jesus Christ, and his Holy Spirit, and that is OK. If you have read and understood (not necessarily agreed) with what has been written before in this work, you may entertain where we are regarding this subject.

It speaks to me through God's Word that God has done all he is going to do-it is finished.

He created all this from the beginning to the end-he has done it all. We are only walking through his already completed will; his creation. God sent his Son, Jesus, to walk among us as a man in order to bear witness of the truth, and reconcile us to God our Father. In order to provide for us in his absence, Jesus sent the Holy Spirit, the Comforter and Teacher, in his stead. It is the Holy Spirit we now deal with-or else deals with us. It speaks to me that praying to God goes around the Spirit, and almost denies his existence. If we accept that God's work is finished, and Jesus Christ completed the Father's work he was given to do on this earth; it seems wrong to pray to God to change what they did. It seems more fitting, correct and proper to claim, believe, and stand fast on God's Word given to us in the Bible; made clear to us through the Holy Ghost. When we do this in faith, the Spirit can give us understanding and comfort, which was what he was sent to do. This can only happen through the Word of God, and not through prayer.

1 John 5:6-8 This is he that came by water and blood, even Jesus Christ; not by water only, but by water and blood. And it is the Spirit that beareth witness, because the Spirit is truth. For there are three that bear record in heaven, the Father, the Word, and the Holy Ghost: and these three are one. And there are three that bear witness in earth, the Spirit, and the water, and the blood: and these three agree in one.

In **1 Corinthians 12:4-10** we are told that God's gifts are given to us by the Holy Spirit-not by God himself (although all things are of God). **1 Corinthians 12:13** For by one Spirit are we all baptized into one body, Let us look at some of the scriptures that talk of the Holy Spirit-the Holy Ghost.

Notes

CONCLUSION

1 Corinthians 12:18 But now hath God set the members every one of them in the body, as it hath pleased him.

1 Corinthians 15:10 But by the grace of God I am what I am:

Colossians 4:17 Take heed to the ministry which thou hast received in the Lord, that thou fulfil it.

1 Corinthians 7:24 Brethren, let every man, wherein he is called, therein abide with God.

Galatians 4:16 Am I therefore become your enemy, because I tell you the truth?

Ephesians 4:7 But unto every one of us is given grace according to the measure of the gift of Christ.

1 Corinthians 3:11 For other foundation can no man lay than that is laid, which is Jesus Christ.

1 Corinthians 3:12 Now if any man build upon this foundation gold, silver, precious stones, wood, hay, stubble;

1 Corinthians 3:13 Every man's work shall be made manifest: for the day shall declare it, because it shall be revealed by fire; and the fire shall try every man's work of what sort it is.

1 Corinthians3:14 If any man's work abide which he hath built thereupon, he shall receive a reward.

1 Corinthians 3:15 If any man's work shall be burned, he shall suffer loss: but he himself shall be saved; yet so as by fire.

Romans 14:5 One man esteemeth one day above another: another esteemeth every day alike. Let every man be fully persuaded in his own mind.

Romans 15:7 Wherefore receive ye one another, as Christ also received us to the glory of God.

John 13:34 A new commandment I give unto you, That ye love one another;

Colossians 3:12 Put on therefore, as the elect of God, holy and beloved, bowels of mercies, kindness, humbleness of mind, meekness, longsuffering;

Colossians 3:13 Forbearing one another, and forgiving one another, if any man have a quarrel against any: even as Christ forgave you, so also do ye.

Matthew 7:1 Judge not, that ye be not judged.

John 8:7 He that is without sin among you, let him first cast a stone at her.

Acts 5:38 And now I say unto you, Refrain from these men, and let them alone: for if this counsel or this work be of men, it will come to nought:

Acts 5:39 But if it be of God, ye cannot overthrow it; lest haply ye be found even to fight against God.

2 Corinthians 5:18 And all things are of God,

TO GOD BE THE GLORY

Hebrews 4:12 For the word of God is quick, and powerful, and sharper than any twoedged sword, piercing even to the dividing asunder of soul and spirit, and of the joints and marrow, and is a discerner of the thoughts and intents of the heart.

Isaiah 55:11 So shall my word be that goeth forth out of my mouth: it shall not return unto me void, but it shall accomplish that which I please, and it shall prosper in the thing whereto I sent it.

Notes

This Manual is a result of the understanding given me through God's Word with the leading of the Spirit. It is understood that much of what you have read here is new to your spirit-you won't hear much of what you have read uttered from traditional pulpits. You may even be in direct opposition to much of what you have been exposed to here-I understand and appreciate how you feel. Isn't it wonderful that you won't be either justified or condemned by my words? Isn't it a blessing, that God's Word promises us comfort, peace and contentment in all things. You are protected by God's loving protection. God says:

1 Corinthians 3:11-15 For other foundation can no man lay than that is laid, which is Jesus Christ. Now if any man build upon this foundation gold, silver, precious stones, wood, hay, stubble; Every man's work shall be made manifest: for the day shall declare it, because it shall be revealed by fire; and the fire shall try every man's work of what sort it is. If any man's work abide which he hath built thereupon, he shall receive a reward. If any man's work shall be burned, he shall suffer loss: but he himself shall be saved; yet so as by fire.

Comment: It is not known to me whether this work will abide, or be burned. All I know is that I had to fulfill the leading, that has brought this work about. Thank God in the Name of Jesus Christ for verse 15 above-if this work is burned, I will suffer loss, but I will be saved-yet so as by fire. All I can say is, Amen and Amen!

In my travels around to various fellowships, I found that in too many instances, believers had escaped one bondage and entered into another. They left the bondage of being unsaved, and entered into a bondage of men's teachings and doctrines. This led to the popular opinion, that at least 80% of Christian believers do not know what is in the Bible. Many believers have not keyed into the true meaning of **Galatians 5:1**-if one stands fast on this verse, the blessings of liberty will surely flow. In my early Christian walk it was easy for me to fall into the comfortable and spectator style of fellowship - being entertained instead of being motivated into

Notes

doing God's Words. The scriptures that fit into my life without making me too uncomfortable and uneasy were the ones I accepted. What happened to me is aptly described in **Matthew 9:16**. It was found "easy" for me to put the new cloth into the old garment. After all, I didn't want the change to be excessively traumatic. What happened to me was typical-I did not want to stand on "yea, yea" or "nay, nay". It was easier (I thought) to ride the fence-it wasn't too long before I discovered that riding a fence could become uncomfortable and painful. In addition to this, my spirit was not at peace. More and more I was led into God's Word-it was there I found the answer (surprise, surprise). Since then the Word of God has been getting daily attention from me, my spirit began finding peace in His wonderful Word. Reading his Word aloud has released a power, that has delivered me from the burdens I had been carrying.

God's Word, the Bible, has all the answers for me. It also has the answers for you. To rightly divide the Word of Truth is to provide a flaming example of "whatsoever a man soweth, that shall he also reap" (**Galatians 6:7**). I was always a happy man; in fact, I used to present a talk program called, "The Happiest Man in the World". After accepting Jesus Christ as Lord and Savior, I discovered what true Joy was. You may not accept how the Holy spirit has guided my understanding in many areas, and that's fine. However, please accept this: God's Word is perfect, pure, and is Truth. Claiming his Word in faith as his promises to us will fill your life with Joy-no matter what is going on around you. Try it - you'll like it!!

2 Pet 1:11-13 For so an entrance shall be ministered unto you abundantly into the everlasting kingdom of our Lord and Saviour Jesus Christ. Wherefore I will not be negligent to put you always in remembrance of these things, though ye know them, and be established in the present truth. Yea, I think it meet, as long as I am in this tabernacle, to stir you up by putting you in remembrance;

Notes

KEY SCRIPTURE VERSES FROM MANUAL SECTIONS
(Aren't they all - key, that is?)

(Fill in spaces)

COUNSEL IS MINE:
* Counsel is _____ (Proverbs 8:14)
* My counsel shall _____ (Isaiah 46:10)
* Thy testimonies are my _____ and my _____
    (Psalm 119:24)
* There are man devices in a man's heart; neverthe-
    less the _____ of the
Lord shall _____. (Proverbs 19:21)

REJOICE:
* _____ evermore. (1 Thessalonians 5:16)
* Rejoice and be _____ _____ (Matthew 5:12)
* Yet I will _____ in the _____, I will ____ in the
    ____ of my _____
(Habakkuk 3:18)
* By whom also we have access by _____ into this
    _____ wherein we _____, and _____ in _____
    of the _____ of God. (Romans 5:2)

JUST WHO ARE WE IN CHRIST JESUS?
* But by the _____ of ____ I __ what I __ (1
    Corinthians 15:10)
* That whosoever _____ in ____ should not
    _____, but have _____ life.
(John 3:16)
* ____, in all _____ _____ we are more than
    _____ through ____ that _____ us.
    (Romans 8:37)
* And they said, _____ on the _____ _____
    _____, and thou _____ be _____, and thy _____
    (Acts 16:31)

PROTECTION:
* The _____ is my _____ and my _____; whom
    shall I _____? the LORD is the _____ of my
    life; of _____ shall I be _____? (Psalm 27:1)
* And the _____ shall _____ me from every _____
    work, and will _____ me (2 Timothy 4:18)

* Behold, I give unto you _____ to _____ on serpents and _____, and over all the _____ of the _____: and _____ shall by any _____ hurt you. (Luke 10:19)
* What shall we ____ ___ to these _____? If ___ be for us, who can be _____ us? (Romans 8:31)

THE TONGUE:
* If any man _____ not in ____, the same is a _____ man, and able also to _____ the whole ____. (James 3:2)
* _____ not thy _____ to _____ thy flesh to ___; (Ecclesiastes 5:6)
* For with the _____ man _____ unto _____; and with the _____ _____ is made unto _____. (Romans 10:10)
* If any ___ _____, let him _____ as the _____ of God (1 Peter 4:11)

WHO SHOULD WE BELIEVE?
* That your _____ should not stand in the _____ __ ___, but in the _____ of God. (1 Corinthians 2:5)
* ____ ye out of the ____ of the ____, and ____ (Isaiah 34:16)
* This is the ____ of ___, that ye _____ on him whom __ ____ ____ (John 6:29)
* And ___ ____, _____ __ ___ ____ ____ ____ (Acts 16:31)

LAW (letter) vs. FAITH ((Spirit)
* for if _____ ____ by the ___, then _____ is ____ in vain.
(Galatians 2:21)
* But if ye be ___ of the _____, ye are not _____ the ___ (Galatians 5:18)
* But ___ we are _____ ____ the law (Romans 7:6)
* For the ___ was _____ by _____, but _____ and truth ____ by _____ _____. (John 1:17)

UNDERSTANDING
* _____ in the ____ with all _____ _____; and ____

Notes

not unto thine own _____ (Proverbs 3:5)

* Through thy _____ I get _____ (Psalm 119:104)
* The _____ of thy words giveth _____; it giveth _____ unto the simple
(Psalm 119:130)
* Then _____ he their _____ that they might _____ the _____ (Luke24:45)

GIFTS
* And they were all_____ the Holy Ghost, and began to _____ with other _____ as the Spirit gave them _____ (Acts 2:4)
* But _____ earnestly the best _____ (! Corinthians 12:31)
* But ____ man hath his ____ ____ of God, one after ____ manner, and another
After _____. (! Corinthians 7:7)
* But unto _____ one of us is given _____ according to the _____of the _____ of _____ (Ephesians 4:31)

ANGER
* _____ from _____, and forsake _____ (Psalm 37:8)
* But now ye also _____ _____ all these; _____ wrath (Colossians 3:8)
* Let all …, and _____, and _____, … be put away from you, (Ephesians 4:31)
* An _____ man stirreth up strife, and a _____ man aboundeth in _____ (Proverbs 29:22)

WORRY
* Let ____ your heart be _____ (John 14:1)
* Be _____ for _____. (Philippians 4:6)
* For I have _____ in whatsoever _____ I am, therewith to be _____ (Philippians 4:11)
* _____ with _____ is great gain. (1 Timothy 6:6)

PEOPLE BUG ME
* Cast thy _____ upon the _____, and he shall _____thee. (Psalm 55:22)
* From _____, let no ___ man _____ me

(Galatians 6:17)

* ____ set the _____ every one of them in the _____, as it hath pleased him. (1 Corinthians 12:18)

* _____ not, that ye be not _____. (Matthew 7:1)

PATIENCE

* Be _____ therefore, brethren, unto the _____ of the ____ (James 5:7)

* In your _____ _____ ye your souls. (Luke 21:19)

* and bring forth _____ with _____ (Luke 8:15)

* then do we ____ _____ wait for it. (Romans 8:25)

LUST

* Teaching us that, denying _____ and worldly _____, we should live soberly, righteously, ___ _____, in this present world; (Titus 2:12)

* But put ye on the ____ _____ _____, and make not provision for the _____, to _____ the _____ thereof. (Romans 13:14)

* Flee also _____ _____ (2 Timothy 2:22)

* Then when ____ hath _____, it bringeth forth ___: and ___, when it is finished, bringeth forth _____. (James 1:15)

HEALING

* by whose _____ ye were _____ (1 Peter 2:24)

* _____ took our _____, and ____ our _____ (Matthew 8:17)

* For they are ____ unto those that ____ ____, and ____ to all their _____

(Proverbs 4:22)

* for I am the ____ that _____ thee (Exodus 15:26)

* Thy _____ hath made thee _____. (Matthew 9:22 & Mark 10:52)

DEATH

* that whosoever _____ in him should not _____, but have _____ life. (John 3:16)

* If a ___ keep my _____, he shall _____ ___ _____ (John 8:51)

Notes

things are possible to ___ that _____ (Mark 9:23)

* To _____ the _____ of _____. (1 Corinthians 12:10)
* I can __ __ _____ through _____ which _____ me. (Philippians 4:13)

COUNSEL IS MINE 11
* Except a man be _____ _____, he cannot ___ the _____ of ___. (John 3:3)
* Enter ye in at the _____ ____: for ____ is the ____, and _____ is the ___, that
That _____ to _____, and ____ there be which __ __ _____:
Because _____ is the ____, and _____ is the ___, which _____ unto ____, and ___ there be ____ ____ __. (Matthew 13:14)
* which they that are _____ and _____ _____, as they do also the other _____, unto their ___ _____ (2 Peter 3:16)
* but the _____ of the _____ shall _____ (Proverbs 10:28)

HOMOSEXUALITY
* For whatsoever is not of _____ is ___. (Romans 14:23)
* Thou shalt ___ ___ with _____, as with _____: it is _____ (Lev. 18:22)
* Know ye not that the _____ shall ___ _____ the _____ __ ___? Be not _____: neither _____, nor _____, nor _____, nor
_____ nor _____ of _____ with _____, (1 Cor. 6:9)
* All _____ is ___. (1 John 5:17)

WINE OR WHINE
* And the ____ said unto them, Should I leave my ____, which _____ ___ and ___? (Judges 9:13)
* Drink no longer _____,but use a little ____ for thy _____ ____ and thine
Often _____ (1 Timothy 5:23)
* I know, and am _____ by the Lord Jesus, that

Notes

there is _____ _____ of _____ (Romans 14:14)

* Let your _____be _____ to all ___. (Philippians 4:5)

THE BUCK STOPS HERE

* And it is the _____ that _____ _____, because the _____ is _____.
(1 John 5:6)

* he shall _____ you with the ____ _____, and with ____: (Matthew 3:11)

* For the ____ _____ shall _____ ___ in the same ____r what ye _____ __ ___.
(Luke 12:12)

* Verily, verily, I say unto thee, Except a ___ be ____ __ _____ and of the ____,
he cannot _____ into the _____ __ ___ (John 3:5)

* For by ___ _____ are we all _____ into ___ ____. (1 Corinthians 12:13)

CONCLUSION

* But now hath ___ set the _____ every ___ __ ____ in the ____, as it hath _____ him (1 Corinthians 12:18)

* But by the _____ of ___, I __ ____ _ am (1 Corinthians 15:10)

* Take ____to the _____ which thou hast _____ in the ____, that thou _____ it (Colossians 4;17)

* Brethren, let _____ ___, wherein he is _____, therein _____ with ___ (1 Corinthians 7:24)

SIMPLICITY

* Owe no ___ ___ _____, but to ____ ___ _____: for he that __ ____ _____ hath _____ the law. (Romans 13:8)

* For all the ___ is_____ in one ____, even in this; Thou _____ ____ thy _____ as _____ (Galatians 5:14)

* For the kingdom __ ___ is not ____ and _____; but _____, and _____, and ___ in the ____ _____ (Romans 14:17)

* Let us hear the _____ of the whole _____: Fear ___, and ____ his _____; for this is the _____ ____ of ___. For God shall bring

Notes

_____ ____ into _____ with every _____ thing, whether it be ____, or _____ it be evil. (Ecclesiastes 12:13-14)

EPILOGUE
* For other_____ can no man ___ than that is ____, which is Jesus Christ (1 Corinthians 3:11)
* for out of the _____ of the _____ the mouth _____. (Matthew 12:34)
* for by thy_____ thou shalt be _____. and by thy _____ thou shalt be _____. (Matthew 12:37)

WHAT (Or Who) IS THE CHURCH
* Likewise _____ the _____ that is in their _____. (Romans 16:5)
* The _____ of Asia _____ you. (1 Corinthians 16:9)
* But he _____ of the _____ of his body.
* What? Know ye not that your ____ is the_____ of the ____ _____? (1 Corinthians 16:19)
* And I saw no _____ therein: for the ____ ___ _____ and the ____ are the _____ of it. (Revelation 21:22)

CAST THY BREAD UPON THE WATERS
* Thus have ye made the _____of ___ of none effect by your_____
(Matthew 15:6)
* I know thy _____, that thou art _____ ____ nor ___: I would thou ____ ____ or ___. (Revelation 3:15)

STRIFE
* Agree with thine _____ quickly (Matthew 5:25)
* Let us walk _____, as in the ___, not in _____ and _____. (Rom. 13:13)
* Let _____ be done through _____ or vain _____. (Philippians 2:3)

SPIRITUAL WARFARE
* And every man that_____ for the mastery is _____in all things (! Cor. 9:25)
* And your ____ shod with the _____ of the

_____ of _____; (Eph. 6:15)
* Let your _____ be known to all _____.
   (Philippians 4:5)
* And the _____ of the Lord must
   not_____ (2 Timothy 2:24)
* Fight the _____ _____ of _____. (1 Timothy 2:24)

JUDGE NOT
* Judge not and ye shall not be _____:
   _____not and ye shall not be
   _____ (Luke 6:37)
* Ye judge after the _____. I _____ no ___. (John
   8:15)
* Therefore thou art _____, O man, whoso-
   ever thou art that _____.
(Romans 2:1)
* Who art thou that _____ another _____
   _____? (Roman's 14:4)
* For if we would _____ _____, we should not
   be _____ (1 Cor. 11:31)
* There is one _____, who is able to _____ and to
   _____: who art _____ that _____ _____?
   (James 4:12)

Notes

in the body of Christ, is it so surprising that we are not walking together? However, regardless of this unfortunate state, we can still rejoice in the Lord always-this will all be to his glory in the end, which actually is the beginning for us.

How does the New Testament treat the area of agreement?

Matthew 15:6 Thus have ye made the commandment of God of none effect by your tradition.

Acts 1:14 These all continued with one accord in prayer and supplication,

Acts 2:42 And they continued stedfastly in the apostles' doctrine and fellowship,

Acts 8:6 And the people with one accord gave heed unto those things

Romans 12:16 Be of the same mind one toward another.

Romans 15:5 Now the God of patience and consolation grant you to be likeminded one toward another according to Christ Jesus:

Romans 15:6 That ye may with one mind and one mouth glorify God, even the Father of our Lord Jesus Christ.

Romans 15:7 Wherefore receive ye one another, as Christ also received us to the glory of God.

1 Corinthians 1:10 Now I beseech you, brethren, by the name of our Lord Jesus Christ, that ye all speak the same thing, and that there be no divisions among you; but that ye be perfectly joined together in the same mind and in the same judgment.

1 Corinthians 2:16 But we have the mind of Christ.

1 Corinthians 3:3 For ye are yet carnal: for whereas there is among you envying, and strife, and divisions, are ye not carnal, and walk as men?

2 Corinthians 13:11 Finally, brethren, farewell. Be perfect, be of good comfort, be of one mind,

Philippians 2:2 Fulfil ye my joy, that ye be likeminded, having the same love, being of one accord, of one mind.

Philippians 2:5 Let this mind be in you, which was also in Christ Jesus:

1 Peter 3:8 Finally, be ye all of one mind,

There is a great temptation to do a lot of sharing my understanding and the underscoring for emphasis here, but if the Word of God doesn't stand on its own in your spirits, the spiritual discernment is lost regardless. We will be still here, and know that he is God (**Psalm 46:10**). We will rejoice in that the Holy Spirit will not be denied-he will open the hearts of those he has already ordained to be opened.

WHAT IS WRITTEN IN THE LAW - HOW READEST THOU?

IS THE ONE-PASTOR SYSTEM SCRIPTURAL?

(Please read it all, and then jump on my "bones.")

(Most of what follows is derived from other works.)

A young man feels called to the ministry. His pastor recommends him to go to a Bible College for three years to become fully equipped for this vocation. At college he is rigorously trained, his trial sermons are assessed and rated, and his final examination papers are passed. At last he is ordained, and he swears to uphold the college's Confession of Faith. He is now a qualified pastor with recognized ordination papers, and his name carries the title prefix "Reverend", or "Pastor" or whatever. (Is there a "glorying in men" here?)

Contact is made with a church that has a vacancy, and he is invited along to take the Sunday services - a try-out, if you will.. The deacons and elders interview him, and ask all the relevant questions. A salary is negotiated. They are happy with him, so they put his name forward for the congregation's vote. He is accepted (by a majority) and becomes the church's pastor; they (the congregation) become what he calls *my* "people". His name goes on the notice board and the advertising literature, and he begins his term of office, which may be reviewed after five years or so.

Notes

Notes

THY WORD IS TRUTH

2 Peter 1:20-21 Knowing this first, that no prophecy of the scripture is of any private interpretation. For the prophecy came not in old time by the will of man: but holy men of God spake as they were moved by the Holy Ghost. **Question:** Is this saying, that scripture (God's Word) is prophecy? How about: **Revelations 19:10** for the testimony of Jesus *is the spirit of prophecy.* ?)

2 Timothy 3:16 All scripture is given by inspiration of God, and is profitable for doctrine, for reproof, for correction, for instruction in righteousness: **Question:** Is this credited to men's words anywhere in the Bible? Is it said in the Bible, that men's words will not return to God void?)

John 17:17 Sanctify them through thy truth: *thy word is truth.*

1 Thessalonians 2:13 For this cause also thank we God without ceasing, because, when ye received the word of God which ye heard of us, ye received it not as the word of men, but as it is *in truth, the word of God*, which effectually worketh also in you that believe. **Question:** Do scriptures say that men's words will "effectually work"?

Hebrews 4:12 For the word of God is quick, and powerful, and sharper than any twoedged sword, piercing even to the dividing asunder of soul and spirit, and of the joints and marrow, and is a discerner of the thoughts and intents of the heart. **Question:** is this said of men's words anywhere in God's Word?

All of the above establishes why it moves in my spirit to share only God's Word(s) as answers to any problems brought to my (His) Christian Counseling Ministry - Stand Fast Ministries.

THE HOLY BIBLE, THE HOLY SCRIPTURES ARE THE WRITTEN WORD OF GOD - AS SPOKEN BY JESUS. THEY WERE GIVEN TO US BY GOD'S DIVINE INSPIRATION THROUGH HOLY MEN OF GOD. THEY WROTE AS THEY WERE LED BY THE HOLY SPIRIT OF GOD. THESE WORDS

Notes

- GOD'S WORD(S) - ARE THE PERFECT REVELATION OF HIS WILL.

GOD THE FATHER, THE SON, AND THE HOLY GHOST

Matthew 28:19 Go ye therefore, and teach all nations, baptizing them in the name of the Father, and of the Son, and of the Holy Ghost:

2 Corinthians 13:14 The grace of the Lord Jesus Christ, and the love of God, and the communion of the Holy Ghost, be with you all. Amen.

Ephesians 4:4-6 There is one body, and one Spirit, even as ye are called in one hope of your calling; One Lord, one faith, one baptism, One God and Father of all, who is above all, and through all, and in you all.

1 Peter 1:2 Elect according to the foreknowledge of God the Father, through sanctification of the Spirit, unto obedience and sprinkling of the blood of Jesus Christ: Grace unto you, and peace, be multiplied.

John 14:16-18 And I will pray the Father, and he shall give you another Comforter, that he may abide with you for ever; Even the Spirit of truth; whom the world cannot receive, because it seeth him not, neither knoweth him: but ye know him; for he dwelleth with you, and shall be in you. I will not leave you comfortless: I will come to you. (Comment: It is said that the Father will give us a Comforter. He gave us Jesus earlier. The Comforter is called "the Spirit of Truth." The Word is the Truth. Jesus Christ is the Word. Jesus said, "I will come to you." I don't know about you, but to me, Jesus said in effect that he will return to us as the Holy Spirit! What thinkest thou? All this coupled with: "I (Jesus Christ) and my Father are one" tells me that the Three are One, and the One is all Three.)

GOD THE FATHER: **Genesis 1:1, Revelations 4:11, 1 Corinthians 15:28, John 3:16, 1 John 4:8, 1 Timothy 1:17, John 14:9, Exodus 34:6-6.**

GOD THE SON: **Isaiah 9:6, John 1:1-3, Colossians 1:13-19, John 10:30, John 14:9, Romans 6:23, 2 Corinthians 5:19, John 5:22,**

Luke 1:35, Philippians 2:5-6 John 14:1.

GOD THE HOLY SPIRIT: Genesis 1:1-2, Luke 1:35, Luke 4:18, Acts 10:38,

2 Corinthians 3:18, Acts 1:8, John 14:16-18, John 14:26, John 16:7-13

HOW ALL OF THE ABOVE SPEAKS TO YOUR SPIRIT IS BETWEEN YOU AND GOD THROUGH THE TEACHING OF THE HOLY SPIRIT BY MEANS OF THE WORD OF GOD. I AM FULLY PERSUADED AND CONTENT.